Early Praise for *Testing Elixir*

This book is sprinkled with excellent testing advice! The breadth of testing topics covered within the Elixir ecosystem makes this book an excellent resource for any Elixir developer! Highly recommend!

➤ **Benjamin Tan**
  Author of *The Little Elixir and OTP Guidebook*

Testing Elixir is an incredible resource for developers of all skill levels. Whether you are beginning your Elixir journey and are designing your first test suite or are an experienced Elixir developer looking for reference material, there is something here for you. This book breaks down a wide range of testing concepts into modular chunks so that you can grab what you need and be on your merry, happily tested way.

➤ **Sundi Myint**
  Co-Host of the *Elixir Wizards* Podcast and Developer, Smart Logic

This is exactly the book that was missing in the Elixir community. It introduces its readers to various testing methodologies from an Elixir lens as well as when to use them. It is loaded with code examples and detailed explanations. A must read!

➤ **Adi Iyengar**
  Back-End Engineer

I would recommend this book to anyone who wants to go beyond basic unit tests. It covers all areas of Elixir apps with examples and information about libraries to leverage in testing.

➤ **Todd Resudek**
  Hex Core Team Member

Testing Elixir

Effective and Robust Testing for Elixir and its Ecosystem

Andrea Leopardi

Jeffrey Matthias

The Pragmatic Bookshelf

Raleigh, North Carolina

For our complete catalog of hands-on, practical, and Pragmatic content for software developers, please visit *https://pragprog.com*.

The team that produced this book includes:

CEO: Dave Rankin
COO: Janet Furlow
Managing Editor: Tammy Coron
Series Editor: Bruce A. Tate
Development Editor: Jacquelyn Carter
Copy Editor: Molly McBeath
Indexing: Potomac Indexing, LLC
Layout: Gilson Graphics
Founders: Andy Hunt and Dave Thomas

For sales, volume licensing, and support, please contact *support@pragprog.com*.

For international rights, please contact *rights@pragprog.com*.

Contents

Acknowledgments

Books don't get published without people reviewing them first. We're deeply grateful to all the folks who spent their time and effort carefully reading and reviewing this book. Thank you to Amos King, Ayomide Aregbede, Devon Estes, Doyle Turner, Geoff Smith, Jonathan Carstens, Justin Smestad, Pedro Medeiros, Solomon White, Todd Resudek, and Zach Thomas.

A special thank you goes to Karl Matthias, who provided thorough and thoughtful comments that challenged our assumptions and pushed us to rethink, reshape, and reword concepts and sentences all over the book. The book's quality wouldn't have been the same without Karl's input.

Another special thank you goes to Kim Shrier, whose reviews were so detailed and neatly organized that it made addressing his comments a breeze.

Most importantly, this book would never have gotten to print without the guidance (and patience) of our Development editor, Jackie Carter. Thank you.

Andrea Leopardi

The biggest thank you goes to the most important person in my life, my wife, Kristina. I can't imagine any other human being so full of support and encouragement. You're the light of my life.

Thank you to my parents for setting up a life for me that made it possible for me to write a book about something. That's pretty crazy. Thank you to my other family, Contrada Cavalli, for filling that life with enough love and fun to give me the energy to learn, work, grow, and write this book.

Thank you to José Valim for creating a beautiful programming language that works the same way my mind does. José, you have been (possibly without even knowing it) an incredible mentor in my career, both in programming as well as in interacting with people.

Thank you to everyone at Community.com who supported me and gave me time and mental space to work on this book while giving me chance after chance to learn and grow professionally.

Thank you to Jeffrey for dragging me into this adventure. You were a friend before this book, but now we share something that will, if you think about it, outlive both of us. Spooky but pretty cool.

Jeffrey Matthias

Before I ever started on this book, several people helped set me up for success. Josh Kaiser and Ted Coleman gave me a trial by fire, making me the testing expert for our team only months into my career. That formed the foundation of everything that I know. Bradley Smith gave me my first opportunity to get paid to work in Elixir and taught me a lot of the foundation of my software knowledge, as well as tolerated my insistence on testing all the things.

I'm thankful to Ben Tan for helping me catch the Elixir bug in 2014 and then years later for supporting me in getting this book out, from pitch to final feedback. Moxley Stratton planted some seeds in my head that showed up as content in this book. The Denver Erlang and Elixir meetup has endured more testing talks than any group should have to. John Unruh deserves a special callout for providing plentiful, helpful feedback as a beta reader.

Getting through this book while working at a quickly growing startup turned out to be a team effort in a lot of ways. I'm grateful to everyone at Community.com. Matt Peltier and Josh Rosenheck created an awesome place to work and supported me from the day I was hired. Tomas Koci and Barry Steinglass consistently made time for me to write. Joe Merriweather-Webb has served as a partner to develop a lot of my Elixir testing techniques. Roland Tritsch helped me climb out of burnout, prioritize the book, and get it over the finish line. Every member of every team I've worked with has worked around my schedule. You're all the coolest.

Thanks to my co-author, Andrea, who let me talk him into this project. I'm glad we're still friends.

My parents have supported me through so many career changes that they likely have whiplash. Thanks for sticking with me until I found one where I am constantly learning and able to give back.

My older brother, Karl, has had an outsized impact. After getting me into software in the first place, he's supported me throughout my career. He inspired me to write a book and then gave me lots of feedback and encouragement the whole way through.

Most of all I want to thank my wife, Amy, and my kids, Noe and Brock, who have been the most patient and supportive of all.

Introduction

Charles Kettering, an American inventor and the longtime head of research for General Motors, has a quote that applies well to our approach to software tests:

> A problem well stated is a problem half-solved.

Think of your tests as stating the problem that your code solves. Once that's done, writing that code becomes easier. Moreover, tests not only state the problem, but they also *verify* that the solution is correct. They're an almost indispensable part of software engineering, and we believe it's important to understand why and how to use them.

Some developers write tests for their software. Some developers don't. There is code running all over the world that doesn't have a single test behind it. So, why do we test? We do it for a plethora of reasons, but they fit into just a few categories.

First of all, we test to increase confidence that our software does what it's supposed to do. Testing gives us *confidence* that our code works as expected. This is true for all kinds of testing, whether for automated tests performed by a machine or for manual tests performed by a human.

The other main reason for testing is to *prevent breaking changes* (also called *regressions*). Imagine you have an existing codebase that you have to work on in order to add a new feature. How can you feel confident that adding the new feature won't break any of the existing features? In most cases, testing is the answer. If the existing codebase is well tested (automated, manual, or both), then you'll feel safer making changes if the testing suite reveals that nothing broke.

In this book we'll focus on *automated testing*. Manual testing, such as QA (Quality Assurance), is fundamental for many reasons, but as developers we often get more value from automated testing. A good automated test suite allows us to have a fast feedback cycle during development and gives us tight control over how we test specific parts of our applications.

Why Do We Need a Book for Testing in Elixir?

Elixir is an interesting and fairly unique programming language. It provides features and concepts that can be hard to test if you've never dealt with anything like them. Some of those features are common in other programming languages but are more prominent in Elixir (and Erlang), such as concurrency and immutability. Other features, such as resiliency or the OTP framework, are more unique to Erlang and Elixir and can be challenging to test effectively.

From a more practical perspective, Elixir is a great language to write a testing book about because the tools and patterns we use when testing Elixir code are pretty consolidated in the Elixir community. One reason for this is that Elixir comes equipped with its own testing framework, *ExUnit*. We'll explore ExUnit inside and out and we'll learn how to use it in many different situations in order to test our applications on different levels.

Elixir is closely tied to its "parent" language, Erlang. As you likely know, Elixir compiles to the same bytecode as Erlang and runs on the Erlang virtual machine (commonly known as the *BEAM*). Elixir code often seamlessly calls out to Erlang code, and Elixir applications almost always depend on a few Erlang libraries. However, testing seems to be an area where the two languages have a bit less in common. The sets of tools and libraries used by the two languages don't intersect much. For these reasons, we won't really talk about testing in Erlang and will focus exclusively on testing in Elixir. We feel this statement is worth clarifying since the two languages are so close to each other.

Who This Book Is For

This book was written for people with a basic Elixir background who want to get better at the testing tools and practices in the Elixir ecosystem. We will skim over most Elixir concepts, such as the language constructs and data types, OTP, Ecto, and Phoenix. Instead of covering those, we'll learn how to *test* those concepts and tools. Whether you've used Elixir just for a bit or you're an Elixir expert, we think you'll learn a few new things throughout the book.

How to Read This Book

Each chapter in the book addresses a different aspect of testing in Elixir.

In Chapter 1, Unit Tests, on page 1, we'll get going and learn about the "smallest" kind of testing: unit testing. We will cover how and when to write unit tests, the tools to write them in Elixir, and techniques to isolate code under test.

In Chapter 2, Integration and End-to-End Tests, on page 35, we'll move on to testing different components of your system that interact with each other. We'll learn how to test components together, as well as how to isolate components to run more focused integration tests. We'll also touch on end-to-end testing, that is, testing the whole system from the perspective of an outside entity.

In Chapter 3, Testing OTP, on page 67, we'll learn about testing one of Erlang and Elixir's most unique features, OTP. OTP and processes in general present quite a few challenges when it comes to testing. We're going to talk about those and learn techniques to make testing these abstractions easier.

In Chapter 4, Testing Ecto Schemas, on page 101, and Chapter 5, Testing Ecto Queries, on page 141, we'll talk about testing code that uses the Ecto framework to validate data and interact with databases. Ecto is a widely used library in the Elixir landscape, and the community has created patterns on how to test code that makes use of it.

In Chapter 6, Testing Phoenix, on page 155, we'll cover Elixir's most used web framework, Phoenix. Phoenix provides several moving pieces. We'll learn how to test those pieces in isolation as well as how to test that the pieces of your Phoenix application work correctly together.

In the last chapter, Chapter 7, Property-Based Testing, on page 187, we'll explore a technique for introducing randomness in your testing suite in order to cover large amounts of inputs to your code and increase the chances of finding inconsistencies.

Note: The chapters in the book don't have to be read in the order they're laid out. For example, if you're particularly interested in testing code that uses the Ecto framework, you can jump directly to Chapter 4, Testing Ecto Schemas, on page 101. Most chapters are self-contained. However, we recommend that you read Chapter 1, Unit Tests, on page 1, and Chapter 2, Integration and End-to-End Tests, on page 35, in order: these chapters lay the foundations for the terminology, tools, and techniques that we'll use throughout the book.

About the Code

A testing book is a strange beast. Most programming books show "application code" when discussing examples and often omit or give little attention to tests. In this book, we want to focus on testing, but we need application code since there's no point in testing if you don't have anything to test. At the same time, we don't want to focus on the application code since it would take away from what we want to talk about, which is testing. As we said, it's a strange beast.

Throughout the book we'll work on two main applications. In the first three chapters, Chapter 1, Unit Tests, on page 1, Chapter 2, Integration and End-to-End Tests, on page 35, and Chapter 3, Testing OTP, on page 67, we'll work on Soggy Waffle. Soggy Waffle is an application that reads the weather forecast for a given area off the Internet and can send SMS alerts in case rain is expected in the next few hours. It's not a broadly useful application, but it helps illustrate many Elixir testing concepts.

In the next two chapters, Chapter 4, Testing Ecto Schemas, on page 101, and Chapter 5, Testing Ecto Queries, on page 141, we'll use a very basic application, called Testing Ecto, to illustrate how to test applications that use the Ecto framework.

Chapter 6, Testing Phoenix, on page 155, will have a single application with examples covering the different interfaces provided in the standard Phoenix library.

The last chapter, Chapter 7, Property-Based Testing, on page 187, won't follow a particular application in order to focus on different concepts related to property-based testing.

We'll have to continuously "escape" these applications over and over again. We made this choice because our focus is testing, and many times we would have had to come up with artificial and forced features for these applications in order to talk about some testing topic. In those cases, we'll just go with self-contained examples that allow us to directly address some testing topics without making our main application a total mess.

Online Resources

You can get the code from the book page on the Pragmatic Bookshelf website.[1] We hope that when you find errors or think of suggestions that you'll report them via the book's errata page.[2]

One online resource we highly recommend is Elixir's excellent documentation. You can find that on Elixir's official website.[3] Particularly interesting for this book is the ExUnit documentation since we'll get to use ExUnit a lot.[4]

If you like the book, we hope you'll take the time to let others know about it. Reviews matter, and one tweet or post from you is worth ten of ours! We're both on Twitter and tweet regularly. Jeffrey's handle is @idlehands and Andrea's is @whatyouhide.[5] [6] You can also drop notes to @pragprog.[7]

Andrea Leopardi and Jeffrey Matthias
July 2021

---

1. https://pragprog.com/book/lmelixir
2. https://pragprog.com/titles/lmelixir/errata
3. https://elixir-lang.org
4. https://hexdocs.pm/ex_unit/ExUnit.html
5. https://twitter.com/idlehands
6. https://twitter.com/whatyouhide
7. https://twitter.com/pragprog

CHAPTER 1

Unit Tests

For most engineers, the testing experience starts with the unit test. Unit tests are the easiest to write since they have a limited focus and therefore usually deal with less complexity than tests that involve large portions of an application, such as integration tests. While unit tests are less complicated, the testing tools and skills we use for them form the basis for all testing, making unit tests the perfect place to start our exploration.

A lot of engineers coming to Elixir have experience with unit testing in some other language with various testing frameworks. Most of that experience transfers over pretty well to Elixir, but implementing some of the concepts in Elixir can be a little different. For example, stubbing, a technique common in interpreted languages is more complex in Elixir, which is compiled. The functional nature of Elixir allows us to open up the definition of what constitutes a "unit," giving us new flexibility in our test design.

The ExUnit tools we use in unit tests are the basis of all of our testing. While integration tests may introduce additional tooling, all of our tests will still be structured similarly to unit tests and use the same assertions. In this chapter, we're going to learn how to define the scope of our tests, write tests for functional code, learn how to structure a test file, and then explore some ways to isolate your code under test.

By the end of the chapter, you'll have a better idea of how to write unit tests in Elixir and will understand how to organize both your application and test code in ways that make it easier to maintain and write effective tests. You'll have a better understanding of how your code organization impacts testing, and you'll start to build a sense of how to define the scope of your unit tests. These skills will transfer to all the tests you write for your Elixir code.

The first thing we need to cover is the scope of a unit test. Since the beginning of software tests, engineers have been discussing how to define the scope of these tests.

Why We Didn't Test-Drive in This Book

Test-driven development, often called TDD, is a development practice that suggests that you write your tests first, have them fail since you haven't implemented your code yet, and then run them continuously as you write your code until those tests pass. It's a common technique that we often like to use. However, we won't practice TDD in this book. Since the focus of our book is testing, we won't pay much attention to the application code, and we'll only use the application code in order to provide context for testing concepts. TDD conflicts with this: if we wanted to practice TDD, we'd have to start with writing the tests but then write the application code in order to make them pass. Instead, we'll usually show you some application code that we already wrote and then you'll write the tests for that code alongside us.

Defining the Unit in Unit Test

A unit test is a software test that focuses on a subset of an application, often removing the overarching context for how the code is used. It's common to find a unit test focused on a single function and just the logic in that function, possibly encapsulating private functions available to it. Sometimes it makes more sense to include code from multiple modules, or processes, inside the scope of your unit tests, expanding the scope of the "unit." Keeping a narrow scope can be beneficial to finding errors faster, but learning when it makes sense to expand the scope can greatly reduce the complexity of your codebase and your tests. If the scope of your unit tests, the unit itself, can be expanded slightly to include other modules, your tests can sometimes end up being simpler and easier to maintain while still providing all the benefits of a traditional, narrowly scoped unit test.

Before we dive into when and how to expand the scope of your unit tests, let's touch on why we test. We need to keep four goals in mind when designing our tests:

- Prove that your code does what it's supposed to do.
- Prevent breaking changes (regressions).
- Make it easy to find where your code is broken.
- Write the least amount of test code possible.

It's likely you're already on board with the first two goals. However, the last two goals are what will guide you in choosing how much of your code should constitute the unit in the scope of your tests. Your tests should draw a *black box* around the code in their scope, which we'll call the code under test or the application code. This black box defines the places where your test code interacts with your application code. In the case of a unit test, this black box would often treat a single function as the unit. The advantage of keeping the scope narrow is that if the code under test has issues, keeping the scope small helps you quickly identify where the issue is. The downside to a narrow scope is that often, in order to isolate the code under test, you need to write more code in your tests, which can make it hard to follow what's happening. Allowing your test scope (black box) to include a well-tested, functional dependency can help you take advantage of the narrow scope while avoiding some of the steps of isolating the code that uses that dependency.

Your tests need to interact with the code under test in two ways. The first is the more obvious one: your test will call a function (or send a message) with parameters and it will get a return value. The second is more complex. Your tests might need to intercept the calls out and return responses, stepping in for a dependency, if your code depends on other code in your codebase. We call this "isolating your code under test." We will cover isolating code later in this chapter, but first we'll look at when we can get away without strict isolation. The following diagram shows the black box drawn around the code under test.

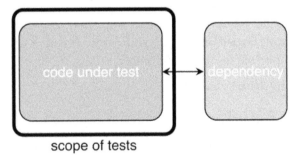

scope of tests

Because the code under test depends on other code in the codebase, the tests will have to address isolating the code. There are different methods of isolating code, but all of them come with costs, typically in terms of time and test complexity. The presence of *purely functional* code can impact what needs to be isolated. A function is "pure" if it returns the exact same answer and has no side effects every single time you call the function with the same parameters. We'll expand on this later in this chapter. When your dependency is purely functional and well tested on its own, you can expand your black box to include that dependency, as seen in the diagram shown on page 4.

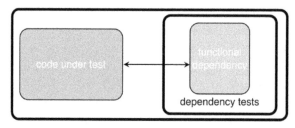

scope of tests

Expanding the black box allows us to skip the extra work of isolating your code while not giving up the ability to easily locate your broken code. Your tests are still narrowly focused on the code under test, and—because your code is purely functional—the environment in which you're testing your code is completely controlled, preventing inconsistent results. When you're able to include dependencies in this fashion, your tests are easier to write, understand, and maintain. Because your dependency is tested on its own, you can write less test code while still being able to identify where your code is broken when a test fails. If your dependency's tests don't fail but you have failures in the tests where you pulled it in, you know that your failures are in the new code and not in your dependency.

The challenge is finding the balance for when you should include your purely functional dependencies in your test scope. Tuning this sense will take some trial and error and learning from pain points. Start off by expanding your black box to include those dependencies and then tighten the scope if you find yourself having issues debugging your code. Practice will help you hone your sense of when this is the right choice.

Now, let's learn to write some tests.

Testing with ExUnit

From the beginning, Elixir was developed with ExUnit, the test framework, as part of the core library. As a result, most of the test tooling we've come to utilize in our production applications is straight out of the Elixir core. This means that if you have Elixir and you're familiar with what's available, you can write effective tests without needing to bring in other libraries.

To learn how to use ExUnit, we're going to start by writing our first test and then discuss some test theory, specifically the stages of testing. We'll look at how to organize test files and then explore using common Elixir to help maximize the effectiveness of our tests. Finally, we'll cover how to design code so that it's well organized and easy to test.

Our First Test

Let's write our first test in our rain alert app, Soggy Waffle. Soggy Waffle makes calls to an API and gets data back from it. It then standardizes the data to its own terms and data structures for the rest of the application to use. While those calls out to the API aren't something we'll focus on in this chapter (but will in *Integration and End-to-End Tests*), the response transformation is a great example of code that can be tested in isolation. Let's look at the code that we'll be testing.

We have included a copy of Soggy Waffle in the code with this book. Most of the application files we'll show in this chapter are from that code. The example test files in Soggy Waffle have the extension .bak.exs so that they won't run when you run your tests, but they're there for reference. If you want to code along with the examples, you should do so inside of the provided Soggy Waffle application, adding test files in the locations we indicate before the examples.

In theory, Soggy Waffle could work with any weather API as long as it returns a timestamp and the weather conditions for that timestamp. As a best practice, our application translates the API response into a list of SoggyWaffle.Weather structs that it defines in lib/soggy_waffle/weather.ex with two fields, one for the timestamp, datetime, and one for whether or not the weather condition translates to rain.

This means that our ResponseParser module will hold a lot of information specific to the API we choose; in this case, that's openweathermap.org. Notice the module attributes in the code as well as the comment about where that information came from.

unit_tests/soggy_waffle/lib/soggy_waffle/weather_api/response_parser.ex
```elixir
defmodule SoggyWaffle.WeatherAPI.ResponseParser do
  alias SoggyWaffle.Weather

  @thunderstorm_ids [200, 201, 202, 210, 211, 212, 221, 230, 231, 232]
  @drizzle_ids [300, 301, 302, 310, 311, 312, 313, 314, 321]
  @rain_ids [500, 501, 502, 503, 504, 511, 520, 521, 522, 531]
  @all_rain_ids @thunderstorm_ids ++ @drizzle_ids ++ @rain_ids

  @spec parse_response(Weather.t()) ::
          {:ok, list(Weather.t())} | {:error, atom()}
  def parse_response(response) do
    results = response["list"]

    Enum.reduce_while(results, {:ok, []}, fn
      %{"dt" => datetime, "weather" => [%{"id" => condition_id}]},
      {:ok, weather_list} ->
        # possible weather codes: https://openweathermap.org/weather-conditions
```

```
        new_weather = %Weather{
          datetime: DateTime.from_unix!(datetime),
          rain?: condition_id in @all_rain_ids
        }

        {:cont, {:ok, [new_weather | weather_list]}}

      _anything_else, _acc ->
        {:halt, {:error, :response_format_invalid}}
    end)
  end
end
```

Our test will need to pass in a response that's shaped like data from the API, and it'll expect the response data to be in the shape of a list of SoggyWaffle.Weather structs that it's defined.

Now let's open up a new test file at test/soggy_waffle/weather_api/response_parser_test.exs in the provided Soggy Waffle code and start writing our first test! Copy the code below into your file.

unit_tests/soggy_waffle_examples/weather_api/response_parser_test.exs

```
Line 1  defmodule SoggyWaffle.WeatherAPI.ResponseParserTest do
          use ExUnit.Case
          alias SoggyWaffle.WeatherAPI.ResponseParser
          alias SoggyWaffle.Weather
   5
          describe "parse_response/1" do
            test "success: accepts a valid payload, returns a list of structs" do
              api_response = %{
                "list" => [
  10              %{"dt" => 1_574_359_200, "weather" => [%{"id" => 600}]},
                  %{"dt" => 1_574_359_900, "weather" => [%{"id" => 299}]}
                ]
              }

  15          assert {:ok, parsed_response} =
                       ResponseParser.parse_response(api_response)

              for weather_record <- parsed_response do
                assert match?(
  20                   %Weather{datetime: %DateTime{}, rain?: _rain},
                       weather_record
                     )

                assert is_boolean(weather_record.rain?)
  25            end
            end
          end
        end
```

This is a pretty basic test, but already a good bit is going on. An assert macro is being called (line 15), and there are assertions inside of a list comprehension (line 18). Let's look at each piece separately.

Functions vs. Macros

 The ExUnit tools are a mixture of macros and functions. From your perspective, you're safe to think of them all as functions, but we've tried to be accurate when describing any specific code. For more information on macros, check out the section in Elixir's Getting Started guide on macros.[1]

The assert call at line 15 works because if the function evaluates to true or something "truthy," the assert will pass. In our case, we're handing it a pattern match. If a pattern match is successful, it returns the data that matched the pattern, which is "truthy." ExUnit also provides the opposite, refute, which will only pass if the expression it's given as a parameter evaluates to false or nil. Be careful, though, as refute doesn't work with a pattern match in the way you'd expect. If a pattern doesn't match, a MatchError is raised. We'll find a way to handle this, if needed, shortly. Also, don't make the common mistake of thinking refute will pass with an empty list (refute []). refute will only pass if the expression it's given evaluates to false or nil. [] is empty, but it's still a list. If you want to assert that a list is empty, use Enum.empty?/1.

The last part for us to look at is the list comprehension at line 18. A couple of things going on here are worth noting. The first is the comprehension itself. The use of a list comprehension here means that we want to apply the same assertions to multiple pieces of data. An Enum.each would work just as well here and the choice of a list comprehension is purely a style choice in this case. Using a list comprehension implies an assertion about the shape of our response—that it's enumerable. If the result can't be iterated through, the test will raise a Protocol.UndefinedError, revealing the bad value. The single element pattern in our anonymous function implies, more specifically, that the response is a list. If our code returned something that couldn't be iterated through, the test would fail with a Protocol.UndefinedError.

Let's now look at the assertions inside the code block. The first one is passing match?(%Weather{datetime: %DateTime{}, rain?: _rain}, weather_record) to assert. match?/2 is the other way of asserting on a pattern match. If you want to use refute with pattern matching, this is how you would do it. Even though match? doesn't bind a value like using = would, you'll still get a compile warning if you don't

---

1. https://elixir-lang.org/getting-started/meta/macros.html

use an _ before the variable in the pattern. This assertion is focused solely on the shape of the data and not on the values provided. Our parser is doing more than one thing, and it's often a best practice to split testing of different responsibilities into multiple tests. If you have a failure in your tests, this approach will lead you to the failing code faster.

The second assertion in the block, assert is_boolean(weather_record.rain?), is still focused on the shape of the data and not on a specific value because converting weather IDs is additional functionality. Unit tests are typically quick to run, and keeping them focused on a single aspect of your code can make finding errors faster and easier. That's OK because we'll add other tests shortly that will focus on specific values in the response.

Our next step is to run the test and see what happens. At the root level of the application, run mix test and look for the response. If the test is written correctly, it'll pass and you'll see a lovely dot representing a passed test. If the test doesn't pass, it's likely that you have a typo somewhere. The errors produced should guide you toward your mistake.

We mentioned before that we'd be adding more tests. But before we do, let's dive into some terminology so that we're set up for success throughout the rest of the book.

Running Tests Without Mix

 While ExUnit works without utilizing Mix, it's very unlikely that you'll find yourself writing many, if any, tests outside of a Mix application. As a result, we'll focus on using Mix and the test flow that it entails.

Anatomy of a Test

As we begin our journey into the land of unit tests, let's establish some basic vocabulary and test theory. Software tests, no matter how complicated they are, are comprised of no more than four stages. They have different names depending on who you ask, so in this book we'll use *setup, exercise, verify,* and *teardown.* Simple tests may only have two of these stages; complex ones might have cycles that repeat phases. Sometimes the order isn't straightforward, but every test can be broken down into these four stages. Let's take a look at each one individually in the order that they "normally" occur.

Depending on the scope of the test, setup can be as simple as preparing data to pass in as parameters to the code under test or it can mean staging data in some sort of shared state, like a database. This stage is very common; but when testing purely functional code, setup is often not needed.

The exercise phase is always present. This is the call to run the code under test. Without it, there'd be nothing to do.

Your tests make their assertions about the behavior of your code during the verify phase. While sometimes inline with the exercise step, the verify stage is always present in a test. Without verifying that your code behaves a certain way, well, your tests would be pointless.

If your setup phase involved any impact on shared state, you'll need to return things to how they were beforehand during the teardown phase. If there's no shared state, like for a database, then this stage isn't necessary. Often tools are used to take care of this step automatically, like Ecto's sandbox, but that doesn't mean this step doesn't happen. Often when there are "random" test failures, it's because a test did not properly tear down the data that was set up.

We mentioned that the order of the stages isn't guaranteed to be setup, exercise, verify, and teardown. Sometimes test code has to be written in a different order than it is executed in. The most common case for this is when a test double (a concept we'll cover later) is used. If that test double utilizes assertions, the code defining it will have to be written *before* the exercise step, even though the actual assertions won't be executed until *after* the exercise step.

Earlier, we stated that complex tests may actually repeat some of these stages. When you're working in unit tests, a sign that your test might be doing too much is if you see a second (or later) recurrence of a phase. User interface tests, though, might need to have repeated stages, mirroring successive steps through a user's experience. We will cover that kind of testing in Chapter 6, Testing Phoenix, on page 155. Within the context of this chapter, and of unit tests, you can think of tests having each stage only once.

Now let's look into how to structure your tests and what tools ExUnit provides to help organize tests, group them, and make your test suite easier to maintain.

Organizing Your Tests

As well as making sure our code works, our test suite serves a secondary purpose. If written well, it becomes a source of documentation for our code, with text descriptions of how we expect the code to work and working examples of how to exercise the code. This sounds like a lofty goal, but with a little organization, it's entirely achievable. Imagine a *future you* looking back at code that you haven't seen in months and trying to remember how it works and how to use it. The more organized your test suite is, the more *future you* will love *past you* for reducing the complexity of this challenge. That alone can serve as motivation to think about the overall design of your tests. Fortunately, ExUnit ships with some useful functions (and macros) that allow us to organize an individual file in a way that's readable and maintainable.

As we build more and more complicated tests, you'll see these organizational tools showing up in our examples. Let's start by looking at those tools and code examples and how you can use them to keep your test suite easier to read and maintain.

Describing Your Tests

While it's possible to have a readable test file with a flat organizational structure, ExUnit gives us a good tool for grouping tests together within a file, describe. This tool allows us to pass a description for the grouping and, as we'll discover shortly, to group tests that share a common setup. It's important to note that, unlike some other testing frameworks, the creators of ExUnit made the decision to only allow one level of grouping, so you can't nest describe blocks. While this may seem counterintuitive at first, it strikes a healthy balance between organizing your tests and avoiding a nesting nightmare for setup.

As a general guideline, grouping your tests by function is a good place to start, as laid out in the following example:

```
unit_tests/misc/describe.exs
defmodule YourApp.YourModuleTest do
  use ExUnit.Case

  describe "thing_to_do/1" do
    test "it returns :ok, calls the function if the key is correct"
    test "it does not call the function if the key is wrong"
  end
end
```

You might have noticed that the description includes a /1 to denote arity (the number of parameters the function takes). This is a style choice. You may group your tests however you feel is most logical. Later in this book, when we tackle integration tests, you may group your tests by something like the endpoint they're hitting. The point is to make it easier to read your tests so you (and your collaborators) can decide what makes the most sense. One guide that can help drive your design is whether or not your functions have a common setup.

Setup Blocks

While an individual test can contain its own setup code, sometimes you realize you're writing the same setup over and over. This situation is an opportunity to consider a setup block instead. The code in a setup block will be executed before each test inside of its scope. Since the code has the same name as the stage in the test design, we'll call the executable code a *setup block* while referring to the stage of testing as *setup*.

A setup block needs to return a value that makes sense for what comes after it. If the setup is to set state elsewhere and none of the values are useful in the tests following it, the return value can be as simple as :ok. More often, the return value from a setup block is passed to the tests it precedes. As Elixir and ExUnit have matured, the common practice has become to have your setup return a map of values that can be used in the subsequent test. When testing purely functional code, this is often the only time you would use a setup block, since there's no shared state to set up. Let's look at an example of a setup block where no state is changed but we've decided that we don't want to redefine the same anonymous functions for each test.

unit_tests/misc/callbacks.exs
```
setup do
  function_to_not_call = fn ->
    flunk("this function should not have been called")
  end

  function_to_call = fn -> send(self(), :function_called) end

  %{bad_function: function_to_not_call, good_function: function_to_call}
end
```

Remember that when you pull logic into a setup block, it makes it a little harder to read an individual test. Not every value in your setup will be used in every test, but if you're pulling a value into your setup block, it should be used in multiple tests. In the preceding example, it's very unlikely that both the bad function and the good function would ever be used in the same tests, since one is used for success cases and the other for failure cases, but since each is going to be used by multiple tests, they're both worth pulling into the common setup.

Accepting values from a setup in your tests requires a slight modification to your test definition:

```
unit_tests/misc/callbacks.exs
test "does not call the function if the key is wrong",
    %{bad_function: bad_function} do
  assert {:error, _} =
          YourModule.thing_to_do(:bad_first_arg, bad_function)
end
```

Adding a pattern as a second parameter to your test allows you to pull in anything passed from the setup. If you have too many things being passed in so that destructuring the map makes your test unreadable, you can always just use a variable and pull what you need from it when you need it.

```
unit_tests/misc/callbacks.exs
test "does not call the function if the key is wrong", context do
  assert {:error, _} =
          YourModule.thing_to_do(:bad_first_arg, context.bad_function)
end
```

Choosing What to Move Into Common Setup

 It can be easy to overreach on what code should be moved into your setup. If you move too much into a common block, the purpose of an individual test is hard to understand. You can avoid this by choosing names that describe the things that you're accepting from the setup block. Instead of user, your variable could be named user_with_completed_profile. Sometimes a long name can save a lot of work for those who come after you.

The scope of your setup is set by the logical grouping of your tests. If your setup is inside of a describe, it'll be run before the tests grouped inside of that describe. If it's at the top of your test file—outside of any describes—it'll be run before all the tests in that file.

Your setups can build on top of each other. If you have a setup that's common to an entire file but also need a setup for your describe block, the setup in your describe can accept values passed to it from the higher-up describe by adding a pattern to the test's parameters.

```
setup context do
  additional_value = "example value"

  Map.merge(context, %{additional_value: additional_value})
end
```

Adding a pattern can be helpful, but be careful that you're selectively choosing what should be moved into the higher-level setup block, since you're starting to spread the logic needed to understand each test to several different areas of your file. There's a lot of value in being able to read and understand a single test without having to look in different places in the file or codebase.

Later we'll discuss test cases, another construct to help reduce duplication in your code. They provide an additional layer of setup, this time across multiple test files. Because that setup is defined *outside* of your current test file, it's definitely worth taking the time to consider how to organize your tests to make sure that everything is easy to follow. Even without nested describe blocks, we're getting close to a readability and maintenance nightmare if we don't think about that balance when organizing our tests.

One other feature of setup can help maintain clarity in your tests while still reducing duplication in your individual tests or multiple setups: setup can accept the name of a function or a list of function names instead of a block. Those functions should conform to a pattern that accepts the existing context (the data passed by previous setup blocks or functions) and returns an updated context so that they can be piped. As you can see in the following example, with_authenticated_user/1 expects a map of the data from previous setup functions, adds more data to that map, and then returns that map.

```
unit_tests/misc/setup_with_helper_functions.exs
def with_authenticated_user(context) do
  user = User.create(%{name: "Bob Robertson"})
  authenticated_user = TestHelper.authenticate(user)

  Map.put(context, :authenticated_user, authenticated_user)
end
```

If you have defined functions that follow that pattern, you can pass a list to setup of the functions to execute:

```
unit_tests/misc/setup_with_helper_functions.exs
setup [:create_organization, :with_admin, :with_authenticated_user]
```

The functions are executed in the order they're listed. This allows you to reuse the same logic in different setup scopes and to keep your setup logic closer (in the file) to where it's being used. This functionality is intended to remove the need for nested describe blocks. As you use it, you'll find it to be a fairly elegant solution.

While setup is the right solution for most scenarios, a couple of additional functions can help organize your tests.

setup_all

Often you need a setup step, but you don't need to repeat it before each test. If your tests will work just fine with those steps being executed just one time for the whole file, you can use setup_all. Except for how often it's run, setup_all works just like setup, meaning that it can be used with a list of functions, a block of code, or a pattern for the context and a block of code. The return should match the pattern you've set up for the rest of your setup functions.

```
unit_tests/misc/callbacks.exs
setup_all do
  function_to_not_call = fn ->
    flunk("this function should not have been called")
  end

  function_to_call = fn -> send(self(), :function_called) end

  %{bad_function: function_to_not_call, good_function: function_to_call}
end
```

Our example isn't doing anything that needs to be repeated for every call. The functions we define won't change between the different tests. As a result, this block is a good candidate for setup_all. Situations where setup_all is not the correct solution include anything time-based where you need a new timestamp for each test, or a setup for tests that require shared state and then alter that state, which would leave it unusable for the next test. While we won't cover it in this chapter, tests that involve a data store are a good example of the latter. When you use both, setup_all will be called first, and the context that it returns will be passed into setup before being passed onto the test. For more about the ordering and the test life cycle, check out Appendix 2, Test Life Cycle, on page 221.

on_exit

We've covered the setup phase of testing and the tools that allow us to reduce setup repetition. But ExUnit also provides us with an on_exit callback that lets us organize the teardown stage in a similar way. This callback can be defined inside your setup block or within an individual test.

```
unit_tests/misc/callbacks.exs
setup do
  file_name = "example.txt"
  :ok = File.write(file_name, "hello")

  on_exit(fn ->
    File.rm(file_name)
  end)

  %{file_name: file_name}
end
```

Notice that the return value of the setup is still the last line of the block. on_exit will return :ok, which is likely not useful for your setup. In this example, the setup has a return of the file name, giving the tests access to a file that's guaranteed to be there. As with all anonymous functions in Elixir, the function you pass to on_exit is a closure, so you can reference any variables defined before the function is defined.

on_exit is powerful because even if your test fails spectacularly, the anonymous function will still be executed. This helps guarantee the state of your test environment, no matter the outcome of an individual test. It isn't as common, but on_exit is available to you in an individual test as well. If you want to keep your setup inside of a single test but need the guarantee that your teardown will be done, no matter the test outcome, use on_exit.

Now that we have more tools for keeping our tests organized, we can jump back to writing more tests utilizing these organizational tools.

Where Are Doctests?

Elixir makes documentation a first-class citizen, something few other languages do. Anyone writing Elixir code is encouraged to add documentation to their public functions. Part of that functionality is doctests. While they have "test" in their name, they're actually a tool to make sure the examples in your documentation are up-to-date. We wholeheartedly encourage you to learn more about doctests, but we felt like they were out of scope for this book, given that doctests aren't part of your test suite and aren't focused on the behavior of your code but on the accuracy of your documentation. Elixir's Getting Started guide does a great job of explaining doctests in more detail if you want to dive deeper.[a]

---

a.   https://elixir-lang.org/getting-started/mix-otp/docs-tests-and-with.html#doctests

Creating Comprehensive Test Coverage

We've covered some of the very basics of testing and delved into a bit of test theory. In order to provide solid coverage of a file, we'll need to build on that knowledge by pulling in some features of Elixir itself, as well as some optional features of ExUnit's assertions. These skills will help you write maximum test coverage with minimal code and without trade-offs.

Using a Setup Block

Let's jump back to where we left our Soggy Waffle test, SoggyWaffle.WeatherAPI.ResponseParserTest. We'll make a modification to our existing test before adding some more tests to our response parser. The data we used in our test was hand-coded. That's a great way to start, but we don't own the original source of the data, the weather API. While it's easy to read the hard-coded data, it's actually a significantly pared down version of the real data from the weather API. It would be nice to be working with data that's as realistic as possible. To do this, we can use a fixture file. A simple curl call to the API can provide an actual JSON response payload. We've saved that to a file in the application, test/support/weather_api_response.json. Let's modify our test to use that data instead of the handwritten values we used earlier:

```
unit_tests/soggy_waffle_examples/test/soggy_waffle/weather_api/response_parser_test.exs
describe "parse_response/1" do
  setup_all do
    response_as_string =
      File.read!("test/support/weather_api_response.json")

    response_as_map = Jason.decode!(response_as_string)
    %{weather_data: response_as_map}
  end

  test "success: accepts a valid payload, returns a list of weather structs",
       %{weather_data: weather_data} do
    assert {:ok, parsed_response} =
             ResponseParser.parse_response(weather_data)

    for weather_record <- parsed_response do
      assert match?(
               %Weather{datetime: %DateTime{}, rain?: _rain},
               weather_record
             )

      assert is_boolean(weather_record.rain?)
    end
  end
end
```

Let's update our test to use a setup block (line 2). In the setup code, you'll see that we're reading the contents of a JSON file (line 3) and then decoding it to an Elixir map (line 6). This leaves us with data parsed just like it would have been by other parts of the application before being passed to ResponseParser.parse_response/1. We now have real data, so let's use it in the test.

Our test has been modified at line 11 to accept a test context. This is how the data gets from the setup block into the test. Note that we destructured the map so that we have immediate access to the variable, weather_data. After that, we need to remove the old data setup and replace the parameter in the exercise call with the new variable (line 12). Run mix test; because our test was focused on the shape of the data and not on specific values, it should pass.

There are trade-offs to writing our test this way. As mentioned earlier, we benefit from the comfort of knowing that our test data is as realistic as it gets. To get there, though, we've sacrificed some of the readability of our test. The data we're passing in is hidden in another file in JSON, a format that isn't as easy to read as a pared-down Elixir map. Additionally, to make the fixture data available to other tests, we've moved it into a setup block.

Setup blocks are wonderful for test organization and for preventing repetition in our test suite, but they remove some of the test setup from the test and move it to another part of the file. Anytime the logic of a test extends outside of the test itself, it's harder to read and understand. That said, like everything we do, we need to make a call on which way to go and which test design gives us the best balance of coverage and readability/maintainability.

Setting Module Attributes in Test Files

Now that our first test is using a fixture, we'll add tests that focus on specific values in the weather API response, meaning we won't use the fixture data because we don't know the specific values. Since the module under test (SoggyWaffle.WeatherAPI.ResponseParser) is focused on translating data specific to an external API into internal data, the module must have a lot of knowledge specific to that API. This shows up in the form of all the various weather condition IDs at the top of the module.

Our tests will have to have that same level of knowledge so that they can test the code thoroughly. This means adding a copy of all of the IDs to our test file. It may seem like a good idea to put them somewhere where both the test and the code under test can access them, but that's discouraged. Any accidental modifications to that list could cause our test to miss a needed case, allowing our code under test to make it to production with a bug. You should avoid using the Don't Repeat Yourself (DRY) principle when the instances are split between your tests and your code under test.[2]

In our case, we know that more than one test will likely make use of those lists of IDs, so we'll add them as module attributes to the top of the test file.

```
unit_tests/soggy_waffle_examples/test/soggy_waffle/weather_api/response_parser_test.exs
@thunderstorm_ids {
  "thunderstorm",
  [200, 201, 202, 210, 211, 212, 221, 230, 231, 232]
}
@drizzle_ids {"drizzle", [300, 301, 302, 310, 311, 312, 313, 314, 321]}
@rain_ids {"rain", [500, 501, 502, 503, 504, 511, 520, 521, 522, 531]}
```

---

2. https://en.wikipedia.org/wiki/Don%27t_repeat_yourself

Leveraging List Comprehensions

Are you ready for something wild? We're going to wrap our new test in a list comprehension. Add the following code to your test file and we'll step through it. Keep the first for at the same level of indentation as the test before it.

```
unit_tests/soggy_waffle_examples/test/soggy_waffle/weather_api/response_parser_test.exs
for {condition, ids} <- [@thunderstorm_ids, @drizzle_ids, @rain_ids] do
  test "success: recognizes #{condition} as a rainy condition" do
    now_unix = DateTime.utc_now() |> DateTime.to_unix()

    for id <- unquote(ids) do
      record = %{"dt" => now_unix, "weather" => [%{"id" => id}]}

      assert {:ok, [weather_struct]} =
               ResponseParser.parse_response(%{"list" => [record]})

      assert weather_struct.rain? == true
    end
  end
end
```

Once you've got the code in, run mix test to make sure that your tests are passing.

Before we talk about the list comprehension, let's look at the data that we're passing into the function at the exercise step. It's a hand-coded map. Now that we've tested that our code handles correctly shaped data by passing a real response, we can trust that if we pass in correctly shaped data, the code will work fine. The payload has been distilled to the parts that our code cares about: a map with "dt" and "weather" keys, with the ID nested in a list of maps under the "weather" key. Keeping the input payload so small will help us keep our tests easier to understand. Additionally, because we're defining the values inside our test file (and inside the test in this case), we're safe to make assertions on specific values without worrying about hard-to-maintain tests.

The list comprehension actually adds three new tests, one for each kind of weather condition that we're interested in: thunderstorms, drizzle, and rain. List comprehensions are useful when you have nearly identical tests but want your errors separated. You'll see that we had to use unquote,[3] a metaprogramming macro, to have access to the information inside the test. This can be especially confusing since it's not inside of a quote block, but it works and it's the only piece of metaprogramming we'll introduce in this book. You'll need

---

3.   https://hexdocs.pm/elixir/Kernel.SpecialForms.html#unquote/1

to have a way to provide a unique test name for each iteration, like the way we're using the condition in the test name. If any of these tests fail, the output from ExUnit will tell you which test it is, making it easier to hunt down the issue.

```
➤ 1) test parse_response/1 success: recognizes drizzle as a rainy condition
     (SoggyWaffle.WeatherAPI.ResponseParserTest)
   test/soggy_waffle/weather_api/response_parser_test.exs:32
```

Writing Custom Test Failure Messages

While list comprehensions allow us to cover more test cases with less test code, they run the risk of obfuscating your errors. If your test fails but you can't tell which values it was asserting against, you'll lose time having to debug the failure. In the test we just wrote, how would we know which ID we were testing when we had the wrong value of rain? Let's update that assertion to use a custom failure message:

```
unit_tests/soggy_waffle_examples/test/soggy_waffle/weather_api/response_parser_test.exs
Line 1 for {condition, ids} <- [@thunderstorm_ids, @drizzle_ids, @rain_ids] do
   2    test "success: recognizes #{condition} as a rainy condition" do
   3      # «test body»
   4
   5      assert weather_struct.rain? == true,
   6            "Expected weather id (#{id}) to be a rain condition"
   7    end
   8 end
```

Adding a custom error message with string interpolation (line 6) now gives us everything we need to know if the test fails. Having this information is very important because otherwise it'll be impossible to see which specific code caused the test to fail. When designing your tests, take time to make sure that the failure message points you straight at the issue. It doesn't take long, and you, or your teammates, will thank you later.

```
  1) test parse_response/1 success:
     recognizes drizzle as a rainy condition
     (SoggyWaffle.WeatherAPI.ResponseParserTest)
   test/soggy_waffle/weather_api/response_parser_test.exs:32
➤ Expected weather id (300) to be a rain condition
   code: for id <- unquote(ids) do
```

Covering All the Use Cases

While we will discuss property-based testing in a later chapter, we often don't need anything outside of ExUnit and Elixir to cover the rest of our cases. We've added a test for the conditions that will return true for rain, but now we need a test to make sure that no other codes will generate a true value. Add another test to your file with the following code:

```
unit_tests/soggy_waffle_examples/test/soggy_waffle/weather_api/response_parser_test.exs
test "success: returns rain?: false for any other id codes" do
  {_, thunderstorm_ids} = @thunderstorm_ids
  {_, drizzle_ids} = @drizzle_ids
  {_, rain_ids} = @rain_ids
  all_rain_ids = thunderstorm_ids ++ drizzle_ids ++ rain_ids
  now_unix = DateTime.utc_now() |> DateTime.to_unix()

  for id <- 100..900, id not in all_rain_ids do
    record = %{"dt" => now_unix, "weather" => [%{"id" => id}]}

    assert {:ok, [weather_struct]} =
             ResponseParser.parse_response(%{"list" => [record]})

    assert weather_struct.rain? == false,
           "Expected weather id (#{id}) to NOT be a rain condition."
  end
end
```

It's time for another test run (mix test) to make sure your tests are green. Running your tests regularly is always a good way to keep from getting too far down a rabbit hole before you realize you have a problem.

These tests are very thorough in that they test all possible positive values. We're able to do that because we have a known, finite list of rainy weather IDs. We don't have as comprehensive a list of non-rainy IDs. As a result, looking at the documentation from the API, we've narrowed the range of codes that we could get back to between 100 and 900. We're using a list comprehension again, but this time we're using the filter function of a list comprehension to, on the fly, build a list of all IDs between 100 and 900 *except* the ones we know to be rain IDs (line 8). Even though this means we're testing a lot of values, because our code is purely functional, the test will still run fairly quickly. We again gave ourselves a custom error message to make sure that if this test fails, we know the ID that caused the failure.

This test could have used a list comprehension in either of the ways we talked about (creating a new test or a new assertion for each value) and there are trade-offs with both. Generating a new test will remove the need for custom error messages, but it'll increase the actual number of tests that are run. It's up to you to decide which makes the most sense for you when you decide that a list comprehension is the appropriate tool to reach for.

Testing Error Cases

Every test we've written has focused on success cases. We add "success" and "error" to the beginning of our test names to help keep them sorted mentally, but that's a style choice in response to not being able to nest describe blocks in our tests. Now let's look at the places where our code might not return a success response, in this case due to bad input data. Since we want to test different functionality in separate tests, let's choose the malformed weather data.

Our application is fairly small and isn't intended for customer-facing production. If it were, we'd have more tests and would leverage Ecto Schema and Changeset functions. We'll cover examples of that in Chapter 4, Testing Ecto Schemas, on page 101. For now, we're going to add some basic coverage with the understanding that once you're done with this book, you'll have better tools to write even better validation tests for payloads. Add a new test inside the same describe block; but this time, it's an "error" test:

```
unit_tests/soggy_waffle_examples/test/soggy_waffle/weather_api/response_parser_test.exs
test "error: returns error if weather data is malformed" do
  malformed_day = %{
    "dt" => 1_574_359_200,
    "weather" => [
      %{
        "wrong_key" => 1
      }
    ]
  }

  almost_correct_response = %{"list" => [malformed_day]}

  assert {:error, :response_format_invalid} =
           ResponseParser.parse_response(almost_correct_response)
end
```

Run your tests again with mix test.

By comparison, this test is almost boring. It's able to be simple because we already have a test that asserts that if we pass good data to the code under test, the code parses it correctly. As a result, we just need to focus on one small thing, a missing "id" key. It's worth noting that, by choosing to name the bad key "wrong_key", we're making our test self-documenting. Small opportunities like this occur everywhere in your tests.

We'll add one more test to our file to cover a missing datetime in the payload. Add this one last test in that same describe block:

unit_tests/soggy_waffle_examples/test/soggy_waffle/weather_api/response_parser_test.exs

```
test "error: returns error if timestamp is missing" do
  malformed_day = %{
    # wrong key
    "datetime" => 1_574_359_200,
    "weather" => [
      %{
        "main" => 1
      }
    ]
  }

  almost_correct_response = %{"list" => [malformed_day]}

  assert {:error, :response_format_invalid} =
           ResponseParser.parse_response(almost_correct_response)
end
```

This test is almost identical to the previous test; but because it's testing a different part of the functionality of the code under test, we'll leave it as a separate test instead of finding a way to use a list comprehension to DRY them up. If you think about your tests as documentation, your test names are the top-level reference, and combining tests that aren't focused on the same thing removes some of your documentation.

Now that we've covered the anatomy of a test and written a comprehensive test file, it's time to start looking at how the design of our code impacts the design of our tests. We'll start by looking at testing purely functional code.

Testing Pure Functions

The simplest code to test is a pure function.[4] A function is "pure" if, every single time you call the function with the same parameters, it returns the exact same answer and if it has no side effects. If a dependency can change the result, the function is not pure. When testing a pure function, the test is able to focus on the data going in—the function parameters—and the response. That's it.

With pure functions, the only setup we need is to prepare the data for the parameters. The exercise step for the test is a function call, passing the input parameters. The verify stage is just assertions on the response, and only the response. There is no teardown because setup was only creating the parameters, which have no impact outside of the test. Let's take a look at some examples of tests on a pure function.

---

4.   https://en.wikipedia.org/wiki/Pure_function

The one function that we've tested so far, SoggyWaffle.WeatherAPI.ResponsePars-er.parse_response/1, is a pure function. Our tests never had to worry about side effects and they consistently get the same response from the code under test, no matter how many times they're run.

While testing pure functions is simple, most applications can't be comprised entirely of pure functions, so we have to look at two strategies for testing code that has state: moving logic into pure functions or designing functions to use one of the available methods of dependency injection, allowing us to isolate our code. We'll explore moving our logic first and then start to delve into code isolation.

Refactoring Toward Pure Functions

When you have a module that's really hard to test, refactoring as much of the logic into pure functions is the easiest way to simplify testing, if you can make it work. We'll deep dive into an example of this in the GenServer section of Chapter 3, Testing OTP, on page 67, but let's make sure we understand the basic ideas before we move on. When code has an external dependency, it rarely acts as a straight pass-through of the values of that dependency. Most of the time, it will make a call to a dependency and then manipulate the response before returning the result of the function call. The more manipulation your code does of that data, the better a candidate it is for refactoring the logic into a pure function.

Let's look at a visual representation of a function that both calls out to a dependency and manipulates that data before returning its response.

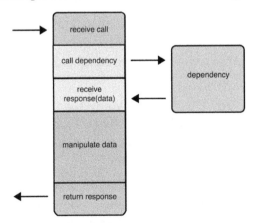

The section of our drawing labeled "manipulate data" is code that changes the data without any external dependencies. If the code has significantly different outcomes, testing this function can be pretty painful, depending on the data returned from the dependency. Each test, for each possible way that logic can behave, will have to use some kind of mechanism to guarantee that the dependency returns a predictable, known response. We'll talk about one of the ways to do that in the next section, but the alternative is to refactor your code so that specifically that portion of logic ("manipulate data") is pulled out of the function and into a new, pure function. That way it becomes a new dependency for our original function, as you can see in the following figure.

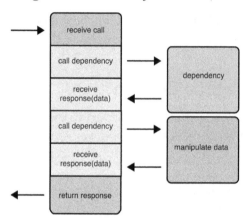

This may seem as though it makes things more complicated, but it doesn't. What we've done is pulled that code into a place where we can test it easily, having multiple tests with either a simple setup or no setup, an exercise phase, and a verify phase. When we learn about isolating code, you'll get a better idea of the complexity we're able to avoid. Once that individual piece of logic is well tested, it can now be considered safe to pull into the testing black box for our original function. We know that code works and that it'll behave consistently every time it's given the same input. We no longer need to figure out how to create scenarios where the original dependency returns different values, and we can reduce the number of tests needed to test the original function.

Refactoring to pure functions works if you want to pull the logic into a new function in your existing module or into a new function in a new module. The only thing to remember is that it needs to be a public function and it needs to be well tested.

Earlier in this chapter, we tested the SoggyWaffle.WeatherAPI.ResponseParser. Then we discussed pure functions and named SoggyWaffle.WeatherAPI.ResponseParser.parse_response/1 as an example. That module is only used by one other module, SoggyWaffle. It would've been very easy for us to have just left all of the response-parsing logic inside of SoggyWaffle. That would've looked something like this:

```
unit_tests/soggy_waffle_examples/overloaded_soggy_waffle.ex
defmodule SoggyWaffle do
  alias SoggyWaffle.Weather

  @thunderstorm_ids [200, 201, 202, 210, 211, 212, 221, 230, 231, 232]
  @drizzle_ids [300, 301, 302, 310, 311, 312, 313, 314, 321]
  @rain_ids [500, 501, 502, 503, 504, 511, 520, 521, 522, 531]
  @all_rain_ids @thunderstorm_ids ++ @drizzle_ids ++ @rain_ids

  def rain?(city) do
    with {:ok, response} <- SoggyWaffle.WeatherAPI.get_forecast(city) do
      weather_data = parse_response(response)

      SoggyWaffle.Weather.imminent_rain?(weather_data)
    end
  end

  defp parse_response(response) do
    # «parsing logic»
  end
end
```

The code organization isn't awful, and the module isn't very large. This would likely be maintainable since this application isn't expected to grow much. In fact, the code looks almost deceptively simple. It's getting data from an API (not purely functional), parsing the data (purely functional), and then checking for rain (purely functional).

From a code design standpoint, this function is coordinating three different types of work. It's good practice to keep functions that coordinate the responses from other functions as light on internal logic as possible. Aside from good software design, testing a function that coordinates multiple kinds of logic is a challenge even when it doesn't contain much of its own logic. If conditions can vary before the internal logic, you'll have to write tests that set up every condition to make sure that code is exercised by your tests correctly. Everything about this scenario points to refactoring toward pure functions, as we did with the SoggyWaffle.WeatherAPI.ResponseParser.

Alas, there are plenty of times where we can't draw clear lines about what can be extracted into a new function. When that's the case, we still have another tool at our disposal to create a controlled environment in which to exercise our code. We can create a replacement for the dependency, isolating our code. Let's take a look at that next.

Isolating Code

We can employ multiple strategies to test our code in a way that removes outside variables, controlling the situation in which our code under test must perform and allowing us to expect a specific outcome. We'll cover the easiest method—injecting dependencies and creating basic substitutes (test doubles)—in order to add another option to your testing tool belt.

Dependency Injection

Before we can leverage dependency injection to isolate the behavior of our code under test, let's take a moment to define dependency injection. A dependency is any code that your code relies on. Dependency injection (often abbreviated as DI) is a fancy name for any system that allows your code to utilize a dependency without hard-coding the name of the dependency, allowing any unit of code that meets a contract to be used. In Elixir, we have two common ways to inject a dependency: as a parameter to a function and through the application environment. Utilizing DI in our tests allows us to create replacement dependencies that behave in predictable ways, allowing the tests to focus on the logic inside the code under test.

Passing a dependency as a parameter is the more common way to inject dependencies in unit testing, which is the style that we'll focus on first. In later chapters, we'll cover dependency injection via the application environment, as well as Mox, a tool that aids in creating test doubles.

Test Double Terminology

 In this chapter, we'll refer to stand-ins for production code for the purposes of testing as "test doubles." This covers code that can return a prescribed result and even assert that it was called, with or without specific parameters. We'll dive deeper into different kinds of doubles in the next chapter.

Passing a Dependency as a Parameter

Passing a dependency as a parameter is as straightforward as it sounds and is often the simplest solution. We can choose to either pass a function or a module as a parameter. When you inject a module as shown in the following code, it must meet an implicit contract. Otherwise calling the code will raise an exception. The SoggyWaffle module has been written to allow a weather forecast function to be passed in:

unit_tests/soggy_waffle/lib/soggy_waffle.ex
```
Line 1  defmodule SoggyWaffle do
   -      alias SoggyWaffle.WeatherAPI
   -      def rain?(city, datetime, weather_fn \\ &WeatherAPI.get_forecast/1) do
   -        with {:ok, response} <- weather_fn.(city) do
   5          {:ok, weather_data} =
```

```
        SoggyWaffle.WeatherAPI.ResponseParser.parse_response(response)

        SoggyWaffle.Weather.imminent_rain?(weather_data, datetime)
      end
10    end
  end
```

Here, at line 3, we're providing a function reference as the default parameter for the injected dependency. This pattern allows us to not have to pass in the real dependency during execution while allowing us to pass in a double during testing. Injecting a function is a tool to reach for when you have a complicated dependency that might return inconsistent results even within the same test setup. Injecting a double allows you to remove unknown factors and give your code under test a consistent environment in which it is tested. Injecting a whole module, which we'll explore in the next chapter, can be useful when your code will call more than one function on that module.

In our code, the other two dependencies, SoggyWaffle.WeatherAPI.ResponseParser and SoggyWaffle.Weather, are purely functional and are separately well tested. As a result, we can save ourselves extra work by not worrying about injecting doubles for those dependencies. They'll never produce a different result. The only part of the code that we need to remove from the test scenario, which is why we call this code isolation, is the call to the weather API at line 4. It very easily could return different results depending on when the code is executed, preventing our test from being able to expect exact results.

Now that we added a mechanism to inject the dependency, let's write a test that can leverage that mechanism to create a scenario where the result should always be the same. Add the following test file (test/soggy_waffle_test.exs) to your application.

unit_tests/soggy_waffle_examples/test/soggy_waffle_test.exs

```
Line 1  defmodule SoggyWaffleTest do
          use ExUnit.Case

          describe "rain?/2" do
5           test "success: gets forecasts, returns true for imminent rain" do
              now = DateTime.utc_now()
              future_unix = DateTime.to_unix(now) + 1
              expected_city = Enum.random(["Denver", "Los Angeles", "New York"])
              test_pid = self()
10
              weather_fn_double = fn city ->
                send(test_pid, {:get_forecast_called, city})

                data = [
15                %{
```

```
                "dt" => future_unix,
                "weather" => [%{"id" => _drizzle_id = 300}]
              }
          ]

          {:ok, %{"list" => data}}
        end

        assert SoggyWaffle.rain?(expected_city, now, weather_fn_double)

        assert_received {:get_forecast_called, ^expected_city},
                        "get_forecast/1 was never called"
      end
    end
end
```

The major feature of this test is the definition and use of a function-style test double, weather_fn_double, at line 11. It matches the contract of SoggyWaffle.Weather-API.get_forecast/1, but, unlike the real function, it'll always return the exact same response. Now our test can assert on specific values, helping us to know that the module under test, SoggyWaffle, is behaving correctly.

Notice, though, that the test double doesn't just meet the contract, it also has a mechanism to report that the function was called and to send the parameter passed to it back to the test, seen at line 12. When the double is called, the module will send the test process the {:get_forecast_called, city} message.

The test code at line 26 makes sure that the function was called, but it also ensures that the correct value was passed to it. We call this style of testing an expectation. This way, if that dependency is never called, the test will fail. This kind of expectation is mostly useful when there's an expected side effect of your code and your tests are concerned with making sure it happens. Admittedly our test is just making a query via the function call, so the expectation isn't totally necessary in this case, but it still illustrates well how to add an expectation to a test double.

Some other features of this test are worth noting before we move on. The code under test uses time comparisons in its business logic, actually found in a functional dependency, SoggyWaffle.Weather. Because we aren't isolating Soggy-Waffle from that dependency, knowledge of the time comparison has now bled up into the knowledge needed to test SoggyWaffle. This ties back to our earlier discussion of defining the unit, or black box, for our test. Because SoggyWaf-fle.Weather is well tested, there is little downside to taking this approach, as it will prove to be easier to understand and maintain in the long run, a very important priority when we design our tests.

The anonymous function is defined inside of the test at line 11, as opposed to a named function in the same file, because it needs to have access to the value bound to future_unix. Additionally, we have to define the test's process ID (or PID) *outside* of the function because self() won't be evaluated until the function is executed, inside the process of the code under test, which could have a different PID than our test. Because anonymous functions are closures in Elixir, the value of future_unix is part of the function when it gets executed. The call to self() is evaluated at the definition of the anonymous function, with the value being the PID of that test process. Leveraging closures is one of the advantages of function-style dependency injection. We'll examine other DI tools later that give us similar power.

One last, notable feature of this test that isn't related to dependency injection is the use of randomized data at line 8. When test data is incidental, meaning it shouldn't change the behavior of your code, try to avoid hard-coded values.

Don't worry about this issue when you're making your first pass on a test. But before you consider that test complete, we suggest you look for places where you can switch from hard-coded values to randomized data. While you aren't looking to try to test your code with every possible value that could be passed to it (that's more in line with property-based testing, covered in Chapter 7, Property-Based Testing, on page 187), it's possible to accidentally write code that only passes with a single specific input. That's obviously not ideal, so it's nice to reach for the low-hanging fruit and add a little variation to what's passed in. In this case, there's no benefit to testing all of the city options because the value of the string itself won't change anything: it's just being passed to the weather function. Our test's concern is that the correct value is passed to the double we injected. While we have a hard-coded list of possible cities, there are libraries that can help generate random data, like Faker.[5] But even handling it locally like we did here will net you the benefits without having to pull in a new dependency.

Be careful, though. The pursuit of dynamic tests like this can go too far, leaving your test hard to understand and hard to maintain. Additionally, the test *must* have a way to know what data it's using, and the assertions should be able to take that into account.

Finer Control over Dependency Injection

An alternative to injecting a whole function is to pass in a single value. An example you might see in code is when the outside dependency is the system

---

5.   https://hex.pm/packages/faker

time. If your code under test needs to do something with system time, it's very difficult for your tests to assert a known response or value unless you can control system time. While controlling your code's concept of system time is easy in some languages, it isn't in Elixir. That makes this scenario a perfect candidate for injecting a single value. The following code allows for an injected value, but it defaults to the result of a function call if no parameter is passed:

```
unit_tests/soggy_waffle/lib/soggy_waffle/weather.ex
defmodule SoggyWaffle.Weather do
  @type t :: %__MODULE__{}

  defstruct [:datetime, :rain?]

  @spec imminent_rain?([t()], DateTime.t()) :: boolean()
  def imminent_rain?(weather_data, now \\ DateTime.utc_now()) do
    Enum.any?(weather_data, fn
      %__MODULE__{rain?: true} = weather ->
        in_next_4_hours?(now, weather.datetime)

      _ ->
        false
    end)
  end

  defp in_next_4_hours?(now, weather_datetime) do
    four_hours_from_now =
      DateTime.add(now, _4_hours_in_seconds = 4 * 60 * 60)

    DateTime.compare(weather_datetime, now) in [:gt, :eq] and
      DateTime.compare(weather_datetime, four_hours_from_now) in [:lt, :eq]
  end
end
```

Looking at our function signature in line 7, we can see that without a value passed in, the result of DateTime.utc_now/0 will be bound to the variable datetime. Our tests will pass a value in, overriding the default, but the code will use the current time when running in production. By allowing our function to take a known time, we can remove the unknown. When running in production, your code will never be passed another value, but testing it just got a lot easier. Our tests can now create a controlled environment in which to test our code.

```
unit_tests/soggy_waffle_examples/test/soggy_waffle/weather_test.exs
defmodule SoggyWaffle.WeatherTest do
  use ExUnit.Case
  alias SoggyWaffle.Weather

  describe "imminent_rain?/2" do
    test "returns true when it will rain in the future" do
```

```
        now = datetime_struct(hour: 0, minute: 0, second: 0)
        one_second_from_now = datetime_struct(hour: 0, minute: 0, second: 1)

10      weather_data = [weather_struct(one_second_from_now, :rain)]

        assert Weather.imminent_rain?(weather_data, now) == true
    end
```

Our code under test is all time-based, with "the future" being very important. By passing in a value, we're able to strictly control the conditions in which our code is executed, isolating our code under test from its dependency, system time (via DateTime.utc_now/0). This is especially important because we need alignment between "now," when the code is executing, and the time in the weather data passed into the function.

Notice the one-second difference between "now" and the weather data. This is a practice called boundary testing. Our code is looking for values in the future, and we have made the future as close to the boundary as we can so that we can be certain that any time more recent than that will also pass the test. While technically our data could have been one microsecond in the future, the data our application will get from the weather API is granular only down to the second, so we'll stick with a unit of time that most people are more familiar with, the second. Whenever you're writing tests for code that does comparisons, you should strive to test right at the boundaries. This is even more important if you're dealing with any time zone–based logic, as testing too far from a boundary can hide bad time-zone logic.

In our test, there are calls to two helper functions, datetime_struct/1 and weather_struct/2. They can be explained fairly easily: datetime_struct/1 returns a %DateTime{} struct where all the values are the same each time except the overrides for hour, minute, and second, while weather_struct/2 returns SoggyWaffle.Weather structs as defined in the module of the same name in our application. These allow us to easily construct test data in a way that improves the readability of the test. Let's see the definitions for these helper functions:

unit_tests/soggy_waffle_examples/test/soggy_waffle/weather_test.exs
```
defp weather_struct(datetime, condition) do
  %Weather{
    datetime: datetime,
    rain?: condition == :rain
  }
end

defp datetime_struct(options) do
  %DateTime{
    calendar: Calendar.ISO,
    day: 1,
```

```
    hour: Keyword.fetch!(options, :hour),
    microsecond: {0, 0},
    minute: Keyword.fetch!(options, :minute),
    month: 1,
    second: Keyword.fetch!(options, :second),
    std_offset: 0,
    time_zone: "Etc/UTC",
    utc_offset: 0,
    year: 2020,
    zone_abbr: "UTC"
  }
end
```

Be careful, though, because helper functions like this can become a maintenance nightmare. When writing helper functions for your tests, try to keep
them defined in the same file as the tests using them, and try to keep them
simple in functionality, with clear, explanatory names. If you design the helper
function's signature to enhance the readability of your tests, all the better.
In the case of our datetime_struct/1, the signature takes a keyword list, letting
the call itself highlight what's important about the return value.

The keys aren't necessary since plain values would have sufficed, but they
make it fairly easy to understand the difference in the return values at lines
7 and 8 of the test body from the SoggyWaffle.WeatherTest code sample on page
30. All the other values will be the same. By contrast, weather_struct/2 only takes
plain values; but intentional parameter naming, both of the variable name
and that atom, still keep the call easy to understand.

For unit testing, injecting dependencies through the API will help keep your
code clean and your tests easy and controlled. As you move on to dealing
with integration testing, you'll need to explore other methods of dependency
injection since you won't necessarily have the ability to pass a dependency
in from your tests like you would with a unit test. Both of these ways of
injecting dependencies are simple and easy to understand. Ultimately, that's
the best argument for using them.

Wrapping Up

After writing our first tests, we dug into how to define the scope of a unit test.
We then explored the tools ExUnit provides us to organize our tests, rounding
out our exploration with ways to design our code to be more testable: refactoring to pure functions or leveraging dependency injection. The foundation
we've created—organizing test files, understanding the stages of a test, combining list comprehensions with assertions, and designing our code to be

testable—will serve as a starting point for all of the additional concepts in this book.

In the next chapter, we'll expand the scope of our testing black box through integration testing. You'll see how most of the patterns can be scaled when testing across large parts of the application.

CHAPTER 2

Integration and End-to-End Tests

In the real world, it's rare that our applications are made only of pure functions. More frequently, a production application is made of many moving pieces that interact with each other and, perhaps most importantly, with external systems as well. We want to be confident that all the pieces work together and that the integrations with external systems work correctly. However, testing becomes more complex in this scenario. For example, say our application consumes the Twitter API for sending status updates as tweets. How do we test this behavior in an automated way without publishing any tweets? How do we avoid going over the rate limits imposed by Twitter? These kinds of problems require us to rethink how we write reproducible and automated tests when the number of moving parts increases.

In this chapter we'll learn how to design tests for Elixir systems with separate pieces interacting with each other and with external systems. This knowledge, alongside what we learned in the previous chapters, will make us able to test a system both from the perspective of simple functions and modules as well as the interactions between the components of the system.

We'll start by having a quick look at integration tests that cover the interaction of different components within the same application. Then we'll move on to the harder stuff, testing the interaction of our application with external systems. We'll talk about different techniques for testing external dependencies and learn about the tools that Elixir and its ecosystem provide to help with that.

What Is an Integration Test?

Tests that cover the integration of different components (be they external systems or different parts of an application) are often referred to as *integration tests*. In this book, when we use the term integration test, we mean a test that covers a piece of code that calls out to two or more parts of a system or external systems. Integration tests are fundamental to testing a system. Unit tests give you confidence that your functions and modules behave correctly; but you'll need to test that your system functions correctly as a whole, and to do that you need to test the glue between the components of the system. Let's start by looking at an example of integration testing.

A common scenario in HTTP-based web applications is having a router that routes requests to different functions based on the request URI. Those functions are usually contained in modules called *controllers*. A controller function is responsible for doing any necessary manipulation on the request data, formulating an output, and sending a response back to the client. The code for the router and the controller could look something like this:

integration_tests/pseudocode_controller_and_router.ex

```
defmodule MyApp.Router do
  route("POST", "/perform_action", {MyApp.Controller, :perform_action})
end

defmodule MyApp.Controller do
  def perform_action(connection, params) do
    parsed_params = parse_params(params)
    action_result = perform_action(parsed_params)
    response = build_response(action_result)
    send_response(connection, response)
  end
end
```

We know how to write unit tests. We can unit-test the single functionalities like the manipulation of the input (parse_params/1), the isolated actions performed by the controller (perform_action/1), and the building of the response (build_response/1). That would give us confidence that the single pieces work correctly, but we're not confident that the pieces work well together: we need to test the *integration* of these pieces. To get in the right frame of mind, think of an airplane. You can test that the metal of the outer shell of the plane resists bending, the engines turn on correctly, and the shape of the plane is correct for flying. But if the plane hadn't been tested to see if it would actually fly, would you hop on it?

The idea behind integration testing is the same. We want to test that our components work together correctly, even if we're confident that the components work by themselves, thanks to unit tests. In our web router and controller example, we want an integration test that simulates an HTTP request to the /perform_action endpoint with raw parameters and then asserts that the response returned by the controller is correct.

integration_tests/pseudocode_controller_and_router_test.exs

```
defmodule IntegrationTest do
  use ExUnit.Case
```

```
test "POST /perform_action" do
  params = %{"some" => "params"}
  response = simulate_http_call("POST", "/perform_action", params)
  assert response.status == 200
  assert response.body == "OK"
end
end
```

Integration tests that deal with the integration of components within the same system, like the router and controller in this example, are the simplest kind of integration tests. Everything happens in a system you have control over, so the behavior is predictable. The difficulties start when we need to test how our system interfaces with *external* components. Let's look at that next.

Testing Against Real External Dependencies

Many applications interface with databases, other services, or third-party APIs. This makes integration testing harder, since we now have to deal with other running systems in order to design and run our integration test suite. There are two main approaches to dealing with an external dependency in tests: we can either use the real dependency, or we can replace it with something that *doubles* as the dependency. In this section, we're going to have a look at how we can test against external dependencies by using the actual dependencies in our test suite, and then we'll look at dependency doubles in the next section. We'll also offer some guidance on when each of these solutions is appropriate.

Say our application is backed up by a database. The database is a dependency that's external to the application, since it's not running inside it. For our purposes, we can see it as a black box that we can assume works correctly if used correctly. Let's imagine that our application uses this database to store blog articles and that it provides an HTTP API as the interface for creating articles. We have an Article struct that represents an article:

integration_tests/real_external_dependencies/article.ex
```
defmodule Article do
  defstruct [:title, :body, :author_email]
end
```

Then we have a router and a controller that handle the POST /create_article route:

integration_tests/real_external_dependencies/router_and_controller.ex
```
defmodule MyApp.Router do
  route(
    "POST",
    "/create_article",
```

```
      {MyApp.ArticleController, :create_article}
  )
end

defmodule MyApp.ArticleController do
  def create_article(connection, params) do
    article = %Article{
      title: params["title"],
      body: params["body"],
      author_email: params["author_email"]
    }

    article_id = Database.create(article)

    send_response(connection, _status_code = 200, %{article_id: article_id})
  end
end
```

We assume that we have a library that interfaces with the database and exposes a Database module. The simplest way of testing this is to start the database (on the machine where the application's test suite is running) when testing the application and actually call out to it when executing the test. This way, we can also call out to the database in order to check that our code created the article correctly in the database.

integration_tests/real_external_dependencies/http_api_test.exs
```
defmodule HTTPAPITest do
  use ExUnit.Case

  test "articles are created correctly" do
    params = %{
      "title" => "My article",
      "body" => "The body of the article",
      "author_email" => "me@example.com"
    }

    response = simulate_http_call("POST", "/create_article", params)

    assert response.status == 200
    assert %{"article_id" => article_id} = response.body

    assert {:ok, article} = Database.fetch_by_id(Article, article_id)
    assert article.title == "My article"
    assert article.body == "The body of the article"
    assert article.author_email == "me@example.com"
  end
end
```

This test works, but we might run into a problem: we keep cluttering the database with identical articles every time we execute it. A good practice is to try to always start from a clean slate when running tests. In this case, that could mean that we delete all articles before running the test.

This test gives us confidence that our code works, since it's calling to the real database and working as it would in a production setting. One drawback of these tests, however, is that they can be much slower than tests that don't call out to any external dependencies.

The database is an example of an external dependency of the system that we have complete control over. We can start it and stop it whenever we want, and we can modify the data inside it however we want. The same isn't true for external services like third-party APIs. For example, if your application uses the Twitter API, then we can't create tweets and hit the API whenever we want since we need to abide by the rules imposed by the API. This distinction between external dependencies that our application owns (like the database) and external dependencies that we don't own (like a third-party API) is a fundamental one. When we have dependencies that we own, it's usually better to test against the running dependency so as to have our test suite be as close as possible to the code that runs in production. In these cases, we trade off the speed of our test suite for the gained confidence that our code works correctly.

In the next section, we'll explore how to deal with external services that we don't have control over.

Dependency Doubles

In this section, we're going to see how to create something that acts as an external dependency that we don't have control over. This will allow us to test the code that interacts with the external dependency without using the dependency at all.

There's one disclaimer to make before diving in deeper: the terminology around dependency doubles is not "standard": different people use these terms in different ways. We'll use the terms double, mock, stub, and others in the way that we think makes the most sense and we'll use them consistently, but you might encounter the same concepts under different names outside of this book. We'll define these terms later on in this chapter. With that out of the way, let's get to it.

The component that acts as the external dependency is often referred to as a *double* of that dependency. The name comes from the fact that, to the callers of the dependency, the dependency double looks exactly like the dependency. The implementations of dependency doubles can vary in complexity. Sometimes, a dependency double just *looks* like the external dependency but doesn't do anything. Other times, the dependency double can be used to gain insight into how the dependency is called and possibly to test the interaction as well. Let's dive into how we can use dependency doubles in our Soggy Waffle application.

Soggy Waffle needs to interact with a weather API (through HTTP) in order to periodically fetch the weather forecast. To our application, the weather API is an external component, so it's good design to isolate our interactions with it into a module that acts as the *interface* between our application and the API.

```
integration_tests/soggy_waffle/weather_api.ex
defmodule SoggyWaffle.WeatherAPI do
  @spec get_forecast(String.t()) ::
          {:ok, map()} | {:error, reason :: term()}
  def get_forecast(city) when is_binary(city) do
    app_id = SoggyWaffle.api_key()
    query_params = URI.encode_query(%{"q" => city, "APPID" => app_id})

    url =
      "https://api.openweathermap.org/data/2.5/forecast?" <> query_params

    case HTTPoison.get(url) do
      {:ok, %HTTPoison.Response{status_code: 200} = response} ->
        {:ok, Jason.decode!(response.body)}

      {:ok, %HTTPoison.Response{status_code: status_code}} ->
        {:error, {:status, status_code}}

      {:error, reason} ->
        {:error, reason}
    end
  end
end
```

The get_forecast/1 function in this module is called by our main SoggyWaffle.rain?/2 function:

```
integration_tests/soggy_waffle/soggy_waffle.ex
defmodule SoggyWaffle do
  def rain?(city, datetime) do
    with {:ok, response} <- SoggyWaffle.WeatherAPI.get_forecast(city) do
      weather_data =
        SoggyWaffle.WeatherAPI.ResponseParser.parse_response(response)

      SoggyWaffle.Weather.imminent_rain?(weather_data, datetime)
    end
  end
end
```

We want to test the rain?/2 function. However, we don't have control over the weather API so it's hard to test against it. If that API is down, our automated tests (which should be reproducible) will fail. We have to find a way to respect the rate limiting of that API so that our developers can run automated tests as frequently as they want. These reasons suggest that we do something to avoid contacting the weather API directly in tests. A common approach would be to swap out the HTTP client we use in the SoggyWaffle.WeatherAPI module with something that we can control during tests. However, this exposes a detail of the implementation of the SoggyWaffle.WeatherAPI module that we might not be interested in when testing the rain?/2 function. Let's step up one level and deal with the interface exposed by SoggyWaffle.WeatherAPI instead.

The simplest thing we can do is use *dependency injection*, as we discussed in Chapter 1, Unit Tests, on page 1. When we used dependency injection before, we passed a function or a value to our function. However, we usually encapsulate interfaces inside modules, like we did with SoggyWaffle.WeatherAPI. In those cases, it makes sense to pass in a module as the dependency we're injecting. Let's modify the rain?/2 function to take a third argument, the "double" module.

integration_tests/soggy_waffle/soggy_waffle_module_di.ex
```
def rain?(city, datetime, weather_api_module \\ SoggyWaffle.WeatherAPI) do
  with {:ok, response} <- weather_api_module.get_forecast(city) do
    weather_data =
      SoggyWaffle.WeatherAPI.ResponseParser.parse_response(response)

    SoggyWaffle.Weather.imminent_rain?(weather_data, datetime)
  end
end
```

In production, the interfacing module will be SoggyWaffle.WeatherAPI. In our tests, it can be SoggyWaffle.FakeWeatherAPI.

integration_tests/soggy_waffle/fake_weather_api.ex
```
defmodule SoggyWaffle.FakeWeatherAPI do
  require Logger

  @spec get_forecast(String.t()) :: {:ok, map()}
  def get_forecast(city) do
    _ = Logger.info("Getting forecast for city: #{city}")

    response = %{
      "list" => [
        %{
          "dt" => DateTime.to_unix(DateTime.utc_now()),
          "weather" => [%{"id" => _thunderstorm = 231}]
        }
      ]
    }

    {:ok, response}
  end
end
```

In production code, we call rain?/2 without a third argument, defaulting to the real weather API. During testing, we can swap that out with the fake module and assert that SoggyWaffle.FakeWeatherAPI.get_forecast/1 has been called correctly by testing that the correct line has been logged.

This approach to dependency injection works but has a drawback: every time we call the rain?/2 function *in tests*, we need to remember to use SoggyWaffle.FakeWeatherAPI as the second argument. This becomes especially painful when we're testing something that internally calls out to rain?/2, because we need to propagate the additional module argument. Luckily for us, Elixir ships with something that makes things easier in this case: the application environment. The application environment is a key-value in-memory global store that's usually used for things like configuration. We can store the weather API module that we're using in the application environment and read it when executing rain?/2.

integration_tests/soggy_waffle/soggy_waffle_module_from_app_env.ex

```
def rain?(city, datetime) do
  weather_api_module =
    Application.get_env(
      :soggy_waffle,
      :weather_api_module,
      SoggyWaffle.WeatherAPI
    )

  with {:ok, response} <- weather_api_module.get_forecast(city) do
    weather_data =
      SoggyWaffle.WeatherAPI.ResponseParser.parse_response(response)

    SoggyWaffle.Weather.imminent_rain?(weather_data, datetime)
  end
end
```

The third argument to Application.get_env/3 is the default value that's returned when the :weather_api_module key isn't set in the application environment. This means that once again by default the behavior is using the real dependency. We can then configure the value of the :weather_api_module just in the test environment so that the fake interface is only used when testing. A common way to configure the application environment is through Mix configuration.

integration_tests/soggy_waffle/config/test.exs

```
import Mix.Config

config :soggy_waffle, :weather_api_module, SoggyWaffle.FakeWeatherAPI
```

Since we're using SoggyWaffle.FakeWeatherAPI in the test environment, we can modify our test so that we assert on the output logged by SoggyWaffle.FakeWeatherAPI:

```
integration_tests/soggy_waffle/test/soggy_waffle_test.exs
defmodule SoggyWaffleTest do
  use ExUnit.Case

  import ExUnit.CaptureLog

  describe "rain?/2" do
    test "success: gets forecasts, returns true for imminent rain" do
      log =
        capture_log(fn ->
          SoggyWaffle.rain?("Los Angeles", DateTime.utc_now())
        end)

      assert log =~ "Getting forecast for city: Los Angeles"
    end
  end
end
```

This works fine now that SoggyWaffle.WeatherAPI only implements one function. However, we may end up adding more and more functions to SoggyWaffle.Weather-API during the development of our application. How do we keep track of all the functions that SoggyWaffle.FakeWeatherAPI has to implement to mirror Soggy-Waffle.WeatherAPI? Let's figure it out in the next section.

Interfacing to External Dependencies with Behaviours

The interface that the SoggyWaffle.WeatherAPI module provides is simple, as it's made of just one function. However, if we expanded the functionalities of the SoggyWaffle.WeatherAPI module, it would be hard to keep SoggyWaffle.FakeWeatherAPI up to datedate to mirror SoggyWaffle.WeatherAPI. This situation is a great use case for *behaviours*, Elixir modules that define a set of functions (an *interface*) that other modules can agree to implement. We can define a behaviour that specifies how we want to interface with the weather API and then implement that behaviour both in the real weather API interface as well as the fake one.

```
integration_tests/soggy_waffle/weather_api_behaviour.ex
defmodule SoggyWaffle.WeatherAPI.Behaviour do
  @callback get_forecast(city :: String.t()) ::
              {:ok, term()} | {:error, term()}
end
```

Now we can add the @behaviour SoggyWaffle.WeatherAPI.Behaviour line to both our SoggyWaffle.WeatherAPI module as well as our SoggyWaffle.FakeWeatherAPI module. Having a behaviour for our interface has two benefits. The first is that the behaviour will be checked at compile time; so if we add a function to SoggyWaf-fle.WeatherAPI.Behaviour but forget to add it to all the modules that implement that behaviour, then we'll get a compile-time warning. The other benefit is that a behaviour will clearly define the boundaries of the external system: the behaviour represents the interface that we use to work with the external system.

Behaviours are a great tool for working with doubles, but there are easier approaches to doubles than manually creating "fake" modules. In the next section, we'll see the different kinds of test doubles and how to use them.

Test Doubles: Stubs, Mocks, and Fakes

Until now, we've just used the term *external dependency double* to refer to something that doubles as the external dependency. However, we can be more precise than that and define three kinds of doubles: stubs, mocks, and fakes. We already saw an example of a *fake* with SoggyWaffle.FakeWeatherAPI. A fake is just something that acts as the external dependency without calling out to the external dependency. A *stub* is a double where function implementations can be replaced on demand to do something in isolation, for example by replacing a function to do something in one test and something else in another. Stubs can be used to provide a different behavior of a given function based on the need of the test. Stubs are most useful when combined with *mocks*. A mock is essentially a stub that can be used for asserting on how and how many times the double is called.

Stubs and mocks require a little more work than fakes, since we have to be able to work with the specific functions of an interface instead of faking the whole interface at once. Luckily, in Elixir we can use a library called Mox.[1] Mox lets us define test doubles based on behaviours and provides functionalities to make mocks or stubs of single functions in the behaviour. The library works by defining dynamic modules on demand that have an interface of functions that implements the behaviour you're building the mock for. It's pretty cool.

The first thing we want to do is add Mox to the dependencies of our application. We add the dependency only to the test environment since we don't want to bring Mox into a production application:

```
integration_tests/soggy_waffle/mix_with_mox.exs
defp deps do
  [
    # «other dependencies»
    {:mox, ">= 0.0.0", only: :test}
  ]
end
```

---

1. https://github.com/plataformatec/mox

To start with Mox, we can use the Mox.defmock/2 function. This function takes a module name and a :for option as the second argument. The module name will be the name of the test double that Mox will generate. In our weather API example, that module name could be SoggyWaffle.WeatherAPIMock. :for should be a module (or a list of modules) that will act as a test double for the first module passed to the function. The modules passed to :for should be behaviours, since that's how Mox will generate a module that provides the correct interface. In our weather API example, we can generate a test double for the SoggyWaffle.WeatherAPI.Behaviour behaviour. A great place to use Mox.defmock/2 is your application's test/test_helper.exs, which is executed by ExUnit when starting the test suite.

integration_tests/soggy_waffle/test/test_helper.exs
```
Mox.defmock(SoggyWaffle.WeatherAPIMock,
  for: SoggyWaffle.WeatherAPI.Behaviour
)
```

Where to Stick Mock Definitions?

To get started, put Mox.defmock/2 calls in test/test_helper.exs. Mix will let Mox define the mocks dynamically right before running the test suite.

However, you might find that defining mocks like this *at runtime* can cause some compilation warnings if you use some of the techniques in this book, such as reading the dependency double module at compile time in your application code. If that's the case, you can choose to define mock modules through Mox at compile time, too. This way, the mock modules will be compiled like other modules in your application before running any of the test suite.

To do that, we suggest you create a file such as test/support/mocks.ex and put all your Mox.defmock/2 calls in there. This file won't automatically be compiled by Elixir because it doesn't live inside the lib directory, so we need to tweak mix.exs. You can tell Elixir where the files you want to compile are by listing the "compilation paths" under the :elixirc_paths options in the project/0 function of your mix.exs file. Usually, you want to choose compilation paths based on the Mix environment so that mocks are only compiled and loaded during testing and won't be included in your production code.

```
def project do
  [
    # «other options»,
    elixirc_paths: elixirc_paths(Mix.env())
  ]
end

defp elixirc_paths(:test), do: ["lib", "test/support"]
defp elixirc_paths(_env), do: ["lib"]
```

Mox provides two main functions to create stubs and mocks of functions in the behaviour. The first one is called Mox.stub/3. This function takes the mock module, the name of the function to be stubbed, and an anonymous function of the same arity of the function to be stubbed. This anonymous function is what will be executed when the stubbed function is invoked on the mock module. Usually, stub/3 is used inside single tests. We can rewrite the test for our weather API example so that instead of using SoggyWaffle.FakeWeatherAPI, it uses an anonymous function that does the same thing that SoggyWaffle.FakeWeatherAPI.get_forecast/1 does:

```
integration_tests/soggy_waffle/test/soggy_waffle_test_with_mox_stub.exs
defmodule SoggyWaffleTest do
  use ExUnit.Case

  import ExUnit.CaptureLog
➤ import Mox

  require Logger

  describe "rain?/2" do
    test "success: gets forecasts, returns true for imminent rain" do
➤     stub(SoggyWaffle.WeatherAPIMock, :get_forecast, fn city ->
➤       Logger.info("Getting forecast for city: #{city}")
➤
➤       response = %{
➤         "list" => [
➤           %{
➤             "dt" => DateTime.to_unix(DateTime.utc_now()) + _seconds = 60,
➤             "weather" => [%{"id" => _thunderstorm = 231}]
➤           }
➤         ]
➤       }
➤
➤       {:ok, response}
➤     end)
      log =
        capture_log(fn ->
          assert SoggyWaffle.rain?("Los Angeles", DateTime.utc_now())
        end)
      assert log =~ "Getting forecast for city: Los Angeles"
    end
  end
end
```

When a function like get_forecast/1 is stubbed, it can be called any number of times on the mock module. Stubs are usually used when you don't really need logic in the stubbed function but you want to return a value. For example, say get_forecast/1 could return {:error, reason} to signal an error when talking to the weather API. In tests that aren't strictly testing the weather API

functionality, we might want to stub out get_forecast/1 to just return :ok, effectively not doing anything.

In our case, where we *are* performing an action in the stubbed function so
that we can test the results of the action later, a better tool than a stub is a
mock. A mock works the same way a stub does, but it lets you assert that
the mocked function is called a specific number of times. In our example, we
want to assert that rain?/2 calls get_forecast/1 only once. Semantically, mocks
are also used when you have some general expectations about the way the
mock module should be called. To create mock functions, Mox provides
Mox.expect/4, which takes the name of the mock module, the name of the
function, the number of times the mocked function can be invoked, and an
anonymous function (similarly to stub/3).

```
integration_tests/soggy_waffle/test/soggy_waffle_test_with_mox_expect.exs
describe "rain?/2" do
  test "success: gets forecasts, returns true for imminent rain" do
➤    expect(SoggyWaffle.WeatherAPIMock, :get_forecast, 1, fn city ->
➤      assert city == "Los Angeles"
➤
➤      response = %{
➤        "list" => [
➤          %{
➤            "dt" => DateTime.to_unix(DateTime.utc_now()) + _seconds = 60,
➤            "weather" => [%{"id" => _thunderstorm = 231}]
➤          }
➤        ]
➤      }
➤
➤      {:ok, response}
➤    end)

    assert SoggyWaffle.rain?("Los Angeles", DateTime.utc_now())

➤    verify!(SoggyWaffle.WeatherAPIMock)
  end
end
```

We changed the call to the stub/3 function with a call to expect/4. We expect
get_forecast/1 to be called only once, so we use 1 as the expected number of
invocations (that's the default, but we like to be explicit). In the anonymous
function passed to expect/4, we're making assertions on how we expect the
mock to be called. By combining the expected number of invocations and the
assertions in the anonymous functions, we're setting clear expectations on
how the weather API interface should be used by rain?/2.

There's one more difference between using stub/3 and using expect/4. When we
use expect/4, we need to call Mox.verify!/1 at the end of the test. verify!/1 takes the

name of a mock module (in this case it's SoggyWaffle.WeatherAPIMock) and verifies the expectations we set on the mock functions. If we call the mock function less or more times than specified in expect/4, we won't get an error unless we call verify!/1.

In this case, a mock is the cleanest solution to testing that the rain?/2 function uses the weather API interface correctly. When using a fake or a stub, we had to resort to a Logger call (which is a *global side effect*) in order to test that the weather API interface was called the correct number of times and with the correct arguments. With a mock, however, we can put the assertions right in the mock function and call it a day.

Let's quickly talk about verifying expectations. A manual call to verify!/1 isn't used very often in real-world code, since Mox provides a few alternatives that are less repetitive. The first one isn't much more concise but it can simplify things a little bit: instead of calling verify!/1 with the mock module name, we can call Mox.verify!/0 with no arguments. When we do that, Mox will verify all the expectations on all the mock modules used in the test where it's called. Another useful function is Mox.verify_on_exit!/1. When invoked, this function sets up an on_exit hook for the current test that will verify all the expectations in the test (similarly to verify!/0) when the test process exits. verify_on_exit!/1 takes an optional argument, which is the test context. This is done for convenience, since a great way to use verify_on_exit!/1 is to use it as a setup callback.

integration_tests/soggy_waffle/test/soggy_waffle_test_verify_on_exit_setup.exs
```
import Mox
```
➤ `setup :verify_on_exit!`

When used in the global test context, Mox will verify expectations at the end of each test. If we want more control, we can always use describe blocks (as mentioned in Describing Your Tests, on page 10) and only use the setup callback in the blocks where we need it.

Allowing Mocks to Be Used from Different Processes

We haven't discussed how Mox decides who's allowed to call the mock or stub functions. When a function of a double is stubbed or mocked, that stub or mock by default only works when that function is invoked from the process that defines the stub or mock. In our weather API example, this doesn't cause any problems since the weather API interface is used directly from the process that calls rain?/2, which is the test process. However, let's slightly change the code for the rain?/2 function so that the weather API interface is invoked in a different process. We'll use Task.async/1 to spawn the new process and Task.await/1 to block until the call to the weather API is done. We're really forcing the code to use another process since it doesn't make sense in this particular case to call the API asynchronously, but it'll help show this Mox functionality, so bear with us for just a second:

```
integration_tests/soggy_waffle/soggy_waffle_async_get_forecast.ex
def rain?(city, datetime) do
  weather_api_module =
    Application.get_env(
      :soggy_waffle,
      :weather_api_module,
      SoggyWaffle.WeatherAPI
    )
➤ weather_api_task =
➤   Task.async(fn ->
➤     weather_api_module.get_forecast(city)
➤   end)
➤
➤ with {:ok, response} <- Task.await(weather_api_task) do
    weather_data =
      SoggyWaffle.WeatherAPI.ResponseParser.parse_response(response)

    SoggyWaffle.Weather.imminent_rain?(weather_data, datetime)
  end
end
```

If we try to run the same test as before, Mox will fail, saying that SoggyWaf-fle.WeatherAPIMock can't be called from outside the test process. For such cases, Mox provides two functions that solve the issue. The first one is Mox.allow/3: it takes the mock module name, the PID of the process that defines the stubs or mocks, and the PID of a process that's then allowed to use the same stubs and mocks defined by the defining process. In practice, this function isn't used very often since it requires you to know the PID of the process that wants to use the mock module. In our case, we don't know the PID of the weather API task from outside the rain?/2 function, so we can't use allow/3. Luckily, Mox also provides the Mox.set_mox_global/1 function. When Mox is set to *global mode*, then mock modules can be called from any process. This is what we want in our example. We could call set_mox_global/1 directly, but this function can be used in the same way that verify_on_exit!/1 can, that is, as a setup callback.

```
integration_tests/soggy_waffle/test/soggy_waffle_test_set_mox_global_setup.exs
import Mox

➤ setup :set_mox_global
  setup :verify_on_exit!
```

To contrast set_mox_global/1, Mox also provides Mox.set_mox_private/1, which sets Mox to private mode (the default). Using Mox's global mode over private mode or allow/3 calls has a disadvantage: the test case cannot be asynchronous. This might make the test suite a bit slower, but in cases such as the rain?/2 one, we don't have an alternative.

Stubbing Entire Interfaces

Often we aren't willing to use the mock module in all of our tests. Imagine we have tests that cover a piece of code that internally calls rain?/2. In that case, we probably don't want to set expectations on functions in the SoggyWaffle.Weather-APIMock module since we don't care about checking how the mock module is called. We want to stub the functions in SoggyWaffle.WeatherAPIMock so that they do the bare minimum to pretend everything went fine when interfacing with the weather API.

However, stubbing all the functions in each test that somehow end up calling get_forecast/1 quickly becomes a pain. For this reason, Mox provides a Mox.stub_with/2 function to stub all of the functions in a mock module with the implementations in another module. For example, we could define a NoOp-WeatherAPI module that implements the SoggyWaffle.WeatherAPI.Behaviour behaviour but does absolutely nothing in the get_forecast/1 function.

```elixir
integration_tests/soggy_waffle/no_op_weather_api.ex
defmodule SoggyWaffle.NoOpWeatherAPI do
  @behaviour SoggyWaffle.WeatherAPI.Behaviour

  @spec get_forecast(String.t()) :: {:ok, map()}
  def get_forecast(city) do
    response = %{
      "list" => [
        %{
          "dt" => DateTime.to_unix(DateTime.utc_now()),
          "weather" => [%{"id" => _thunderstorm = 231}]
        }
      ]
    }

    {:ok, response}
  end
end
```

Once we have SoggyWaffle.NoOpWeatherAPI, we can use it as a stub of the SoggyWaffle.WeatherAPIMock module in every test where we don't care about asserting how SoggyWaffle.WeatherAPIMock is called. To do that, it's enough to call stub_with/2 for those tests:

```elixir
Mox.stub_with(SoggyWaffle.WeatherAPIMock, SoggyWaffle.NoOpWeatherAPI)
```

If we want to default to the no-op module for all our tests and only use the mock module in a few tests that assert how the interface is used, we can use the application environment directly. For example, we can set our application to use the no-op module in the configuration for the test environment:

```
import Mix.Config

config :soggy_waffle, :weather_api_module, SoggyWaffle.NoOpWeatherAPI
```

Then, in the tests where we want to use the mock to verify expectations, we can set the value of :weather_api_module to SoggyWaffle.WeatherAPIMock:

```
integration_tests/soggy_waffle/test/soggy_waffle_test_app_env_setup.exs
defmodule SoggyWaffleTest do
  use ExUnit.Case

  setup do
    current_weather_api_module =
      Application.fetch_env!(
        :soggy_waffle,
        :weather_api_module,
        SoggyWaffle.WeatherAPI
      )

    Application.put_env(
      :soggy_waffle,
      :weather_api_module,
      SoggyWaffle.WeatherAPIMock
    )

    on_exit(fn ->
      Application.put_env(
        :soggy_waffle,
        :weather_api_module,
        SoggyWaffle.NoOpWeatherAPI
      )
    end)
  end

  # «tests»
end
```

The application environment is a global storage; so if we take this approach, we can't make the test case asynchronous and we have to remember to set the value of :weather_api_module in the application environment back to the original value after the tests.

Before taking a step back and discussing the benefits of dependency doubles in general, let's look at one last pattern to fix a small code smell that we introduced into the code.

Improving Performance at Compile Time

The patterns we discussed are powerful and flexible, and they let us have fine-grained control over testing interactions with external services. However, there's still one principle we're going against: we're introducing a runtime call to decide which double to use *in production code*. That is, every time we'll call the rain?/2 function, we'll call Application.get_env/3 (which is essentially a read from an ETS table) to get the double module we want to use. Changing production code to accommodate for testing is often a necessary evil, but it should be limited as much as possible, especially when it comes with a performance cost. In this case, the performance hit is negligible compared to the cost of the HTTP call to the API when running in production. However, you can imagine cases where you might want to shave off even the handful of microseconds it takes to read from the ETS table in Application.get_env/3.

To solve this problem, a likely initial approach is to read the module at compile time using Application.compile_env/3. compile_env/3 works like get_env/3, but this function enforces that it's used at compile time and allows Elixir to track configuration values that change between runtime and compile time. We won't focus on this feature in particular here, but it's good practice to use compile_env/3 in cases such as this one.

```
integration_tests/soggy_waffle/soggy_waffle_compile_time_di.ex
defmodule SoggyWaffle do
  @weather_api_module Application.compile_env(
                        :soggy_waffle,
                        :weather_api_module,
                        SoggyWaffle.WeatherAPI
                      )

  def rain?(city, datetime) do
    with {:ok, response} <- @weather_api_module.get_forecast(city) do
      weather_data =
        SoggyWaffle.WeatherAPI.ResponseParser.parse_response(response)

      SoggyWaffle.Weather.imminent_rain?(weather_data, datetime)
    end
  end
end
```

This approach works well in a few cases, but it has a critical drawback: you can only use one double module throughout your testing environment. The reason for this is that we read the application environment *at compile time*, so our code will be compiled with a specific double module as the value for @weather_api_module. What this all means is that you won't be able to test both the actual SoggyWaffle.WeatherAPI module *and* use doubles to isolate tests like we discussed in this chapter.

To address this issue, we came up with a pattern that takes advantage of Mox.stub_with/2. The idea might sound confusing but here it goes: use a double as the default module during testing, and stub it with the *real module* when you need to test the actual interaction with the external system. Essentially, you're using a double and stubbing the double with the real module. Crazy pants. Let's see it in action.

We'll keep reading from the application environment at compile time and storing the weather API module in @weather_api_module. In the dev and prod environments, this module will be SoggyWaffle.WeatherAPI, the real module. In the test environment, we'll set the module to SoggyWaffle.WeatherAPIMock. However, when we want to test some code through real interactions with the API, we'll call stub_with/2:

```
integration_tests/soggy_waffle/test/soggy_waffle_test_stub_with.exs
describe "rain?/2" do
  test "success: using the real API" do
    Mox.stub_with(SoggyWaffle.WeatherAPIMock, SoggyWaffle.WeatherAPI)

    # «rest of the test»
  end
end
```

In this test, the weather API mock will "route" function calls to the real Soggy-Waffle.WeatherAPI module, letting us test that.

This pattern has *zero runtime impact* in the dev and prod environment, which is where performance matters the most. By using this trick you'll effectively be as close as you can to not changing your production code to accommodate for tests while still using dependency injection and being able to test in isolation.

Now that we have learned about the different kinds of dependency doubles, let's discuss the benefits that doubles bring to the design of your system.

The Hidden Benefits of Dependency Doubles

Let's take a step back. We talked about integration tests from the perspective of external dependencies. As we saw in the previous sections, it's usually a good rule of thumb to use external dependencies directly in tests if we own the dependencies and go with dependency doubles otherwise.

Dependency doubles are a great tool for testing, but their benefits extend to the design of our applications as well. If we look back at the changes we made to be able to use a double for the weather API interface, there were two key points: making the interface swappable at the call site (in rain?/2) and defining a behaviour for the interface. Both of these things end up making our application less tightly coupled and better architected. Now, we have a clear point of separation between our system and the external system. The interface with the external system is clearly defined by the behaviour, which forces us to reason about *how* we interface with the dependency.

Finally, making the interface to the external system swappable means that we can be flexible and change it to whatever is appropriate for a specific environment. For example, we might want to use SoggyWaffle.WeatherAPIMock in tests, SoggyWaffle.FakeWeatherAPI when developing the application and trying it out locally, and the real SoggyWaffle.WeatherAPI module when in the acceptance, staging, or production environments.

Testing the Actual Interaction with Services

When working with third-party APIs like the weather API, we push the code that integrates with the API to the outside of our application in a lightweight wrapper. When we're testing our application, we're able to swap out that small part with a double to run the rest of our application. At some point, though, we also need to make sure that the code that talks to the API works. In this section, we'll learn about the different approaches to do that.

In our weather API application, the code that talks to the weather API is this:

integration_tests/soggy_waffle/weather_api.ex
```
defmodule SoggyWaffle.WeatherAPI do
  @spec get_forecast(String.t()) ::
          {:ok, map()} | {:error, reason :: term()}
  def get_forecast(city) when is_binary(city) do
    app_id = SoggyWaffle.api_key()
    query_params = URI.encode_query(%{"q" => city, "APPID" => app_id})

    url =
      "https://api.openweathermap.org/data/2.5/forecast?" <> query_params

    case HTTPoison.get(url) do
      {:ok, %HTTPoison.Response{status_code: 200} = response} ->
        {:ok, Jason.decode!(response.body)}

      {:ok, %HTTPoison.Response{status_code: status_code}} ->
        {:error, {:status, status_code}}

      {:error, reason} ->
        {:error, reason}
    end
  end
end
```

We're using HTTPoison as our HTTP client. The get/1 function lets us send a GET HTTP request to the URL we pass to it and returns an {:ok, response} tuple. However, we still want to make sure that the URL is correct for our request, that the request is performed correctly, and that the response is actually a 200 status code with a body that we're able to parse. There's no way out of this other than to send the real request to the weather API, but there are a few approaches on how to do it reliably and in a reproducible way.

Sending Real Requests

The simplest approach is to send the real request to the weather API in the tests and assert on the response sent back by the API. The advantage of this approach is that we test the real API directly, so if the API changes or if the code that interacts with it changes, the tests will possibly fail. However, there are some important disadvantages. First of all, our tests now depend on the availability of a third-party system, which we don't control. If the weather API goes down or we don't have access to the Internet, our tests will fail even if the code is correct, which means that our tests are brittle and not reproducible. Another disadvantage is that the API could change some returned data that the test relies on without breaking the contract. In that case, the test might start failing without signaling a real issue. The other main disadvantage of this approach is that making real HTTP requests can cause problems in many use cases. For example, the weather API we're using is rate-limited (as most APIs are in some way), which means that our tests could affect the rate limiting of the API without providing a service to the users.

The disadvantages of the real requests approach can be mitigated in some cases. For example, some third-party APIs provide a "staging" or "sandbox" API with the same interface as the real API but with different behaviour. For example, with a weather API like the one we're using, the sandbox API could always return the same weather data without actually talking to any forecasting service. This would significantly reduce the load on the weather API itself, allowing its developers to possibly lift the rate limiting in this environment. However, many third-party APIs don't provide anything like this, so we have to come up with ways to avoid making real requests in tests but still test the code that makes those requests. Let's see the two most common approaches next.

Building an Ad-hoc HTTP Server

The first approach we're going to examine is building an ad-hoc HTTP server we can send requests to that runs alongside our test suite. We'll have control over the server itself, so we'll be able to control its behaviour and send as many requests to it as we want during testing.

Let's go back to the weather API use case. The weather API exposes a GET /data/2.5/forecast endpoint that we hit from our application. This endpoint accepts two parameters in the query string: q, which is the *query*, and APPID, which identifies the credentials of our application. The endpoint returns a 200 OK HTTP response with a JSON body containing information about the weather forecast. Let's build an HTTP server that mimics this API.

The Elixir ecosystem has established libraries to build HTTP servers. For now, we're going to use Plug.[2] Plug is a library that provides a common interface over different Erlang and Elixir web servers. A commonly used web server is Cowboy.[3] The first thing we'll need is to add Plug and Cowboy to our dependencies, which can be done by adding the :plug_cowboy dependency. We'll only add this dependency in the :test environment so that it won't be shipped with our application (assuming our application doesn't use Plug and Cowboy itself):

```
integration_tests/soggy_waffle_actual_integrations/mix_with_plug_cowboy.exs
defp deps do
  [
    # «other dependencies»
    {:plug_cowboy, ">= 0.0.0", only: :test}
  ]
end
```

Now let's define a Plug that exposes the endpoint. We'll use Plug.Router, which provides an intuitive DSL for writing simple HTTP endpoints:

```
integration_tests/soggy_waffle_actual_integrations/test/support/weather_api_test_router.exs
defmodule SoggyWaffle.WeatherAPITestRouter do
  use Plug.Router

  # We need to manually import the assertions since we're not
  # inside an ExUnit test case.
  import ExUnit.Assertions

  plug :match
  plug :dispatch
  plug :fetch_query_params

  get "/data/2.5/forecast" do
    params = conn.query_params

    assert is_binary(params["q"])
    assert is_binary(params["APPID"])
```

---

2. https://github.com/elixir-plug/plug
3. https://github.com/ninenines/cowboy

```
      forecast_data = %{
        "list" => [
          %{
            "dt" => DateTime.to_unix(DateTime.utc_now()),
            "weather" => [%{"id" => _thunderstorm = 231}]
          }
        ]
      }

      conn
      |> put_resp_content_type("application/json")
      |> send_resp(200, Jason.encode!(forecast_data))
    end
end
```

We have a server that exposes an endpoint that behaves exactly like the weather one but performs some assertions on the incoming request. We need to start the server. Do that in the setup callback of the SoggyWaffle.WeatherAPI test case:

integration_tests/soggy_waffle_actual_integrati ... st/soggy_waffle/weather_api_test_plug_cowboy.exs

```
setup do
  options = [
    scheme: :http,
    plug: SoggyWaffle.WeatherAPITestRouter,
    options: [port: 4040]
  ]

  start_supervised!({Plug.Cowboy, options})
  :ok
end
```

We started an HTTP server on port 4040 that we can use throughout the tests by hitting http://localhost:4040/data/2.5/forecast. However, the real weather API URL (https://api.openweathermap.org/data/2.5/forecast) is hard-coded in the SoggyWaffle.Weather-API module. We need to make that configurable. We can use the same approach we used when passing a module as an optional argument when we were dealing with doubles. Let's change SoggyWaffle.WeatherAPI:

integration_tests/soggy_waffle_actual_integrations/lib/soggy_waffle/weather_api.ex

```
defmodule SoggyWaffle.WeatherAPI do
  @default_base_url "https://api.openweathermap.org"

  @spec get_forecast(String.t(), String.t()) ::
          {:ok, map()} | {:error, reason :: term()}
➤ def get_forecast(city, base_url \\ @default_base_url)
➤     when is_binary(city) do
    app_id = SoggyWaffle.api_key()
    query_params = URI.encode_query(%{"q" => city, "APPID" => app_id})
➤   url = base_url <> "/data/2.5/forecast?" <> query_params
```

```
    case HTTPoison.get(url) do
      {:ok, %HTTPoison.Response{status_code: 200} = response} ->
        {:ok, Jason.decode!(response.body)}

      {:ok, %HTTPoison.Response{status_code: status_code}} ->
        {:error, {:status, status_code}}

      {:error, reason} ->
        {:error, reason}
    end
  end
end
```

Now we can add a test for SoggyWaffle.WeatherAPI that hits the ad-hoc test server:

integration_tests/soggy_waffle_actual_integrati ... st/soggy_waffle/weather_api_test_plug_cowboy.exs
```
test "get_forecast/1 hits GET /data/2.5/forecast" do
  query = "losangeles"
  app_id = "MY_APP_ID"
  test_server_url = "http://localhost:4040"

  assert {:ok, body} =
           SoggyWaffle.WeatherAPI.get_forecast(
             "Los Angeles",
             test_server_url
           )
  assert %{"list" => [weather | _]} = body
  assert %{"dt" => _, "weather" => _} = weather
  # «potentially more assertions on the weather»
end
```

This test will hit the test server every time it's run and assert that the Soggy-Waffle.WeatherAPI.get_forecast/1 function hits the correct endpoint. Writing our own server from scratch works fine, but there's room for improvement. For example, in our test server we're only asserting that the "q" and "APPID" parameters are strings, but we're not checking that they're the same strings as specified in the test. To do that, we would have to hard-code those strings in the test server code, which in turn means that we'd have to build new test servers to test different scenarios. There's a tool called Bypass that helps in this situation.

Bypass is a library that lets you define Plug-based servers on the fly with an API similar to the one provided by Mox that we saw in the previous sections. Let's see how we can use it to improve our tests.[4] First of all, add the library to your dependencies in place of :plug_cowboy:

---

4. https://github.com/PSPDFKit-labs/bypass

```
integration_tests/soggy_waffle_actual_integrations/mix_with_bypass.exs
defp deps do
  [
    # «other dependencies»
    {:bypass, ">= 0.0.0", only: :test}
  ]
end
```

Bypass provides Bypass.expect_once/4 to set up an expectation for a request. To use this function, we need to open a Bypass connection in our tests.

Do that in the setup callback:

```
integration_tests/soggy_waffle_actual_integrations/test/soggy_waffle/weather_api_test_bypass.exs
setup do
  bypass = Bypass.open()
  {:ok, bypass: bypass}
end
```

We return a bypass data structure from the test that will contain information like the port the server was started on. We'll pass this data structure around in tests through the test context, and we'll then pass it into the functions we invoke on the Bypass module so that they know how to interact with the test.

Now we can rewrite the test for get_forecast/1 using a Bypass expectation:

```
integration_tests/soggy_waffle_actual_integrations/test/soggy_waffle/weather_api_test_bypass.exs
test "get_forecast/1 hits GET /data/2.5/forecast", %{bypass: bypass} do
  query = "losangeles"
  app_id = "MY_APP_ID"
  test_server_url = "http://localhost:4040"

  forecast_data = %{
    "list" => [
      %{
        "dt" => DateTime.to_unix(DateTime.utc_now()) + _seconds = 60,
        "weather" => [%{"id" => _thunderstorm = 231}]
      }
    ]
  }

  Bypass.expect_once(bypass, "GET", "/data/2.5/forecast", fn conn ->
    conn = Plug.Conn.fetch_query_params(conn)

    assert conn.query_params["q"] == query
    assert conn.query_params["APPID"] == app_id

    conn
    |> Plug.Conn.put_resp_content_type("application/json")
    |> Plug.Conn.resp(200, Jason.encode!(forecast_data))
  end)
```

```
  assert {:ok, body} =
           SoggyWaffle.WeatherAPI.get_forecast(
             "Los Angeles",
             test_server_url
           )
  assert body == forecast_data
end
```

Bypass.expect_once/4 expects the specified request to be issued exactly once. The function passed to it takes a conn data structure (a Plug.Conn struct) that we can use to make assertions and to send a response. As you can see, this API is similar to what Mox provides and allows us to have fine-grained control over the test server and set different expectations in each test.

This "real requests" approach has the advantage of letting us send as many real HTTP requests as we want during testing so that we can exercise the code that interfaces with the real HTTP API as well as the HTTP client we're using. However, this approach has a disadvantage as well. When building the test server and setting request expectations, we're effectively copying what the third-party API does, and by doing so we're tying ourselves to a specific behaviour of that API. If the weather API were to change and we were only relying on test-server-based tests, we wouldn't notice the change when running the test suite. This is important to keep in mind, as there's no clear and straightforward solution for this problem. The only way around it is to periodically check that the weather API still behaves in the same way as the test server. We can do that either manually or by running the code against the real weather API once in a while.

In the next section, we'll see an alternative approach to the same problem that compromises on some things for the sake of making it easier to keep the tests up to date.

Recording Requests with Cassettes

So far, we've explored two alternatives for testing the interaction with a third-party API: issuing requests to the real API or building a test server to mimic the third-party API during testing. In this section we'll explore one last approach, which consists of recording and replaying requests through a library called ExVCR.[5]

The idea behind ExVCR is to issue a request to the real third-party API the first time and record the response into a file called a *cassette*. Then, when we

---

5.   https://github.com/parroty/exvcr

need to make that same request to the third-party API, ExVCR will *replay* that request and return the response from the cassette without making any real HTTP calls. By now you probably get why it's called ExVCR: cassettes, recording, replaying.... It makes sense.

The way ExVCR works is by creating implicit mocks of widely used Erlang and Elixir HTTP clients, such as the built-in httpc or hackney.[6][7] These mocks intercept requests and record them if there's no cassette for them, or replay the requests from the respective cassette. This approach is limiting in cases where you don't use one of the HTTP clients supported by ExVCR, since ExVCR won't work. However, many applications do use clients supported by ExVCR so it's still worth exploring.

Let's see how to change the SoggyWaffle.WeatherAPI test to make use of ExVCR. Start by adding :ex_vcr as a dependency:

integration_tests/soggy_waffle_actual_integrations/mix_with_ex_vcr.exs

```
defp deps do
  [
    # «other dependencies»
➤   {:ex_vcr, ">= 0.0.0", only: :test}
  ]
end
```

The get_forecast/1 function uses HTTPoison as its HTTP client and HTTPoison uses :hackney under the hood, so ExVCR will work. Now we need to call use ExVCR.Mock to make the ExVCR DSL available in our tests and we'll have to use the ExVCR.Adapter.Hackney adapter.

integration_tests/soggy_waffle_actual_integrations/test/soggy_waffle/weather_api_test_ex_vcr.exs

```
use ExVCR.Mock, adapter: ExVCR.Adapter.Hackney
```

ExVCR provides a use_cassette/2 macro that takes a cassette name and a block of code. Requests executed in the block of code are recorded to and replayed from the specified cassette. Let's rewrite the get_forecast/1 test to use use_cassette/2.

integration_tests/soggy_waffle_actual_integrations/test/soggy_waffle/weather_api_test_ex_vcr.exs

```
test "get_forecast/1 hits GET /data/2.5/forecast" do
  query = "losangeles"
  app_id = "MY_APP_ID"

  use_cassette "weather_api_successful_request" do
    assert {:ok, body} =
             SoggyWaffle.WeatherAPI.get_forecast("Los Angeles")
  end
```

---

6. http://erlang.org/doc/man/httpc.html
7. https://github.com/benoitc/hackney

```
  assert %{"list" => [weather | _]} = body
  assert %{"dt" => _, "weather" => _} = weather
  # «potentially more assertions on the weather»
end
```

The first time this test is run, the request is issued against the real weather API. After the weather API returns a response, that response is recorded into a cassette called weather_api_successful_request. We use a descriptive and unique name so that it won't conflict with other cassettes. When the same test is run again, no HTTP requests are made and the response recorded into the cassette is returned to the HTTP client.

This approach differs from a test server because it focuses less on asserting that the request is made correctly. The main goal of a cassette is to behave exactly like the real third-party service without having to write code to emulate that third-party service. The workflow is, in fact, simpler than the test server: we just wrap our code with use_cassette/2 and go on about our day. However, cassettes present a similar problem to the test server, which is that they can get out of sync with the actual API. The solution for cassettes is somewhat simpler though, since we only have to delete the stale cassette and rerun our tests in order to re-create an up-to-date cassette.

To push the idea of keeping cassettes up to date further, we can always force real requests to be made when running tests in a continuous integration (CI) server. This way, we'll avoid making real HTTP requests when developing on our local machine, but the CI server (which usually runs much less frequently) will make sure that the cassettes haven't gotten out-of-date. This approach heavily depends on what making a request to the real API implies. In the weather API example, making real requests to /data/2.5/forecast is feasible: if it's only done in CI then it's unlikely that we'll negatively affect our rate limiting. In other cases, making requests might cost money or break things, so making real requests on every CI run might not be ideal. Furthermore, we usually want CI to be reproducible and consistent between runs, and depending on the availability of an external API might not be feasible.

Our favorite use case for cassettes is an external service that allows you to set up and tear down resources through its API. For example, the weather API could expose endpoints to register and delete named queries. Now, if we wanted to test that we can query the forecast through a named query, we could create the named query, test the appropriate functions, and delete the named query all in the same test. In this use case, the cassette merely becomes a "cache" of HTTP requests. Even when not using cassettes (such as in CI), the test would create and destroy all necessary resources to run the test, leaving the external service's state unchanged.

One important practice to keep in mind when working with ExVCR is to *never reuse cassettes*. If you have two tests that make the same request, you might be tempted to use the same cassette, but there's a good chance that at some point the request made in one of the two tests will change slightly and then things won't work anymore. If you use a different cassette in each test, you're guaranteed to not mess things up in this regard.

Let's recap what we discussed in this section and see which approach is best for different use cases.

What Approach Is Best for Testing External Services?

We saw three possible approaches to testing third-party HTTP services: making real requests, running a test server that mocks the service, or recording real requests and replaying them. As is often the case in our industry, there's no definitive best approach among these. Each one fits some use cases better.

If you can get away with making real requests to a service, then it's often a good idea to do that. Many HTTP services provide sandbox environments specifically for testing or are idempotent, meaning that you can make requests without affecting the state of the service. Even in these cases, though, you might want to avoid the real requests approach if you don't want to rely on an Internet connection in your tests. Nowadays it's rare to not have an Internet connection available, but there are situations (like being on a flight) that take your Internet connection away. Relying on an Internet connection can also cause all sorts of weird problems if the connection is unstable. Personally, we're fans of a workaround that gives you a nice way to deal with this: we tag our tests that use the Internet as @tag :requires_internet. This way, if you don't have a connection available, you can run mix test --exclude requires_internet and still run all the tests that don't require the connection. This is a good workaround if you're rarely without a connection. One thing to consider is that this approach doesn't necessarily let you test different kinds of responses from an external service (such as temporary errors), so you might have to mix this in with other approaches.

If you want tight control over how the third-party API should behave, then building a test server is the way to go. This lets you test different responses from the API and gives you flexibility. However, the trade-off is that you have to build the test server and then keep it up to date with the real API.

If you want to mimic the API perfectly and use one of the supported HTTP clients, then ExVCR is a good alternative. The trade-off is that you have to keep cassettes up to date, but that's something that you can only avoid by going with the real requests approach anyway.

Testing Non-HTTP Services

In the previous sections, we mostly talked about testing HTTP-based third-party services. We explored how to build doubles for those services and then how to test the interaction with the actual services. The concepts we discussed mostly apply to non-HTTP services as well. If you're talking with a service that exposes a binary protocol, for example, you can build an interface (with a behaviour) that specifies how to interact with the service. Then you can use dependency doubles to test components that talk to the service through the interface. However, testing the actual interaction with a service that doesn't expose an HTTP interface is a bit more complex because fewer tools are available. If you want to build a test server, you'll often have to implement that yourself on top of lower-level protocols like TCP. If you want cassettes, you'll have to implement all of the infrastructure needed for them yourself because there isn't an ExVCR counterpart for protocols other than HTTP.

Luckily, most third-party services provide HTTP APIs. Usually, the external systems that do not provide HTTP APIs are the ones we have control over, such as databases or message queues.

Now that we have a good mental image of how to test external services, let's quickly discuss end-to-end tests.

End-to-End Tests

End-to-end tests are tests that sit one level higher than integration tests. Instead of testing the integration between components of the system or between the system and external dependencies, end-to-end tests exercise the whole system *from end to end* as it might be used by the final user.

Let's look at the weather API example from a wider perspective and think about the whole system. End-to-end tests should test the system from the perspective of a user. In this case, an end-to-end test would spin up the system and perform assertions on the observable changes. For example, the end-to-end test could start the system and then wait for an alert about rain.

The principle behind end-to-end tests is to test the real system, so using dependency doubles rarely makes sense. However, the architecture induced by dependency doubles is still useful, since we can swap the doubles for the real external dependencies when running end-to-end tests.

Unfortunately, it's hard to find patterns for end-to-end tests when it comes to interfacing with external dependencies, since finding patterns often depends on the nature of the external dependency as well as how the system's allowed to use it.

It's also hard to find patterns when it comes to an end-to-end test pretending to be a user of the system under test. As with the interaction with external systems, this heavily depends on the nature of the system we're testing. For example, if we're testing a system that exposes an HTTP API, then we might want to use an HTTP client in the end-to-end tests and perform actual requests to the systems like a client of the API would. If our system is a website that you can visit from the browser, we'd use tools that can script human-like browser interactions. We'll have a deeper look at some of these approaches in Chapter 6, Testing Phoenix, on page 155.

Wrapping Up

We had a look at the practice of integration testing and end-to-end testing. We discussed in-depth ways to write integration tests for parts of the system that interface with external systems, and we looked at some Elixir-specific tooling for doing so. In the next chapter, we'll look at testing one of the most peculiar tools in the Elixir and Erlang landscapes, the OTP set of abstractions. There we'll see some of the things mentioned in this chapter being used in more practical scenarios.

CHAPTER 3

Testing OTP

In the previous two chapters, we established a mental framework to think and work with different levels of testing. We now have the tools to test isolated pieces of code through unit testing, test parts of the system that interact together through integration testing, and test the whole system through end-to-end testing. We covered many patterns that are specific to Elixir but also talked about testing practices in general. In this chapter, we're going to focus on something that's specific to Elixir: the OTP set of abstractions. We're going to dive deeper into testing a few OTP abstractions, such as GenServers and supervisors, as well as talk about some patterns and things to pay attention to when testing asynchronous code.

We're going to start this chapter by discussing how to test GenServers, which are usually considered the *fundamental* abstraction in OTP.

Testing a GenServer

Let's refresh our memory: a GenServer is a process that holds state and optionally provides an interface to read or update that state. OTP abstracts all of the common parts of a GenServer, like spawning the process, having a receive loop, and sending messages. What's left to the user is to implement *callbacks* that implement code that's specific to a particular GenServer.

We'll see how we can make use of a GenServer in the Soggy Waffle application, but we'd like to start off with a self-contained example. It's going to make things easier when illustrating some concepts. We'll use a GenServer that provides a simple rolling average of the last N numeric measurements given to it. We can start with a simple implementation by looking at the public API exposed by the GenServer:

```
testing_otp/rolling_average/overloaded_genserver.ex
def start_link(max_measurements) do
  GenServer.start_link(__MODULE__, max_measurements)
end

def add_element(pid, element) do
  GenServer.cast(pid, {:add_element, element})
end

def average(pid) do
  GenServer.call(pid, :average)
end
```

We have a function to start the GenServer, a function to store a new element in the GenServer, and a function to get the average of the elements that the GenServer is storing at a given time. From the public API, we know that this is going to be a GenServer (because of the calls to GenServer functions), but we don't know what the internal state of the GenServer or the implementation of the add_element/2 and average/1 functionalities will look like.

Let's examine them now.

The internal state is going to be a struct with two fields: the maximum size of measurements that the GenServer will store at once and the measurements themselves.

```
testing_otp/rolling_average/overloaded_genserver.ex
defmodule RollingAverage do
  use GenServer

  defstruct [:size, :measurements]
```

Let's look at the implementation of the init/1, handle_call/3, and handle_cast/2 callbacks next.

```
testing_otp/rolling_average/overloaded_genserver.ex
@impl GenServer
def init(max_measurements) do
  {:ok, %__MODULE__{size: max_measurements, measurements: []}}
end

@impl GenServer
def handle_call(:average, _from, state) do
  {:reply, Enum.sum(state.measurements) / length(state.measurements), state}
end

@impl GenServer
def handle_cast({:add_element, new_element}, state) do
  measurements =
    if length(state.measurements) < state.size do
      [new_element | state.measurements]
    else
```

```
      without_oldest = Enum.drop(state.measurements, -1)
      [new_element | without_oldest]
    end

  {:noreply, %__MODULE__{state | measurements: measurements}}
end
```

Great. Let's move on to testing this.

Writing the Tests

How do we go about testing this GenServer? We mentioned three different options: initialization, adding a number to the queue, and getting the current average. We'll test these three. Our first test is focused on initialization:

```
testing_otp/rolling_average/overloaded_genserver_test.exs
defmodule RollingAverageTest do
  use ExUnit.Case

  describe "start_link/1" do
    test "accepts a measurement count on start" do
      max_measurements = 3
      assert {:ok, _pid} = RollingAverage.start_link(max_measurements)
    end
  end
```

We're testing that initializing the GenServer with an integer list size doesn't cause problems and returns a {:ok, pid} tuple. From a testing perspective, we don't know whether the size is actually used by the GenServer yet (and used correctly for that matter), but this test helps us know that the GenServer at least starts without causing issues.

Now we need to test that calling add_element/2 adds an element to the queue. Let's see the test itself first and then unpack what's going on.

Disclaimer: The test we're about to show you is a bit nasty. We'll explain why in just a second.

```
testing_otp/rolling_average/overloaded_genserver_test.exs
Line 1  describe "add_element/2" do
   -      test "adding an element to a full list rolls a value" do
   -        max_measurements = Enum.random(3..10)
   -        {:ok, pid} = RollingAverage.start_link(max_measurements)
   5
   -        # "Fill" the measurements with 4s.
   -        for _ <- 1..max_measurements do
   -          RollingAverage.add_element(pid, 4)
   -        end
  10
   -        assert %{size: ^max_measurements, measurements: measurements} =
   -                 :sys.get_state(pid)
```

```
     expected_measurements = List.duplicate(4, max_measurements)
15   assert measurements == expected_measurements

     # We add an element that we know causes an "overflow".
     RollingAverage.add_element(pid, 1)

20   assert %{size: ^max_measurements, measurements: measurements} =
             :sys.get_state(pid)

     expected_measurements = [1 | List.duplicate(4, max_measurements - 1)]
     assert measurements == expected_measurements
25   end
   end
```

First notice that the test is set up to work with a dynamic-size list. When given the option of static versus dynamic values in your tests, always tend toward dynamic ones. This choice makes it less likely that you'll miss edge cases due to your test forcing your code to work only with specific values. In this case, we're starting with a list of 4s, as long as the maximum number of measurements we pass to start_link/1 (this number is dynamic). Then, we fill the state of the GenServer under test with this list and peek at the GenServer's state to assert on the expected state. After that, we add a 5 to the GenServer, which causes the list of measurements to "overflow," deleting the first added element (a 4). Finally, we once again peek at the GenServer state and verify that the oldest measurements have indeed been dropped and the new measurement added to the state.

When using dynamic values, it's important to make sure they show up in the feedback on a failed test. In this case, you can see that max_measurements is pinned and will be part of the failure feedback. This makes it easier to reproduce the same conditions when debugging.

The add_element/2 test is doing a lot, but the biggest issue is that it can't test anything without using a system call to peek into the GenServer and grab its state, seen at line 12. Our test has to know that the GenServer is storing the measurements as a list. This violates the concept of a black box around your code: the test code has to know the internal details of the code in order to pass. However, we want our tests to still pass if we change the internal details of our code but leave the public API unchanged. That would not happen here if we, for example, moved from a list to an Erlang queue (see :queue[1]) for the internal state representation. We warned you the test would be a bit nasty.

---

1.   https://erlang.org/doc/man/queue.html

Our third test is a little simpler. In combination with the test before it, we have confidence that our "rolling" behavior works, so here we're focusing just on the cast callback returning the average. Again, though, setting up state in our GenServer is a large part of the test.

testing_otp/rolling_average/overloaded_genserver_test.exs

```
describe "average/1" do
  test "it returns the average for the elements" do
    max_measurements = 2
    {:ok, pid} = RollingAverage.start_link(max_measurements)

    RollingAverage.add_element(pid, 5)
    RollingAverage.add_element(pid, 6)
    assert RollingAverage.average(pid) == 5.5

    RollingAverage.add_element(pid, 7)
    assert RollingAverage.average(pid) == 6.5
  end
end
```

Having robust tests requires a little bit of dynamic setup and, as mentioned, we're using a call that's normally better to avoid (:sys.get_state/1), to allow the branching behavior to be tested without trying to interpret the results of the average/1 function. Violating the black box model is a test smell, but without it our tests would have to be numerous, because they'd have to set up various different states and interpret the values returned from average/1. That approach doesn't just create a lot of tests to maintain; it also requires a decent-sized mental load for anyone trying to understand what the tests are doing.

This example is basic, but the more complex the internal logic, the harder it is to understand the tests. It becomes very tempting to start reaching into the GenServer for its state more and more. In the next section, we'll take a look at how we can rethink our code so that it becomes more robust and at the same time easier to test.

Isolating a Functional Core

An easier solution to this problem would be to move the logic out of the GenServer's module and into a new, purely functional module. This allows you to take advantage of the ease of testing purely functional code while leaving the GenServer tests focused on what GenServer does best: maintaining state and presenting an API.

First, let's look at the tests and code for the purely functional module, which we'll call the RollingAverageMeasurements because it'll now handle the majority of our code logic. This module is concise and clearly scoped:

```
testing_otp/rolling_average/measurements.ex
Line 1  defmodule RollingAverageMeasurements do
          def new(max_measurements) do
            {[], max_measurements}
          end
5
          def add_element({measurements, max_measurements}, new_element)
              when length(measurements) < max_measurements do
            {[new_element | measurements], max_measurements}
          end
10
          def add_element({measurements, max_measurements}, new_element) do
            without_oldest = Enum.drop(measurements, -1)
            {[new_element | without_oldest], max_measurements}
          end
15
          def average({measurements, _max_measurements}) do
            Enum.sum(measurements) / length(measurements)
          end
        end
```

We moved all the pure data structure logic to this module. The new/1 function
(line 2) returns a brand new set of measurements. Here, we're designing
the *measurements* data structure as a two-element tuple, with the list of
measurements as the first element and the maximum number of allowed
measurements as the second element. We're storing both these values in
the data structure so that the data structure contains all the necessary
information to perform the operations that our GenServer needs to do. By
"hiding" this data structure inside a module and providing a set of functions
to work with it, we'll be able to change the internal representation without
touching the GenServer.

The add_element/2 (line 6) and average/1 (line 16) functions contain essentially
the same logic that the GenServer used to handle the respective cast and call,
but they hide the internal representation of the data structure from the
GenServer itself by accepting our tuple data structure as their first argument.
Keeping the boundaries of the black box intact leads to code that's easily and
safely refactored.

Testing this purely functional code is much easier than testing the whole
GenServer. Our first test focuses on adding an element to the rolling average
data structure when there's space for that element.

```
testing_otp/rolling_average/measurements_test.exs
defmodule RollingAverageMeasurementsTest do
  use ExUnit.Case

  describe "add_element/2" do
```

```
    test "adds an element when there are fewer elements than the size" do
      measurements = RollingAverageMeasurements.new(_max_measurements = 3)

      measurements =
        measurements
        |> RollingAverageMeasurements.add_element(1)
        |> RollingAverageMeasurements.add_element(2)

      assert RollingAverageMeasurements.add_element(
               measurements,
               3
             ) == {[3, 2, 1], 3}
    end
  end
end
```

Because we're testing stateless code, our test only needs to focus on passing in arguments and asserting on return values. No complex setup of state is required. From reading this first test, you can see that we're now able to focus only on the *exercise* and *verify* stages of testing, showing that we've shifted toward testing patterns for purely functional code. You'll see that this test inspects the internal data structure representation (the tuple). That's okay since we're *inside* the black box here, so to speak, and external users of this data structure still won't need to know what it looks like.

In our previous tests, verifying that the "rolling" part of the rolling average was working was difficult because it was hidden behind the interface of the GenServer, requiring state to be set up and, ultimately, encouraging us to violate the boundaries of the black box in order to keep the number of tests to a minimum. Instead, with all the parts explicit, we can functionally test the rolling behavior of our code, too:

```
test "adding an element to a full list rolls a value" do
  initial_measurements =
    RollingAverageMeasurements.new(_max_measurements = 3)

  measurements =
    RollingAverageMeasurements.add_element(measurements, 1)

  measurements =
    RollingAverageMeasurements.add_element(measurements, 1)

  measurements =
    RollingAverageMeasurements.add_element(measurements, 1)

  assert RollingAverageMeasurements.add_element(measurements, 3) ==
           {_list = [3, 1, 1], _max_measurements = 3}
end
```

With the complexity of the test reduced, it's almost fun to figure out how to make the input dynamic. The tests are pretty straightforward and easy to read, even with the dynamic list size. This is a good example of *setup* with functional code. It doesn't impact the state of anything, so no *teardown* is required. But we do need to do a little work to create the right parameters for the test.

We only have one more test that needs to be in our measurements module: averaging a list. If Elixir (or Erlang) shipped with a mean average function, we would potentially be able to skip this, but it's simple enough to add a test and a function:

```elixir
describe "average/1" do
  test "it returns the average of the list" do
    max_measurements = Enum.random(1..100)
    measurements = RollingAverageMeasurements.new(max_measurements)

    input_list = Enum.take_random(1..1_000, max_measurements)

    measurements =
      Enum.reduce(input_list, measurements, fn input, acc ->
        RollingAverageMeasurements.add_element(acc, input)
      end)

    expected_average = Enum.sum(input_list) / length(input_list)

    assert RollingAverageMeasurements.average(input_list) ==
             expected_average
  end
end
```

In this case, the code in the test to build the expected return value is going to look a whole lot like the logic in our code itself. This isn't ideal, because the code is pretty basic. So why have a test at all? This test will help prevent regressions. It's likely that the code under test will be worked on at some point, and having this test will make sure that no one accidentally breaks that functionality.

Our GenServer still needs to be tested but its purpose has now been reduced significantly. It only keeps state and calls out to the measurements module. This is an example of where we might want to expand our testing black box to include the well-tested, purely functional RollingAverageMeasurements module, as shown in the figure on page 75.

Because the measurements code is well tested and consists of truly pure functions, there is very little risk in allowing the GenServer to call it. (Refer back to our discussion of defining the scope of your unit tests in Chapter 1, Unit Tests, on page 1, for more information.) While the risk is low, the reward is that we don't need to alter our code or our tests in a heavy-handed way to make sure that the GenServer is calling out to the utility and verifying that

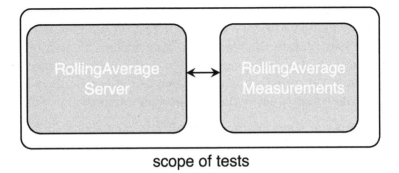

scope of tests

the data it's sending is what's expected. Instead, we can write some lightweight tests that just make sure that the outside behavior is there, knowing that the logic is separately tested.

```elixir
testing_otp/rolling_average/thin_genserver_test.exs
defmodule RollingAverageServerTest do
  use ExUnit.Case

  describe "initialization" do
    test "accepts a measurement count on start" do
      assert {:ok, _pid} =
               RollingAverageServer.start_link(max_measurements: 3)
    end
  end

  describe "adding and averaging" do
    test "it returns the rolling average for the elements" do
      assert {:ok, _pid} =
               RollingAverageServer.start_link(max_measurements: 2)

      RollingAverageServer.add_element(pid, 5)
      RollingAverageServer.add_element(pid, 6)

      assert RollingAverageServer.average(pid) == 5.5

      RollingAverageServer.add_element(pid, 7)

      assert RollingAverageServer.average(pid) == 6.5
    end
  end
end
```

We're now down to two tests: one to make sure the initialization is correct and one to make sure that the basic operations work as expected. Our first test (line 5) is the same as before, but it was pretty small and easy to understand to begin with. Normally, we would break out the tests for the two behaviors, adding elements and averaging the list into two separate tests. However, as we found earlier, it's not easy to test the addition of elements in a way that doesn't violate the black box. This is okay, though, since we've already tested the logic around that through the measurements module. Our second test (line 12) runs through the basic use of the GenServer, making just enough assertions to verify that it's working correctly.

The implementation code for the GenServer is now significantly easier to understand as well:

```
testing_otp/rolling_average/thin_genserver.ex
defmodule RollingAverageServer do
  use GenServer

  defstruct [:measurements]

  def start_link(options) do
    max_measurements = Keyword.fetch!(options, :max_measurements)
    GenServer.start_link(__MODULE__, max_measurements)
  end

  def add_element(pid, element) do
    GenServer.cast(pid, {:add_element, element})
  end

  def average(pid) do
    GenServer.call(pid, :average)
  end

  @impl true
  def init(max_measurements) do
    measurements = RollingAverageMeasurements.new(max_measurements)
    {:ok, %__MODULE__{measurements: measurements}}
  end

  @impl true
  def handle_call(:average, _from, state) do
    average = RollingAverageMeasurements.average(state.measurements)
    {:reply, average, state}
  end

  @impl true
  def handle_cast({:add_element, new_element}, state) do
    measurements =
      RollingAverageMeasurements.add_element(
        state.measurements,
        new_element
      )

    {:noreply, %__MODULE__{state | measurements: measurements}}
  end
end
```

By designing our code to pull the logic into a purely functional module, we have taken code that was hard to test and hard to reason about and broken it into two test files and modules that are easier to test and easier to understand. When possible, moving toward testing purely functional code is a big win. Sometimes it's not as easy as our example here and sometimes your code has dependencies that are not purely functional. In those cases, the ideas discussed in Chapter 2, Integration and End-to-End Tests, on page 35, come in handy.

Now let's quickly take a look at a nice tool in ExUnit's toolbox to help start and stop GenServers (and other "OTP processes") in our tests.

Controlling the Life Cycle of OTP Processes in Tests

Until now, when we needed to start a GenServer in our tests, we always called the GenServer's start_link/1 function directly. We even went as far as having assertions on the return value of this function.

```
assert {:ok, pid} = RollingAverageServer.start_link(max_measurements: n)
```

This kind of assertion might be useful to test that the start_link/1 function behaves properly, but it has a few drawbacks. The most important one is that the process that we start is tied to the life cycle of the test process but not in a *clean* way. The processes are just *linked*. When the test finishes executing, the test process will terminate (peacefully); and since our GenServer process is linked to it, the GenServer will die too. However, the test process doesn't know that it has to wait for the process we started with start_link/1 to properly shut down. In other words, the GenServer process we start could still be shutting down when the next test starts, potentially leading to some nasty bugs and race conditions.

You can imagine why this situation is problematic: if we have two tests that start the same process and register it using the same name, for example, there might be name clashes if there's not enough time between the first test finishing and the next one starting up. Let's see an example of this and imagine that our RollingAverage server takes a :name option when starting, which registers it with a name:

```
testing_otp/rolling_average/server_with_name_start_link_test.exs
test "some test" do
  assert {:ok, _pid} =
           RollingAverageServer.start_link(
             name: :my_server,
             max_measurements: 3
           )
```

```
  # «assertions»
end

test "some other test" do
  assert {:ok, _pid} =
           RollingAverageServer.start_link(
             name: :my_server,
             max_measurements: 3
           )

  # «other assertions»
end
```

In both tests, the server is started with the same name: :my_server option. When
ExUnit finishes running one of the tests and starts the other one, there's no
guarantee that the server registered under the :my_server name (started in the
previous test) has terminated. Thus, there's a chance that the second test
fails because another server registered with same :my_server name can't be
started.

Lucky for us, ExUnit provides a useful workaround: ExUnit.Callbacks.start_super-
vised/1. This function takes a *child specification* to start your process under
an on-the-fly supervisor that it sets up for you. Let's first see it in action:

testing_otp/rolling_average/thin_genserver_test_with_start_supervised.exs
```
defmodule RollingAverageServerTest do
  use ExUnit.Case

  describe "initialization" do
    test "accepts a measurement count on start" do
      assert {:ok, _pid} =
               start_supervised(
                 {RollingAverageServer, max_measurements: 3}
               )
    end
  end
end
```

start_supervised/1 still returns {:ok, pid} if successful, or {:error, reason} if unsuccess-
ful. Behind the scenes, it sets up an on-the-fly supervision tree with the given
process as one of its children. For what we've seen so far, it works almost
identically to our manual start_link/1 assertion. The magic happens when the
test shuts down. Since ExUnit knows you started this process under its on-
the-fly supervisor, it also knows that it has to shut the child process down
when the test finishes executing and the test process exits. When the test
finishes executing, ExUnit will gracefully shut down all the processes you
started with start_supervised/1, using the proper supervisor shutdown semantics.

That means it will wait for the processes to shut down before starting the next test.

When you have to repeatedly start a process in many of your tests, there's no point in having assert {:ok, pid} every time, since you're not effectively testing that the process starts correctly *every time*. That is, it should start correctly every time, but that's not the *focus* of your test. We can see this happening exactly as we just described in our original RollingAverageServerTest on line 14, where we assert that start_link/1 returns {:ok, pid}, even though that's not the focus of the test. In those cases, ExUnit provides another helpful utility, start_supervised!/1. It works the same as start_supervised/1, but raises an exception if the process fails to start. We can use that in our test to make sure that we start the process but without the need to assert on the {:ok, pid} tuple:

testing_otp/rolling_average/thin_genserver_test_with_start_supervised.exs
```
describe "adding and averaging" do
  test "it returns the rolling average for the elements" do
    pid = start_supervised!({RollingAverageServer, max_measurements: 2})

    RollingAverageServer.add_element(pid, 5)
    RollingAverageServer.add_element(pid, 6)

    assert RollingAverageServer.average(pid) == 5.5

    RollingAverageServer.add_element(pid, 7)

    assert RollingAverageServer.average(pid) == 6.5
  end
end
```

Although not as commonly used, ExUnit also provides a helper to shut down processes started with start_supervised/1 (or start_supervised!/1) *before* the test finishes executing. Such helper is ExUnit.Callbacks.stop_supervised/1 (with the mirroring stop_supervised!/1). The next test we'll show is contrived and not the most useful, but it'll help us show stop_supervised/1 in action, so bear with us.

testing_otp/rolling_average/thin_genserver_test_with_start_supervised.exs
```
describe "error cases" do
  test "asking for the average if the server has stopped crashes" do
    pid = start_supervised!({RollingAverageServer, max_measurements: 2})

    RollingAverageServer.add_element(pid, 5)
    RollingAverageServer.add_element(pid, 6)

    stop_supervised!(RollingAverageServer)

    assert {:noproc, _} = catch_exit(RollingAverageServer.average(pid))
  end
end
```

Ignore the call to catch_exit/1. We address that in the sidebar on catch_exit and catch_throw. As you can see, in this test we needed to shut down our GenServer before the end of the test. stop_supervised!/1 to the rescue! stop_supervised/1 and stop_supervised!/1 still shut down the started processes gracefully, so we don't really have to worry about race conditions. One peculiarity to note is that these helpers take the *child ID* of the process to shut down and not its PID. This is in line with the APIs in the Supervisor module to shut down children, which tend to use the children's IDs rather than their PIDs. In our case, the defaults in use GenServer mean that the child ID of our GenServer is its module name, TestingElixirCodeSamples.RollingAverageServer.

catch_exit and catch_throw

In the previous test, we used a macro that we haven't used before: catch_exit/1. ExUnit provides two similar self-explanatory macros called catch_exit/1 and catch_throw/1. They run the expression you give to them and assert that that expression *exits* or *throws* something, respectively.

We won't cover these two assertion helpers here. The main reason is that having a public interface where you exit or throw something is highly discouraged in Elixir. We absolutely don't want you to use exits or throws as a control flow mechanism to expose to users of your code (which might include other parts of your system itself). Throwing can be useful for control flow, especially in deeply nested loops and recursive functions, but you should always catch without exposing the thrown terms to users of the code. Exits are different: they might make sense for cases where your process doesn't know what else to do. Mostly though, they're Erlang heritage. In our test above, the GenServer module exits if the GenServer.call/3 is issued against a server that's not alive. Nowadays, an Elixir developer would have probably used raise in that context instead and you could've used assert_raise to test for that. Well, it is what it is. Sometimes, we have to deal with exits and throws. In those cases, catch_exit/1 and catch_throw/1 are there for you.

One last thing. You might be wondering why on earth these are macros. Why aren't they functions that take an anonymous 0-arity function, like catch_exit(fn -> ... end)? Well, as it turns out, there's no real reason. These were added to ExUnit at a time when the Elixir team was happy to sprinkle macros around. Too late to change it!

In this section, we looked at how to test a GenServer that has a "normal" interaction with its clients, that is, synchronous or asynchronous requests. However, GenServers can also be used as background processes that hold state. A common use for GenServers is as processes that do something *periodically* based on their state. Testing those is nasty. Let's go through it together.

Testing Periodic Actions

At last we can get back to our beloved Soggy Waffle application. We saw how to test a GenServer whose job is essentially to *hold some state*. Another common use for GenServers is to have a process in your system that performs an action *periodically*. For example, you could have a GenServer that resets a cache every five minutes or a GenServer that looks for changes to system environment variables every few seconds and updates other parts of your system when that happens.

For Soggy Waffle, we need something like what we just described. Soggy Waffle's purpose is to alert us in case there's going to be rain in the next few hours. To do that, the application needs to *periodically* call out to the weather API to check if there's rain in the forecast for a given location. Remember the weather API we worked with in Chapter 1, Unit Tests, on page 1, and Chapter 2, Integration and End-to-End Tests, on page 35? We'll finally be able to put that to real use.

Performing weather API calls periodically and alerting if there's rain in the next few hours isn't enough to make this work properly. The application also needs to avoid alerting us every time the forecast says it's going to rain in two hours: if we check the API every 30 minutes and the forecast says it'll rain in two hours, we can't alert every thirty minutes. We already get alerted by too much stuff in this world. We need to store some data somewhere that'll help us avoid useless alerts. That sounds like keeping state.

So our use case is clear: perform some periodic action and store some state. Seems like our best tool to solve this is exactly a GenServer—what a plot twist.

We have one more detail to cover. We want Soggy Waffle to alert us through SMS. To send SMSs, we'll just use a third-party integration such as Twilio.[2] Soggy Waffle will talk to Twilio via HTTP and Twilio will deal with the nitty-gritty details of sending SMSs. Instead of diving into the details of how the code to interact with Twilio would look like, we'll only show you the *interface* to Twilio that we'll use. The idea is the same as that discussed in Chapter 2, Integration and End-to-End Tests, on page 35: when isolating parts of our system, we mostly care about the interfaces that those isolated parts expose. The internals are a different concern. Here's the interface we'll have available:

---

2. https://www.twilio.com

```
testing_otp/periodic_actions/twilio_interface.ex
defmodule SoggyWaffle.Twilio.Behaviour do
  @callback send_sms(phone_number :: String.t(), text :: String.t()) ::
              :ok | {:error, reason :: term()}
end

defmodule SoggyWaffle.Twilio do
  @behaviour SoggyWaffle.Twilio.Behaviour

  @impl true
  def send_sms(phone_number, text)
      when is_binary(phone_number) and is_binary(text) do
    # Make calls to the Twilio API here
  end
end
```

We'll once again use Mox to create a double for this interface.[3] That's why we added the SoggyWaffle.Twilio.Behaviour behaviour. We'll use the double later on to ensure that the weather checker process calls the Twilio interface (and maybe check *how* and *how many times* the checker calls it, but let's not get ahead of ourselves here).

```
testing_otp/periodic_actions/twilio_double.ex
Mox.defmock(SoggyWaffle.TwilioMock, for: SoggyWaffle.Twilio.Behaviour)
```

Now that we have a plan for how to send alerts, let's start with a naive GenServer that satisfies our requirements so that we can look at the challenges of testing something like this.

Starting Simple: A GenServer That Doesn't Keep State

We'll write the simplest GenServer that we can think of. In this phase, we don't even care about storing the alerts we'll send: we want to focus on the periodic action part. The action itself that we want to perform consists of calling the weather API to get the weather forecast, checking if there'll be rain in the next few hours, and potentially alerting through SMS in case rain is expected. We'll call our periodic-action GenServer SoggyWaffle.WeatherChecker:

```
testing_otp/periodic_actions/first_iteration_weather_checker.ex
Line 1  defmodule SoggyWaffle.WeatherChecker do
  -       use GenServer
  -
  -       @twilio_module Application.fetch_env!(:soggy_waffle, :twilio_module)
  5
  -       def start_link(opts) do
  -         GenServer.start_link(__MODULE__, opts)
  -       end
```

---

3.   https://github.com/plataformatec/mox

```
10   @impl GenServer
     def init(opts) do
       interval = Keyword.fetch!(opts, :interval)

       state = %{
15       city: Keyword.fetch!(opts, :city),
         phone_number: Keyword.fetch!(opts, :phone_number),
       }

       :timer.send_interval(interval, self(), :tick)
20
       {:ok, state}
     end

     @impl GenServer
25   def handle_info(:tick, state) do
       # TODO: figure out how to actually use the weather API.
       if SoggyWaffle.rain?(state.city, DateTime.utc_now()) do
         @twilio_module.send_sms(state.phone_number, "It's going to rain")
       end
30
       {:noreply, state}
     end
   end
```

This GenServer works by periodically sending itself a "tick," which is an Elixir
message. We use the :timer.send_interval/3 Erlang function on line 19 to send the
:tick message to the GenServer itself (self()) every time interval milliseconds have
passed.[4] Then, we handle the :tick message in a handle_info/2 callback (on line
25). To handle a tick, the GenServer hits up the weather API; if the weather
API says it's going to rain, then the GenServer sends an SMS to the provided
phone number with a rain alert.

One more thing to note: on line 4 we use a pattern we showed in Chapter 2,
Integration and End-to-End Tests, on page 35, to read the module to use
when calling the Twilio interface. In tests, this will allow us to swap SoggyWaf-
fle.Twilio for its double, SoggyWaffle.TwilioMock.

:timer.send_interval/3 or Process.send_after/3?

The use of :timer.send_interval/3 is discouraged for periodic actions that you have to do
at most a given number of times every given interval. The reason is that the timer will
fire off at the same intervals, but if your process is taking an unusually long time to
do some actions or is blocked by other factors, then it could end up "piling" up tick
messages and then executing them without enough time between them. A more
common approach in these scenarios is to use Process.send_after/3 to send one tick

---

4. http://erlang.org/doc//man/timer.html#send_interval-3

> message at a time. Then you can call Process.send_after/3 after you handle every tick
> message so that you're sure that at least the given interval will pass between handling
> subsequent tick messages. For our example, the interval is long, so we chose to not
> complicate the code and used :timer.send_interval/3 instead, but we wanted to highlight
> that :timer.send_interval/3 is not always the best choice.

How would we go about testing this? As it turns out, it's not really that straightforward. Let's look at the code and then walk through it:

testing_otp/periodic_actions/first_iteration_weather_checker_test.exs

```elixir
defmodule SoggyWaffle.WeatherCheckerTest do
  use ExUnit.Case, async: true

  import Mox

  setup [:set_mox_from_context, :verify_on_exit!]

  test "when the process \"ticks\", the Twilio interface is called" do
    interval_in_ms = 5
    phone_number = "+1 111 11 1111"

    stub(SoggyWaffle.TwilioMock, :send_sms, fn to, text ->
      assert to == phone_number
      # TODO: assert on text
      :ok
    end)

    start_options = [
      interval: interval_in_ms,
      city: "Los Angeles",
      phone_number: phone_number
    ]

    start_supervised!({SoggyWaffle.WeatherChecker, start_options})

    Process.sleep(interval_in_ms * 2)
  end
end
```

The test starts the SoggyWaffle.WeatherChecker GenServer with a low interval (five milliseconds), so that the GenServer calls the Twilio interface "soon enough," and then checks that the Twilio interface is called. As we learned in Chapter 2, Integration and End-to-End Tests, on page 35, we can use Mox.stub/3 to check that the send_sms/2 function of the interface is called. Remember that Mox.stub/3 doesn't guarantee that the double is called; it only provides a way to execute code when the stub function is called. Since our GenServer "ticks" after starting, we also need to make sure that we wait for the first tick to happen. Since we control the ticking interval, we could use Process.sleep/1 in the test and sleep enough (say, double the interval) to feel confident that the stub has been called.

This works, but it's a pretty bad test. Relying on Process.sleep/1 is usually a big red flag, since it can make tests either brittle when the timeout is too short or slow if the timeout is too long. Instead, we can use a fairly common Elixir trick to get the timing just right: in the stub function, we can send a message to the test process right before returning :ok. This way, the test process can use assert_receive/1 to wait on the message sent from the stub function. This will at least guarantee that the stub function is called (at least once). It doesn't guarantee that when we get the message, the stub function has returned. Solving that is more problematic since we don't want to break the black box model and inspect what the GenServer is doing. Luckily for us, we know our GenServer isn't doing much after calling the stub function, so we're fine with this small inconsistency. Here's the updated code that uses message-passing:

```elixir
defmodule SoggyWaffle.WeatherCheckerTest do
  use ExUnit.Case, async: true

  # «same setup as before»,

  test "when the process \"ticks\", the Twilio interface is called" do
    interval_in_ms = 5
    phone_number = "+1 111 11 1111"
➤   test_pid = self()
➤   ref = make_ref()

    stub(SoggyWaffle.TwilioMock, :send_sms, fn to, text ->
      assert to == phone_number
      # TODO: assert on text
➤     send(test_pid, {:send_sms_called, ref})
      :ok
    end)

    start_options = [
      interval: interval_in_ms,
      city: "Los Angeles",
      phone_number: phone_number
    ]

    start_supervised!({SoggyWaffle.WeatherChecker, start_options})

➤   assert_receive {:send_sms_called, ^ref}
  end
end
```

It's good practice to include a reference (generated with make_ref/0) with this sort of message so that we're *positive* that the message we assert on is the one we mean to assert on. The reason we're so certain is that references are terms that are unique enough for practical purposes (each one reoccurs after approximately 2^{82} calls to make_ref/0). We want to stress that the message-sending technique above is quite commonly found in Elixir tests that cover asynchronous code. There isn't always a better alternative, so it's a good tool to have in our tool belt.

This GenServer and its test both work. However, there's a problem with the test: it'll happily pass if we decide to refactor our GenServer so that it sends two or more messages when it ticks. This happens because we use Mox.stub/3, which allows you to call the stub function as many times as possible and doesn't make assertions on how many times it's called. Let's try to fix this shortcoming in the next section.

Compromising Between the Black Box Model and Practical Needs

Mox provides the perfect function for what we want: Mox.expect/4. We can use expect/4 to make sure that the send_sms/2 function is called exactly once. However, our problem persists because of the nature of our test subject. Since the GenServer performs its action periodically, we don't really know how many times it'll tick in our tests. For example, if our machine is particularly slow, then the GenServer might tick a few times during the course of a single test, if we use a fast interval like we did in the previous section. So the problem is in the foundations of our test.

As it turns out, it's quite hard to escape the hole we find ourselves in. In a moment, we'll see that this situation well summarizes a whole category of test problems related to periodic actions. In this book, we always try to strictly follow testing principles such as treating application code as a black box, as well as avoiding changes to application code just for the sake of making testing easier. However, we already bent the rules slightly before: for example, reading the @twilio_module attribute at compile time in order to swap the Twilio interface double during testing is surely a change that we made to application code in order to favor testing. In this case, we'll take a similar but slightly more invasive approach and make a logic change to SoggyWaffle.WeatherChecker to make testing easier. We're walking the line between clean tests that are *practical* and *effective* at the same time.

The fundamental problem we have is that our GenServer performs a periodic action in the background that, once set off, keeps repeating until we stop the GenServer itself. Well, what if we didn't perform the action periodically but "on demand"? Our current SoggyWaffle.WeatherChecker doesn't support that, but it's something we can change. We'll add support for a :mode option when starting the GenServer. This option controls whether the GenServer will behave like it does now and perform the tick periodically (:periodic mode) or whether we'll trigger each tick manually (:manual mode).

```
testing_otp/periodic_actions/weather_checker_with_mode.ex
defmodule SoggyWaffle.WeatherChecker do
  use GenServer

  # «same module attribute and start_link/1 as before»

  @impl GenServer
  def init(opts) do
    mode = Keyword.get(opts, :mode, :periodic)
    interval = Keyword.fetch!(opts, :interval)

    state = %{
      city: Keyword.fetch!(opts, :city),
      phone_number: Keyword.fetch!(opts, :phone_number),
    }

    case mode do
      :periodic ->
        :timer.send_interval(interval, self(), :tick)

      :manual ->
        :ok
    end

    {:ok, state}
  end

  @impl GenServer
  def handle_info(:tick, state) do
    # «exactly the same code as before»
  end
end
```

As you can see, the changes we made are minimal. Now, if we pass mode: :manual when starting the GenServer, the GenServer won't initiate the ticking loop. That means we need a way to manually tick. This is going to sound horrible, but we think the best way is to send the GenServer a :tick message to simulate exactly what mode: :periodic would do. It sounds bad because it breaks the black box model by relying on an internal implementation detail of our GenServer. However, we believe that it's a simple and practical solution that achieves the purposes of testing: if we change the internal implementation, the test will break, which is not ideal but at least will signal that there's something to fix and won't slip through the cracks instead. We could come up with more elegant ways of hiding this implementation detail, such as exposing a tick/0 function in the GenServer, but we believe that keeping the changes to the application code to a minimum yields more benefits than hiding this detail.

Now our test can start the GenServer in :manual mode and use Mox.expect/4 to assert that send_sms/2 is called exactly once during the test:

```
testing_otp/periodic_actions/weather_checker_with_mode_test.exs
defmodule SoggyWaffle.WeatherCheckerTest do
  use ExUnit.Case, async: true

  # «same setup as before»,

  test "when the process \"ticks\", the Twilio interface is called" do
    interval_in_ms = 5
    phone_number = "+1 111 11 1111"
    test_pid = self()
    ref = make_ref()

    start_options = [
      # The :mode option is set explicitly for testing.
      mode: :manual,
      interval: interval_in_ms,
      city: "Los Angeles",
      phone_number: phone_number
    ]

    pid = start_supervised!({SoggyWaffle.WeatherChecker, start_options})

    expect(SoggyWaffle.TwilioMock, :send_sms, fn to, text ->
      assert to == phone_number
      # TODO: assert on text
      send(test_pid, {:send_sms_called, ref})
      :ok
    end)

    send(pid, :tick)

    assert_receive {:send_sms_called, ^ref}
  end
end
```

There's one last problem we need to solve: what if we want to start our GenServer in our application's supervision tree? That's pretty likely, but it'll mean that our tests can't rely on starting another SoggyWaffle.WeatherChecker in the test, because both the application-level GenServer and the test-level GenServer would call the same test double, making our Mox.expect/4 assertions unreliable.

This problem is more general and is related to *singleton resources*, which are components of your application that are singletons and started by your application at startup. Those tend to cause different kinds of problems in tests because usually you either can't start other instances of those resources in tests (after all, they're singletons) or, if you can start other instances in tests, they'll fight for the same resources against the singleton instance. Let's explore singleton resources more in the next section.

Testing Singleton Resources

It's quite common in Elixir and Erlang applications to have *singleton resources*. A singleton resource exists in your application as a single and unique unit. For example, a process with a globally registered name is a singleton resource, since no other process with that same name can exist in the system at the same time. That example is a bit oversimplified.

A more common and realistic example is a process that does something that should be done by at most one process at a time—for example, a process that needs exclusive access to a file on the file system or a process that periodically notifies users via SMS that it's going to rain soon. See where we're going with the latter? If we have more than one of this kind of process, we're going to have a bad time because each of those processes will try to send text messages, resulting in users getting notified more than once. The solution could be to have a list of the notified users shared between the processes, for example in an ETS table. However, we're just moving the problem around: the singleton resource is now the ETS table. Ouch. So, how do we test these scenarios?

We truly believe singletons often are one of the nastiest things to test. *Writing* singleton resources isn't usually challenging, since you'll have one instance of the resource running at any given time. However, when you want to *test* these instances, you'll usually want to spin up additional instances of the singleton resource in order to test them in isolation. We're going to cover a few workarounds to test singleton resources, but don't expect strong recommendations on clean and established testing patterns. In this landscape, testing might have to be thought out on a case-by-case basis, and it seems that the Elixir community hasn't found a widely accepted solution yet.

In general when testing a singleton resource, we suggest you identify *what makes it a singleton resource* in the first place. Is it the registered name? Is it the fact that it's the only thing allowed to work with a particular file? Maybe it's the only connection to an external system? Let's see how to find this out and how to go about testing.

Making the Essence of a Singleton Resource Customizable

In the previous sections, when we added the mode: :manual option to SoggyWaffle.WeatherChecker, we broke our core belief that application code shouldn't be changed just to make testing easier. Well, we'll have to break that belief again.

One of the easiest, simplest, and most efficient ways to test singleton resources is to make whatever makes them singleton resources *customizable*.

Since we already worked with a singleton resource in the previous sections (SoggyWaffle.WeatherChecker), we'll use that as our case study. In this case, the thing that makes SoggyWaffle.WeatherChecker a singleton resource is the fact that it's the only thing allowed to send SMS messages to users (in order to avoid multiple messages to the same user). In code, we can translate that idea to this statement: SoggyWaffle.WeatherChecker is the only thing allowed to use Soggy-Waffle.Twilio.send_sms/2 at any given time.

The contents of Chapter 2, Integration and End-to-End Tests, on page 35, are going to apply well here. Our weather checker GenServer already reads the module to use for the Twilio interface from the application environment at compile time.

As we mentioned when discussing integration testing, and in particular in Stubbing Entire Interfaces, on page 50, a useful and flexible technique with dependency doubles is to use a no-op fake in most tests that make up the testing suite but use an actual mock during the specific test that exercises the behavior we're interested in.

In this case, we can use a Twilio fake that doesn't do anything in all tests except for the ones for the weather checker GenServer. The code for the fake is short and sweet:

```
testing_otp/periodic_actions/no_op_twilio.ex
defmodule SoggyWaffle.NoOpTwilio do
  @behaviour SoggyWaffle.Twilio.Behaviour

  @impl true
  def send_sms(_phone_number, _text), do: :ok
end
```

Then, whenever we need to spin up a weather checker process without it interfacing with Twilio or the double, we can use Mox.stub_with/2:

```
Mox.stub_with(SoggyWaffle.TwilioMock, SoggyWaffle.NoOpTwilio)
```

We'll also have to use mode: :manual when starting the weather checker in the application's supervision tree, to avoid the weather checker running in the background.

When testing our GenServer, we'll now be able to switch to the SoggyWaffle.TwilioMock mock and test that the weather checker does the right calls to Twilio.

Dirtier Solutions to the Singleton Problem

Sometimes you might feel as though you're in a situation where you have a singleton resource that you just can't start in the test environment. Let's come up with a crazy example: your application needs to forcibly restart the whole VM every hour at the thirty-seventh-minute mark, because that is the business requirement. You'd do something like this with a cron job, but we said *crazy example*, so let's say you implement a GenServer that performs a check every minute to see if the current minute is the thirty-seventh in the hour. If it is the thirty-seventh minute, the GenServer restarts the VM. How do you test something like this?

A solution that some people come up with is to use a *different application supervision tree* in the test environment. For example, your Application.start/2 callback might look like the one below:

```
testing_otp/singleton_resources/different_sup_tree_for_testing/application.ex
@mix_env Mix.env()

def start(_type, _args) do
  Supervisor.start_link(children(@mix_env), strategy: :one_for_one)
end
```

As you can see, we call children(@mix_env) in order to determine the children of the application's top-level supervisor based on the Mix environment. This way, we can have different sets of children for the test environment than we do for the dev and prod environments. Why read Mix.env() at compile time and store it in @mix_env, you say? Well, because the Mix module (and the :mix application) aren't available at runtime in Elixir releases,[5] so we want to read the Mix environment when compiling our code. Good catch!

Now back to our code. The children/1 function could look like this:

```
defp children(:test) do
  [
    MyApp.OtherChild
  ]
end

defp children(_env) do
  [
    MyApp.VMRestarter,
    MyApp.OtherChild
  ]
end
```

---

5. https://hexdocs.pm/mix/Mix.Tasks.Release.html

We only start the MyApp.VMRestarter GenServer in the dev and prod environments but not in the test environment. However, if we don't start the GenServer in the test environment, how do we test the GenServer itself? Well, in this case, you wouldn't. Not being able to test the GenServer is the main reason why we highly discourage doing something like this.

In our experience, there are no situations where a carefully placed dependency double (a fake, a mock, or a stub) can't save the day. In cases like the one described above, though, you might have to get a bit off the high road and be flexible with what a "dependency double" is. For example, in this case, the GenServer would probably have to call something like the Erlang function :init.reboot/0 in order to restart the VM.[6] Well, then you could wrap an interface module around this function and create a dependency double for that:

```
testing_otp/singleton_resources/different_sup_tree_for_testing/rebooter.ex
defmodule MyApp.RebooterBehaviour do
  @callback reboot() :: :ok
end

defmodule MyApp.Rebooter do
  @behaviour MyApp.RebooterBehaviour

  @impl true
  defdelegate reboot(), to: :init
end

Mox.defmock(RebooterFake, for: MyApp.Rebooter)
```

Here you'd use the RebooterFake module in tests and use MyApp.Rebooter in dev and prod, like we showed in the previous sections.

We understand how "unclean" this practice can feel. Luckily, during our professional careers we haven't encountered too many cases where we had to resort to such extreme measures. In those few cases, though, we found this approach to be the "least terrible" solution, and we like it much more than the different-supervision-trees solution. Least terrible is far from best, but it's better than most terrible, right?

The truth is, the more intertwined and complex the code gets and the more it interacts with complex parts of the world (like the host machine, or *time itself* when talking about periodic actions), the harder it gets to have control over those parts of the world and make testing clean. The good news is that there are some workarounds to these problems. The bad news is that they aren't always nice and tidy.

---

6. https://erlang.org/doc/man/init.html#reboot-0

Now that we've covered how to test GenServers, periodic actions, and singleton resources, let's move on to testing another not-test-friendly Elixir and Erlang feature, *resiliency*.

That is, let's talk about testing what happens when things go bad at the process level.

Testing Resiliency

Let's start this section with a bold statement: we are not fans of testing process crashes. We'll get philosophical. Why does a process crash? Most of the time, because of an *unexpected error*. In some cases, the best thing to do might be to raise an exception or exit from a process for an error condition that we know can happen (an *expected error*). However, we find that tends to be the exception rather than the rule, because if the error is expected then you likely want to handle it gracefully (think of TCP connections dropping or user input error). In cases where you're raising or exiting on purpose, it might make sense to test that behavior.

Regardless of that, one of the most powerful features of the OTP architecture is that if a process bumps into an unexpected error and crashes, there will likely be a supervisor bringing it back up. That's not behavior we want to test; supervisors work and have been tested with automated and on-the-field techniques for decades now. At the same time, we don't really want to test that processes *can crash*. But if they crash because of an unexpected error, how do we test that if the error itself is unexpected? If you can test an unexpected error, we believe that error is by definition not unexpected. There's your philosophy right there.

So, we don't want to test that processes are restarted if they crash and we don't want to test that processes can crash because of unexpected errors. So what do we test? Well, one interesting thing to test about processes crashing is the *aftermath* of a crash: the *crash recovery*, so to speak. Most of OTP is designed in a way so as to have most things automatically cleaned up when a process crashes, using things like links between processes and ports. For example, if a GenServer starts a TCP socket using :gen_tcp, that socket will be linked to the GenServer. If the GenServer were to crash, the socket would be closed thanks to the existing link.

However, there are some cases where your processes start or open resources aren't automatically stopped or closed when their "parent process" dies. A straightforward example could be a GenServer process that creates and opens a file when starting and uses it to dump some internal state during its life cycle. It's likely that you would want this file to be deleted and cleaned up if the GenServer were to crash unexpectedly. This is something that we believe is worth testing, so we'll explore it a bit later in this section.

When it comes to supervision trees, we believe the thing that *might* be worth testing is that your supervision tree is *laid out correctly*. However, we'll be frank here: that's hard and messy to test. We'll explore some solutions and alternatives toward the end of this section, but we want to set the expectations pretty low.

Testing Cleanup After Crashes

If you want to perform some cleanup after a process crashes in order to ensure that the crash doesn't leave anything behind, your best option will often be a different and *very straightforward* process that monitors the first process and whose job is to perform only the necessary cleanup when the first process crashes. Let's go back to the example we mentioned at the end of the last section: a GenServer that dumps some terms to a file during its life cycle to avoid keeping such state in memory:

```
testing_otp/cleanup_after_crashes/genserver_that_uses_file.ex
defmodule GenServerThatUsesFile do
  use GenServer

  def start_link(opts) do
    GenServer.start_link(__MODULE__, opts, name: __MODULE__)
  end

  def store(pid, term) do
    GenServer.cast(pid, {:store, term})
  end

  @impl true
  def init(opts) do
    path = Keyword.fetch!(opts, :path)

    File.touch!(path)

    pid = self()
    ref = make_ref()
    spawn_link(fn -> monitor_for_cleanup(pid, ref, path) end)

    # Wait for the cleanup process to be ready, so that if this process
    # crashes before the cleanup process is trapping exits then we don't
    # leave a zombie process.
    receive do
      {^ref, :ready} -> :ok
    end

    {:ok, path}
  end
```

```
@impl true
def handle_cast({:store, term}, path) do
  new_content = "\n" <> :erlang.term_to_binary(term)
  File.write!(path, new_content, [:binary, :append])
  {:noreply, path}
end

defp monitor_for_cleanup(pid, ref, path) do
  Process.flag(:trap_exit, true)
  send(pid, {ref, :ready})

  receive do
    {:EXIT, ^pid, _reason} ->
      File.rm_rf!(path)
  end
end
end
```

This GenServer doesn't do anything useful, but you can imagine how it could have an API to retrieve particular terms that it adds to the file, for example. Let's keep this possible API in our imagination for the sake of writing less code.

There's no reliable way to make sure that if this GenServer crashes it'll clean up the file. So, what we do is write a little "cleanup process." This process could also crash, yes, but it's less likely to do so given how simple its code is. We spawn this process directly from the GenServer's init/1 callback. The code isn't the most straightforward, but it's just taking care of possible race conditions and ensuring the following:

- The GenServer process dies if—because of some freak accident—the cleanup process dies, and

- The cleanup process only removes the file when the GenServer process dies and then peacefully terminates.

Now that we have this process in place, testing the aftermath of it crashing is straightforward. We can just kill the GenServer process and make sure that the file isn't there anymore:

testing_otp/cleanup_after_crashes/genserver_that_uses_file_test.exs
```
test "no file is left behind if the GenServer process crashes" do
  path =
    Path.join(
      System.tmp_dir!(),
      Integer.to_string(System.unique_integer([:positive]))
    )

  pid = start_supervised!({GenServerThatUsesFile, path: path})
```

```
  assert File.exists?(path)

  Process.exit(pid, :kill)

  wait_for_passing(_2_seconds = 2000, fn ->
    refute File.exists?(path)
  end)
end
```

The test generates a random path in the system's temporary directory (using System.tmp_dir!/0), then starts the GenServer and asserts that the file is there, kills the GenServer brutally (with Process.exit/2 and reason :kill), and finally asserts that the file isn't there anymore. You'll notice the use of a function called wait_for_passing/2. This is a little function we find ourselves writing pretty often when working on Elixir code. Its purpose is to avoid fancy message-passing in order to know *when* we can run an assertion.

wait_for_passing/2's job is to run an assertion repeatedly for a maximum given interval of time (two seconds in this case), *allowing it to fail* during that interval. After the time interval, the assertion is run one last time without rescuing any exceptions so that if the assertion fails after the given time interval, then the test will fail. We need wait_for_passing/2 in this test because if we were to assert the non-existence of the file *right after* we killed the GenServer, we'd have a race condition that could result in the file not having been deleted yet when the assertion is run. By waiting for a couple of seconds and trying the assertion over and over, we're giving what's likely more than enough time to the cleanup process to delete the file. If after two seconds the file is still there, it means that we probably have a problem. Note that we could bump the interval to ten or twenty seconds or even more if we didn't feel comfortable: wait_for_passing/2 returns as soon as the assertion passes, so our tests would remain fast unless the assertion would fail (which is unlikely to be our normal test run since we'd hopefully fix the bug and make it pass again!).

Let's look at the code for this little helper function:

testing_otp/cleanup_after_crashes/genserver_that_uses_file_test.exs
```
defp wait_for_passing(timeout, fun) when timeout > 0 do
  fun.()
rescue
  _ ->
    Process.sleep(100)
    wait_for_passing(timeout - 100, fun)
end

defp wait_for_passing(_timeout, fun), do: fun.()
```

The implementation is straightforward and uses recursion. It decreases the given timeout until it "runs out." In this implementation, we're hard-coding Process.sleep(100) and timeout - 100, which means that the assertion is run every 100 milliseconds during the given interval, but we could change this value or turn it into an argument to the wait_for_passing function to make it customizable. wait_for_passing/2 isn't the most efficient function since it repeatedly runs the assertion and "wastes" a few hundred milliseconds between runs, but it's a good and effective tool that in the real world we've ended up using in more than a few places.

This section has turned out to be more about the code to test than the tests themselves, but we believe it serves the purpose of showing what it means to test cleaning up after crashes. In this instance, the test was small and simple enough. If things become more complicated, you'll have the tools we learned about in the previous chapters to help you architect your tests using things like dependency doubles and message passing.

Let's move on to the final enemy of easy testing in the OTP landscape: supervisors.

Testing Supervision Trees

Supervisors are one of the strongest selling points of Erlang/Elixir and the OTP set of abstractions. They allow you to structure the life cycle of the processes inside your application in a resilient way, and they make isolating failures a breeze. However, supervisors are one of the toughest things to test that we've come across. The reason for this is that their main job is to allow your application to recover from complex and cascading failures that are hard to trigger on purpose during testing.

Imagine having a complex and "deep" supervision tree (with several levels between the root of the tree and the leaf processes). Now imagine that a child in a corner of the tree starts crashing and doesn't recover just by being restarted on its own. OTP works beautifully and propagates the failure to the parent supervisor of that child, which starts crashing and restarting *all of its children*. If that doesn't solve the problem, then the failure is propagated up and up until restarting enough of your application fixes the problem (or the whole thing crashes, if it's a really serious problem). Well, how do you test this behavior? Do you even *want* to extensively test it?

It's hard to inject a failure during testing that isn't solved by a simple restart but that also doesn't bring down the whole application. At the same time, we know that supervisors work: that is, we know that the failure isolation and "bubble up" restarting behavior work. We know that because supervisors have been battle-tested for decades at this point. As already discussed, that's not what we want to test because it falls in the antipattern of "testing the abstraction" instead of testing your own logic.

Our advice? In practice, we tend to just not have automated testing for supervision trees. We test the individual components of our applications, and sometimes those components are made of a set of processes organized in a "subtree" of the main application supervision tree. In order to stay true to the black box testing model, we often test the component as a whole regardless of whether it's made of multiple processes living inside a supervision tree. If components are unit-tested and integration tested, then we happily rely on OTP to make sure that supervisors behave in the right way.

However, we don't fly completely blind. Most of the time, we spend some time every now and then manually firing up our application and just doing some manual testing. We kill processes in the running application and make sure that the supervision tree isolates failures and recovers things as expected. Let's talk about this approach some more.

Exploratory Manual Testing

As it turns out, we find that in practice there is a way of testing supervision trees that strikes a nice balance between increasing your confidence in the resiliency of your application without having to write complex, convoluted, and fragile test suites. We're talking about *exploratory manual testing*. We're using this terminology exclusively to sound fancy, because what we really mean is this: fire up observer, go right-click on random processes in your application, kill them without mercy, and see what happens.

As crude as it sounds, this method is pretty efficient and practical. What we do is start our application and simulate a situation in which it's operating under normal conditions. We could generate a constant flow of web requests if we're building an application with an HTTP interface, for example. Then, we kill random processes in the supervision tree and observe what happens. Of course, the expected outcome of a process being killed depends on the process: if we kill the top-level supervisor, we'll surely see our application stop replying to HTTP requests. However, what happens if we, say, kill a process handling a single web request? We should see one dropped request but nothing else. This isn't hard to observe. What happens if we kill the whole pool of database connections? We'll probably start to see a bunch of requests return some 4xx or 5xx HTTP status codes. In most cases you should know what happens when a part of the supervision tree crashes, because that exact knowledge should drive how to design the shape of the supervision tree in the first place. If you want your database connections to fail in isolation while your application keeps serving HTTP requests, for example, then you need to isolate the supervision tree of the database connections from the supervision tree of the HTTP request handlers, and maybe make them siblings in their parent supervision tree.

Let's talk about the downsides of this testing technique. The main one is that this type of testing isn't automated. You need to have a human do all the steps manually: start the application, generate some work for it to perform, run observer, kill processes, and observe the behavior. We're all about automated testing, as you can imagine, so we aren't big fans of this. However, in our experience, the supervision trees of many applications tend to be changed relatively rarely compared to the rest of the code. As such, this kind of manual testing might be required only a few times during the life cycle of the application. When comparing the time it takes to run such manual tests to the time it would take to build automated testing for the failure behavior, it might make practical sense to just run those manual tests a few times.

Another observation that we have from experience is that many Elixir and Erlang applications have a relatively "flat" supervision tree, with only a handful of children. The exploratory manual testing technique works significantly better with smaller and simpler supervision trees since, well, there are fewer failure cases to manually test in the first place. Testing a flat supervision tree tends to be easier than testing a nested tree.

Property-Based Testing for Supervision Trees

Property-based testing is a technique that we'll discuss more extensively in Chapter 7, Property-Based Testing, on page 187. In short, it revolves around generating random input data for your code and making sure your code maintains a given set of properties regardless of the (valid) input data. This might sound alien, but you'll have time to dig in and understand these ideas in the chapter. However, we just wanted to get slightly ahead of ourselves and mention a library called sups by Fred Hebert.[7] This library is experimental but can be used with a couple of different Erlang property-based testing frameworks to programmatically run your application, inject random failures in the supervision tree, and monitor some properties of the application that you define.

The library's README explains this in the best way:

---

7.   https://github.com/ferd/sups

In a scenario where the supervision structure encodes the expected failure semantics of a program, this library can be used to do fault-injection and failure simulation to see that the failures taking place within the program actually respect the model exposed by the supervision tree.

We have never used this library in real-world projects ourselves because we've never felt the need to have complex automated testing for our supervision trees (for the reasons mentioned in the previous sections). However, we know Fred and trust his work, so we are referencing this library here for the curious reader that wants or needs a bullet-proof testing suite for their supervision trees. We want to stress that the library is experimental, so use at your own risk.

We feel that the lack of more widely used or prominent tooling around testing supervisors is a good sign that the Erlang and Elixir communities aren't so keen on having robust automated testing of supervision trees either. Maybe one day the communities will figure out a good way of having simple and effective testing for supervision trees. But as far as we can tell, it's not that day yet.

Wrapping Up

This was a hard chapter to write. OTP is undeniably one of the features that most draws developers to Erlang and Elixir. However, while the abstractions in OTP are often simple and effective, testing asynchronous and "background" code remains one of the hardest things to do in the testing landscape.

This chapter was less "preachy" compared with the other chapters in the book as a direct result of the complexity often involved in testing code that uses OTP. Our aim was to give you options and ideas to address common problems when testing OTP abstractions and asynchronous code in general. For example, we saw how to isolate the functional core of a GenServer, which is often a great approach to simplifying testing but not always possible to do. We talked about techniques for testing asynchronous code, periodic actions, and singleton resources. We finished the chapter by discussing philosophies and ideas around testing failure recovery, resiliency, and supervision trees. We hope you'll be able to use some of these concepts and apply them to your own test suite.

Next we're going to look at testing the most widely used libraries and frameworks in the Elixir ecosystem, Ecto and Phoenix.

CHAPTER 4

Testing Ecto Schemas

As Elixir matures, the community is settling on certain libraries as *the* libraries for certain use cases. Both because of the involvement of José Valim and due to its inclusion in Phoenix, the de facto Elixir web framework, Ecto has found itself positioned as *the* relational database library for Elixir. Due to Ecto's composition of a few discreet parts, Ecto.Schema has found a second purpose, that of a casting and validation library separate from database-related needs. This leaves us with the two most common use cases of Ecto: validation and database interactions. Both uses have their own sets of tests, and we'll cover both in this chapter.

The common saying "Don't test your framework" often leads people to undertest their database code. Before we begin testing our Ecto code, let's examine this saying and identify what practical implications it brings. Ecto is one of the most used libraries in the Elixir community and has a great team behind it who are putting out very solid work. The library "just works." If there are bugs, they're discovered very quickly. When we write our tests, we *should not* test the actual functionality of the library, but we *should* test that our code uses that library's functionality correctly.

This can be confusing, but we can provide you a heuristic that'll help you know whether or not to test code: is it in your codebase? If yes, then generally you should test it. If not, then generally you shouldn't. That means that you *should not* test that a function in Ecto works correctly, but you *should* test that that function is called correctly from your codebase to the library code. If you think about the code that uses Ecto, your tests should actually be focused on the interface presented by that code. That means that your tests should, in theory, not know or care if you're using the library. They should just be focused on input, return values, and side effects (in this case, changes to the data in the database).

During our journey through testing Ecto, we'll start by testing it as a validation library and as a database schema. Then we'll move on to testing your database interactions. Finally, we'll look at tooling, factories, and test cases that can drastically speed up writing your tests. As a bonus, we'll also hit on some test tips and tricks that can be used in other tests as well.

Ecto's Second Use Case

 As of Ecto 3.0, the Ecto team has tipped their hat to Ecto's secondary purpose as a validation library. They've actually separated the library into two parts, allowing the use of schemas without having to pull the database-specific code into your application if you don't need it. This separation of concerns is a great example of discreet, composable parts being used to build a flexible library.

Testing Your Schema Through Changesets

As we mentioned, Ecto can be used for more than just database interactions, the most common case being as a validator of data. Either way you use it, there's a common core of code in the schema file and therefore there are common tests. We'll start by testing that common code, and then we'll make some refactors to make our tests easier to maintain. After that, we'll branch out and refactor our code and tests twice, once for each use case. We'll call it out when it happens. This means that we'll be working in very similar code but switching between file names to keep the concepts separate.

Our Ecto-based code and tests are going to be written to reflect the belief that schema files should contain a bare minimum of logic, usually just the schema definition and functions that are focused on translating data to or from that schema definition. If you like to put more logic in your modules, you'll be on your own for testing it.

Ecto provides two modules, Ecto.Schema and Ecto.Changeset, that we'll use to define our basic schema and core validation behavior. Ecto.Schema allows us to define (Ecto) structs and their types using a domain-specific language (DSL). Ecto.Changeset is code that, among other things, provides type casting and validation logic. When you define a schema with Ecto.Schema, you're defining a container for data, but code tests are focused on behavior. On our first pass, we'll test code using Ecto.Changeset functions under the hood to allow our tests to explore and validate both the definition of the schema as well as the behavior of a single function.

Let's start with a basic schema and then look at how it can be tested. We'll make a generic Ecto schema for a user and build onto it as we learn. Create a new Mix project called testing_ecto with a supervision tree ($ mix new --sup testing_ecto). Next, add {:ecto, "~> 3.0"} to the deps section of the mix.exs file. Run mix deps.get to make sure you have pulled a local copy of Ecto for your project. Now let's create a file called lib/schemas/user_basic_schema.ex and add the following code:

```
testing_ecto/lib/schemas/user_basic_schema.ex
defmodule TestingEcto.Schemas.UserBasicSchema do
  use Ecto.Schema
  import Ecto.Changeset

  @optional_fields [:favorite_number]

  @primary_key false
  embedded_schema do
    field(:date_of_birth, :date)
    field(:email, :string)
    field(:favorite_number, :float)
    field(:first_name, :string)
    field(:last_name, :string)
    field(:phone_number, :string)
  end

  defp all_fields do
    __MODULE__.__schema__(:fields)
  end

  def changeset(params) do
    %__MODULE__{}
    |> cast(params, all_fields())
    |> validate_required(all_fields() -- @optional_fields)
  end
end
```

If you've worked with Ecto before, you're likely to notice that we did something a little funny: we used embedded_schema instead of schema. This means that this schema can't be used to interact with the database because it isn't associated with a table. Don't worry, we'll cover associating it with a database later, but remember that right now we're focused on the core parts of the schema.

We also have a private function that uses the Ecto.Schema reflection functions.[1] The advantage of this function is that it always returns an up-to-date list of the fields (as atoms), even when a new field is added. Since for now we cast all the fields in the changeset, this can be helpful.

---

1. https://hexdocs.pm/ecto/Ecto.Schema.html#module-reflection

That's Not How I Write Schemas!

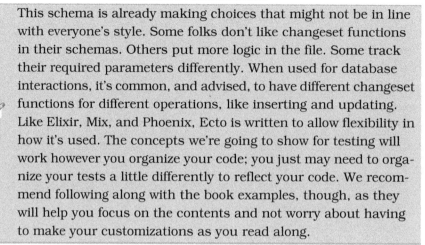

This schema is already making choices that might not be in line with everyone's style. Some folks don't like changeset functions in their schemas. Others put more logic in the file. Some track their required parameters differently. When used for database interactions, it's common, and advised, to have different changeset functions for different operations, like inserting and updating. Like Elixir, Mix, and Phoenix, Ecto is written to allow flexibility in how it's used. The concepts we're going to show for testing will work however you organize your code; you just may need to organize your tests a little differently to reflect your code. We recommend following along with the book examples, though, as they will help you focus on the contents and not worry about having to make your customizations as you read along.

Let's examine the code we have and discuss what aspects of it need to be tested. Our basic schema defines five fields: date_of_birth, favorite_number, first_name, last_name, and phone_number, with favorite_number being the only optional field. Beyond the definition of the schema, we have a single function, changeset/1, that has two lines of code logic in it. Our tests need to cover the basic schema fields (and their types) as well as the two lines of logic in changeset/1, casting and validating the presence of the required fields. We can test all of that through the interface of changeset/1.

Let's go ahead and start by writing a success test. Create a test file at test/schemas/user_basic_schema_1_test.exs in your project. Note that we've appended a 1 in the file name since, in order to provide you with refactored versions with the included code, we had to version our test files. That breaks a convention of having your test file name match the name of the code under test (but with a trailing _test.exs).

You're welcome to skip this test file if you plan to do the upcoming refactors in place instead of in a new file.

testing_ecto/test/schemas/user_basic_schema_1_test.exs
```
Line 1  defmodule TestingEcto.Schemas.UserBasicSchema1Test do
          use ExUnit.Case
          alias Ecto.Changeset
          alias TestingEcto.Schemas.UserBasicSchema
     5
          @schema_fields [
            :date_of_birth,
            :email,
```

```
         :favorite_number,
10       :first_name,
         :last_name,
         :phone_number
     ]

15   describe "changeset/1" do
       test "success: returns a valid changeset when given valid arguments" do
         params = %{
           "date_of_birth" => "1948-02-28",
           "email" => "example@example.com",
20         "favorite_number" => 3.14,
           "first_name" => "Bob",
           "last_name" => "Matthews",
           "phone_number" => "555-555-5555"
         }
25
         changeset = UserBasicSchema.changeset(params)
         assert %Changeset{valid?: true, changes: changes} = changeset

         mutated = [:date_of_birth]
30
         for field <- @schema_fields, field not in mutated do
           actual = Map.get(changes, field)
           expected = params[Atom.to_string(field)]
           assert actual == expected,
35                 "Values did not match for field: #{field}\nexpected: #{
                     inspect(expected)
                   }\nactual: #{inspect(actual)}"
         end

40       expected_dob = Date.from_iso8601!(params["date_of_birth"])
         assert changes.date_of_birth == expected_dob
       end

     end
45 end
```

We have a test file with a module attribute listing the fields on the schema and a happy path test. We chose to use a local (in the test) list of the fields instead of referencing the schema somehow, because it gives us basic protection against regressions. If someone accidentally deletes a line from the schema defining a field, some of our tests will catch it. We'll see that in a later test, but for now we can file it away.

Our test is a happy path test. We have some hard-coded, known-good parameters. It's worth noting that our parameters have string keys, as this is common since Ecto casting and validation often happen on external input (such as deserialized JSON). We exercise the test at line 26, passing those parameters to changeset/1 and asserting that we're getting back a valid changeset. We could just have that line bind the response to a variable and make the assertion on a subsequent line, but the error that'll result if it fails is clear enough—especially if you have color test output—that we don't need to.

The following test failure output shows us that the two changesets vary on the value of :valid?. If you have color output in your shell, it'll be highlighted.

```
1) test changeset/1 success: returns a valid changeset when given valid
     arguments                         (TestingEcto.Schemas.UserBasicSchema1Test)
test/schemas/user_basic_schema_1_test.exs:16
match (=) failed
code:  assert %Changeset{valid?: true, changes: changes} = changeset
left:  %Ecto.Changeset{changes: changes, valid?: true}
right: %Ecto.Changeset{
         changes: %{date_of_birth: ~D[1948-02-28], first_name: "Bob",
                    last_name: "Matthews", phone_number: "555-555-5555"},
         valid?: false,
«rest of test output»
```

Assuming the response is a valid changeset, we want to make sure that the expected new values are present in the changes field of the returned changeset. We leverage a list comprehension, using the module attribute @schema_fields to provide the fields to check. We have to exclude the date of birth, though, because the data itself will have changed when it was cast to Ecto's :date type. As a result, we need an additional assertion to validate that the correct date is present in the changes.

Our test is a happy path test, but it tells us more than just that things work when given the right data. As we mentioned before, since tests can only focus on behavior (return values and side effects), we can't directly test the description of the schema. But this test, and the ones that follow, will only pass if the schema is defined correctly. While no individual test can provide that guarantee, all of the tests for changeset/1 will together provide that coverage. We'll look at another approach to this when we work on our refactor.

Our happy path test, in theory, only passes if the values are being cast, so this is a success test for the cast/3 call in the changeset/1 function. Let's lock down our coverage of that line by adding an error test for that same line. We'll pass values that can't be cast correctly and then look for the errors on the changeset. Add this test inside of the same describe block, under your last test:

```
Line 1  test "error: returns an error changeset when given un-castable values" do
   -      not_a_string = DateTime.utc_now()
   -
   -      params = %{
   5        "date_of_birth" => "not a date",
```

```
        "email" => not_a_string,
        "favorite_number" => "not a number",
        "first_name" => not_a_string,
        "last_name" => not_a_string,
10      "phone_number" => not_a_string
      }

      changeset = UserBasicSchema.changeset(params)

15    assert %Changeset{valid?: false, errors: errors} = changeset

      for field <- @schema_fields do
        assert errors[field], "expected an error for #{field}"
        {_, meta} = errors[field]
20
        assert meta[:validation] == :cast,
              "The validation type, #{meta[:validation]}, is incorrect."
      end
    end
```

The setup is similar to the success test, but you'll see that we've found different data types that we know Ecto can't cast to the types defined in the schema. Our line to exercise is the same, and the following pattern match and assertion only differ in that they expect valid? to be false. But then we hit a different list comprehension. Using our list of expected fields, @schema_fields, we have a two-part assertion for each field. The first, at line 18, is to make sure there's an error for that field. The second (line 22) is to make sure it's a cast error. When you write assertions like this, it's helpful to make sure your custom error messages are different. Even though test output tells you the line where the error occurred, having the same message will make it too easy to accidentally debug a failure at the wrong assertion. Ultimately, we only care that a cast error is present, but because there are slight differences in the errors for each field, as shown in the following code sample, we have to jump through a couple of hoops. The following snippet shows the errors from our changeset:

```
[
  favorite_number: {"is invalid", [type: :float, validation: :cast]},
  date_of_birth: {"is invalid", [type: :date, validation: :cast]},
  last_name: {"is invalid", [type: :string, validation: :cast]},
  phone_number: {"is invalid", [type: :string, validation: :cast]}
]
```

Each error has a different type, which causes the need for the multistep assertions. Another approach to this would be to process the errors ahead of time and remap the list to only contain the field name and the validation type. Phoenix provides a function, called errors_on, that remaps errors to just be the field name and the error message (the string). It's a small function,[2] and one that can be copied straight into your non-Phoenix codebase, but we aren't fans of matching on strings when they aren't needed. Later in this chapter we'll present an alternative. For now let's leave the two-step assertion in place.

Between the success test and the error test, we've covered both that cast/3 is present in the changeset function and that we've been able to make assertions about data types in the field definitions. Let's move on to testing the required fields. When writing this next test, it's important to know that Ecto treats nil, empty strings (""), and missing keys as violations of validate_required/2. Let's add one more test, an error case, to that same describe block.

```
test "error: returns error changeset when required fields are missing" do
  params = %{}

  assert %Changeset{valid?: false, errors: errors} =
           UserBasicSchema.changeset(params)

  optional_params = [:favorite_number]
  expected_fields = @schema_fields -- optional_params

  for field <- expected_fields do
    assert errors[field], "Field #{inspect(field)} is missing from errors."
    {_, meta} = errors[field]

    assert meta[:validation] == :required,
           "The validation type, #{meta[:validation]}, is incorrect."
  end

  for field <- optional_params do
    refute errors[field],
           "The optional field #{field} is required when it shouldn't be."
  end
end
```

The format of this test should feel familiar by now. The following explains some notable changes in the preceding code:

- We're passing an empty map of parameters to force the violation of the required validation.

- We're removing the optional parameter fields (in this case, just :favorite_number) from the list comprehension.

- The type of error that we're expecting is :required and not :cast.

There's an additional assertion at the bottom to make sure that there isn't an error for :favorite_number. We could have assertions to guarantee that there

---

2. https://github.com/phoenixframework/phoenix/blob/cc261a67a83649555841b92c3cbc1df024888cc8/installer/templates/phx_ecto/data_case.ex#L48

are no errors on optional parameters, but because we're passing an empty map of parameters, there should be no way for an error to show up on a parameter we didn't pass.

When testing for the presence of Ecto errors, try to identify how to make sure that your test covers what it needs with the bare minimum of assumptions about the data it's examining. This test is focused on the presence of required errors. We didn't assume we knew the size of the error list, a practice that you'll come across often. While it seems on the surface that such an assertion might be helpful, it can lead to a brittle test. We know from our success test that if we pass in good data, things are good. This test confirms that we're getting the right errors for missing data that is required. If we make any other assumptions about what the errors on the changeset should look like, we run the risk of having a test failure on the presence of an error that isn't the focus of the test. This situation could happen if there was more logic written in the changeset/1 function that inserted a different error on :favorite_number. The error would be present, but it isn't the concern of this test. A good practice for all unit tests, not just Ecto focused ones, is to ensure failures are caused by problems in the code being tested, and not by the testing code.

We've now written the tests to cover a schema definition and a simple changeset function. Our tests check every aspect of the return values, and we can be confident that our code works as intended. If you were to make changes to the schema, the tests we wrote would either need to be updated (if new fields are added) or supplemented with new tests (if new validations are added). Later in this chapter, we'll branch the code and tests we just wrote to specialize our schema for either input validation or for database interactions. Before we do that, though, we're going to make another pass at the tests we just wrote to identify patterns and changes we can make to specialize our tests for code that uses Ecto.Schema.

Refactoring to Increase Test Maintainability

Most applications that use Ecto have more than one schema, and over time each schema grows to have more fields or more logic in its changeset functions. We're going to refactor our existing test file to allow our code to be easier to maintain, but that means we're going to tread into some territory that makes some folk uncomfortable: we're going to refactor our tests to be self-updating. We'll build safety into the way we test to avoid a lot of the typical caveats that leave most people burned by writing self-updating tests.

We want to make it clear that we don't promote this style of testing wholesale across your application. We're working in a section of our code that's fairly predictable and limited in scope. Our schemas only carry the definition and changeset functions.

We're going to create a new test file, testing_ecto/test/schemas/user_basic_schema_2_test.exs, but we're going have it test the same schema code as our previous test file. We mentioned earlier that we were adding numbers into the test file names that would break the convention of matching the test and application file names. Even though we called this a refactor, it's probably best to create a second file, too, because doing so will make it easier to follow along with the book.

Adding Safety Into Your Schema Tests

Open your new test file and add the following code. You'll see that we're testing the same module as our previous file, TestingEcto.Schemas.UserBasicSchema:

```
testing_ecto/test/schemas/user_basic_schema_2_test.exs
Line 1  defmodule TestingEcto.Schemas.UserBasicSchema2Test do
          use ExUnit.Case
          alias Ecto.Changeset
          alias TestingEcto.Schemas.UserBasicSchema
     5
          @expected_fields_with_types [
            {:date_of_birth, :date},
            {:email, :string},
            {:favorite_number, :float},
    10      {:first_name, :string},
            {:last_name, :string},
            {:phone_number, :string}
          ]
          describe "fields and types" do
    15      @tag :schema_definition
            test "it has the correct fields and types" do
              actual_fields_with_types =
                for field <- UserBasicSchema.__schema__(:fields) do
                  type = UserBasicSchema.__schema__(:type, field)
    20            {field, type}
                end

              assert MapSet.new(actual_fields_with_types) ==
                       MapSet.new(@expected_fields_with_types)
    25      end
          end

        end
```

Aside from the module name, the first real change is that instead of having a module attribute, @schema_fields, we have an attribute called @expected_fields_with_types. This attribute contains a keyword list with the field names and the expected field type for our schema. Our previous test did give us confidence that the schema defined the correct types for the field, but having this information duplicated in the test file is a major component of the safety we promised to give you for this refactor. We'll come back to why it's important after we've added more to our file.

The describe block at line 14 doesn't follow the convention of a function name because we aren't testing a public function. Instead, our exercise code is a little unusual. Instead of calling a function, we're building a keyword list of field names and types similar to that in our @expected_fields_with_types module attribute. To do this, we're leveraging two calls to reflection functions from Ecto.Schema. If you recall, we first saw reflection in the schema file itself. We're already familiar with __schema__/1 (line 18). __schema__/2 (line 19) returns a single atom for the field type. Our generator is just a call to UserBasic-Schema.__schema__(:fields). Each iteration then calls UserBasicSchema.__schema__(:type, field), which returns an atom representing the type, which will be exactly what was set in the schema file itself. Our list comprehension returns a keyword list of field names and types that comes from the schema definition itself, but it's formatted in the same way as the data stored in @expected_fields_with_types.

This test then checks that the test's expectation of the field names and types (@expected_fields_with_types) matches what's really defined in the file. Again, we didn't do this in our first pass on the file because we didn't need to. Our tests provided coverage for this without us being so explicit. It's important to note that since we're using == for the comparison in our assertion, both lists must be in the same order for the assertion to pass. To address that, we call MapSet.new/1 on both lists. Sets are unordered, and comparing two sets only takes elements into consideration, making it perfect for this use case.

One last new feature of this test is the addition of a test tag, :schema_definition, at line 15. At this point, our tests haven't evolved enough for this to be useful. Later in this chapter, we'll leverage this tag to only run this test.

We stated that this test adds safety to the rest of the refactoring work we're about to do. Let's play with this for a moment. Comment out one of the fields from your schema; let's say field(:first_name, :string). Now run your tests and check the output. It should look something like the following.

```
1) test fields and types it has the correct fields and types
                          (TestingEcto.Schemas.UserBasicSchema2Test)
   test/schemas/user_basic_schema_2_test.exs:16
   Assertion with == failed
   code:  assert MapSet.new(actual_fields_with_types) ==
          MapSet.new(@expected_fields_with_types)
   left:  #MapSet<[{:date_of_birth, :date}, {:favorite_number, :float},
                  {:last_name, :string}, {:phone_number, :string}]>
```

```
right: #MapSet<[{:date_of_birth, :date}, {:favorite_number, :float},
                {:first_name, :string}, {:last_name, :string},
                {:phone_number, :string}]>
stacktrace:
  test/schemas/user_basic_schema_2_test.exs:23: (test))
```

If you have color output from your tests, you'll see immediately that {:first_name, :string} is extra in the expected fields. A failure similar to this would happen if you were to add a new field to your schema. We now have very fast validation feedback that something isn't right, which points us back to the schema definition. @expected_fields_with_types is also going to be used in our upcoming tests as a reference for how the schema is defined. The test we just wrote will help us make sure it's always accurate. If you need to add or remove fields from your schema, you just need to update the list stored in @expected_fields_with_types as well.

There's an added bonus to having this definition at the top of our test file. We've mentioned previously in this book that well-written tests serve as documentation for your code. In this case, we've taken it a step further by making sure there's an accurate description of the schema basics sitting at the top of the file. We don't recommend doing this solely for the sake of having extra reference information in your tests, but it can be nice to have when working in the test file.

Now that we have guaranteed its accuracy, let's write a test to take advantage of @expected_fields_with_types. Before we continue, uncomment the field for first name to get our code back to the correct state.

Creating a Self-Updating Test

Before we write our first test, we're going to write a helper function at the bottom of our test file, after all describe blocks. The new function will be called valid_params/1. Define it with the following code:

```
defp valid_params(fields_with_types) do
  valid_value_by_type = %{
    date: fn -> to_string(Faker.Date.date_of_birth()) end,
    float: fn -> :rand.uniform() * 10 end,
    string: fn -> Faker.Lorem.word() end
  }

  for {field, type} <- fields_with_types, into: %{} do
    {Atom.to_string(field), valid_value_by_type[type].()}
  end
end
```

We'll address the introduction of Faker shortly, but let's discuss what this function does first. The return value of this function is a map functionally identical to the params we had in our success test in our previous iteration of this file. It's just a string-keyed map of valid parameters, but it's built dynamically based off of the list of fields and types passed to it. We'll evolve this concept later on. For now, we have a way to get a list of valid parameters in a repeatable way. The values provided are randomized because the values themselves shouldn't impact the results of the test. We're using anonymous functions so that we get different values for the new field. This isn't strictly necessary, but it makes our data slightly more realistic. We're using a new library, Faker, to provide some of that data. Faker's sole purpose is to provide realistically shaped data. In our case, we're using the module Lorem to generate random words. In order to keep our code compiling and running, you'll need to add Faker into the project dependencies. In the deps section of the mix.exs file, you'll need to add the line {:faker, "~> 0.13.0", only: [:test, :dev]}. We've limited it to the test and dev environments because we don't intend to use Faker in production code. We've left it in :dev because it's nice to be able to drop into a shell session (iex -S mix) to explore the functionality.

Now that we have our helper function, we're ready to write our test. Add this new describe block and test to your test file. You'll notice that it's almost the same, except that our list comprehension is using the @fields_and_types for its generator (but dropping the type) and that the valid parameters are coming from the helper function instead of being hard-coded.

```elixir
describe "changeset/1" do
  test "success: returns a valid changeset when given valid arguments" do
    valid_params = valid_params(@expected_fields_with_types)

    changeset = UserBasicSchema.changeset(valid_params)
    assert %Changeset{valid?: true, changes: changes} = changeset

    mutated = [:date_of_birth]

    for {field, _} <- @expected_fields_with_types, field not in mutated do
      actual = Map.get(changes, field)
      expected = valid_params[Atom.to_string(field)]
      assert actual == expected,
             "Values did not match for field: #{field}\nexpected: #{
               inspect(expected)
             }\nactual: #{inspect(actual)}"
    end

    expected_dob = Date.from_iso8601!(valid_params["date_of_birth"])
    assert changes.date_of_birth == expected_dob
  end
end
```

Now that you've added the test, run the test file to make sure it's passing. Once you've got it passing, let's explore the benefit of this refactor. Think of the first test, asserting on fields and types, as a control. Any changes you make to your file will require an intentional update to that control. So, let's imagine that our code is being upgraded and that we're going to add a new field to our schema. Add a new middle name field (field(:middle_name, :string)) into the schema definition. Now run your tests again, using mix test test/schemas/user_basic_schema_2_test.exs. You'll see more than one test failing.

While it's easy to pick out the test failure to focus on when you have a fairly new and small test file, you may have more test failures in a scenario like this as your schema grows. Remember that tag we added to the test? Since we know we changed the fields on the schema, it seems like a good time to isolate the test that focuses on the schema definitions. Rerun your tests, but this time we'll pass the tag as well, mix test --only schema_definition test/schemas/user_basic_schema_2_test.exs. You should see a single failure similar to the following:

```
1) test fields and types it has the correct fields and types
                              (TestingEcto.Schemas.UserBasicSchema2Test)
   test/schemas/user_basic_schema_2_test.exs:16
   Assertion with == failed
   code:  assert Enum.sort(actual_fields_with_types) ==
          Enum.sort(@expected_fields_with_types)
   left:  [{:date_of_birth, :date}, {:favorite_number, :float},
          {:first_name, :string}, {:last_name, :string},
          {:middle_name, :string}, {:phone_number, :string}]
   right: [date_of_birth: :date, favorite_number: :float,
          first_name: :string, last_name: :string, phone_number: :string]
   stacktrace:
     test/schemas/user_basic_schema_2_test.exs:23: (test)
```

We've seen similar failed output before when we commented out a field, but now the test is telling us that more fields are on the schema than the test expects, instead of a field missing on the schema. All we have to do is update the test's expectation of the definition to include the new field:

```
@expected_fields_with_types [
  {:date_of_birth, :date},
  {:favorite_number, :float},
  {:first_name, :string},
  {:last_name, :string},
  {:middle_name, :string},
  {:phone_number, :string}
```

After adding the field for middle name, rerun the whole test file. All of the tests should pass. What did this bring us? We intentionally added a new field and our tests immediately informed us that they were out-of-date. From their feedback, we were able to update a single location in our test file, and now the test for fields and types is passing, letting us know that our test and schema have the same definition. Given that we didn't have the test in the first version of our file, this doesn't really feel like a win. The value comes from the fact that the second test, checking for success with valid params, updated itself. The new field is automatically included in the test coverage by updating @fields_and_types.

It's important to note that if, like with :date_of_birth, the data is mutated by the cast function in the changeset, you'll need to add it to the list of mutated values and add explicit assertions for the value in the changes in the changeset. While it isn't entirely self-updating in that case, you still have the advantage that tests are making sure you update them, reducing the effort of maintenance.

Before we write any more code, take your schema back to its previous state by removing the middle name field from the definition in your schema and from the @fields_and_types in your test file.

First we'll update the test for the cast errors. To do this, we'll add one more helper function, similar to valid_params/1 but this time called invalid_params/1. It'll work similarly but will return values that can't be cast for the field's type. Open your test file and add this function below your other helper function:

```
defp invalid_params(fields_with_types) do
  invalid_value_by_type = %{
    date: fn -> Faker.Lorem.word() end,
    float: fn -> Faker.Lorem.word() end,
    string: fn -> DateTime.utc_now() end
  }

  for {field, type} <- fields_with_types, into: %{} do
    {Atom.to_string(field), invalid_value_by_type[type].()}
  end
end
```

The function is clearly constructed to work like valid_params/1 but to return values that can't be cast to the matching types. With this added, we can now write an updated version of our error test for casting. You can either write the following test or copy the test from the old file and update it:

```
Line 1  test "error: returns an error changeset when given un-castable values" do
          invalid_params = invalid_params(@expected_fields_with_types)

          assert %Changeset{valid?: false, errors: errors} =
    5             UserBasicSchema.changeset(invalid_params)
```

```
    for {field, _} <- @expected_fields_with_types do
      assert errors[field], "The field :#{field} is missing from errors."
      {_, meta} = errors[field]

      assert meta[:validation] == :cast,
             "The validation type, #{meta[:validation]}, is incorrect."
    end
  end
end
```

Just like our previous test, this test is almost identical to the previous version, but now it includes a call to the helper function to get the bad data on line 2. Since this test makes assertions on all of the fields for the schema, just like the success test we already wrote, our work is done. You're welcome to repeat the process of adding a new field to the schema to see that it has the same results we had previously. If you do so, you'll see both the "fields and types" test and the success test failing. The test we just wrote won't fail because it isn't using the new field yet, but as soon as you update the test's @fields_and_types definition, all tests should pass and will be testing the new field.

The last refactor for us will be the error test for required fields. Let's look at the code from the previous version of this test again:

```
test "error: returns error changeset when required fields are missing" do
  params = %{}

  assert %Changeset{valid?: false, errors: errors} =
           UserBasicSchema.changeset(params)

  optional_params = [:favorite_number]
  expected_fields = @schema_fields -- optional_params

  for field <- expected_fields do
    assert errors[field], "Field #{inspect(field)} is missing from errors."
    {_, meta} = errors[field]

    assert meta[:validation] == :required,
           "The validation type, #{meta[:validation]}, is incorrect."
  end

  for field <- optional_params do
    refute errors[field],
           "The optional field #{field} is required when it shouldn't be."
  end
end
```

This test makes sure it only tests for errors on the required parameters by maintaining an internal list of which parameters are optional. There are always trade-offs to having something like this list. When your test file is small and organized, it's not too bad to maintain that list. When you add a new field that's optional, you need to remember to update the list, but it's usually manageable.

In our refactor, we can continue to keep and maintain the list in the test like that. But instead, let's explore moving it to the top of the file, just under the @fields_and_types attribute. Update your attribute definitions to now have an @optional module attribute.

Your attribute definitions should now look like the following:

```
@expected_fields_with_types [
  {:date_of_birth, :date},
  {:email, :string},
  {:favorite_number, :float},
  {:first_name, :string},
  {:last_name, :string},
  {:phone_number, :string}
]
@optional [:favorite_number]
```

Moving the test file's list of optional parameters serves two purposes. The most important is that it's present, right under the definition of the fields and types. That makes it way more likely that when you're adding an optional field to your schema, your tests will inform you that they don't match the schema and you need to update the types and fields. The second purpose, which is more of a bonus, is that it adds just a little more documentation to your test file. If you have different changesets with different required fields, you'll keep multiple lists like this. Just make sure to give them clear names so that they're helpful instead of confusing.

Now that we have that module attribute set, we'll leverage it in our refactor. Again, you can grab the following test from the old test file and modify it, or you can type it all in. Add the following test into your file:

```
Line 1  test "error: returns error changeset when required fields are missing" do
          params = %{}

          assert %Changeset{valid?: false, errors: errors} =
   5              UserBasicSchema.changeset(params)

          for {field, _} <- @expected_fields_with_types, field not in @optional do
            assert errors[field], "The field :#{field} is missing from errors."
            {_, meta} = errors[field]
  10
            assert meta[:validation] == :required,
                   "The validation type, #{meta[:validation]}, is incorrect."
          end

  15      for {field, _} <- @optional do
```

```
    refute errors[field],
          "The optional field #{field} is required when it shouldn't be."
  end
end
```

Since the test setup still requires an empty set of parameters, the only changes we need to make to update our test are around filtering out the optional parameters so that we only assert that there are errors for each of the required parameters. We've updated our list comprehension similar to the previous tests, where the type is being ignored. The other major update to the test is that the list comprehension is now filtering out fields that are optional, leveraging the filter functionality of list comprehensions and the new @optional attribute.

Run your tests and they should all pass. We've now refactored our test file to improve the maintainability of the file in two ways. The first is that some of the tests actually update with changes to the file they test, and they do so in a safe way. Most attempts at writing self-updating tests fail to provide a mechanism to guarantee they work, and as a result end up creating way more headaches than they remove. We're comfortable doing this here specifically because our pattern has a very limited scope (Ecto schemas) and because we've written enough of these same files over and over again to be confident in the patterns. Be very careful if you try to apply this style of testing anywhere else.

The second benefit of this style of testing is that it raises alerts when things have changed, instead of allowing new code to be untested. It's very common for a new field on a schema to not be tested correctly when it's added after the fact. These tests won't let that happen.

Now that we've refactored our schema tests, let's branch out and start to specialize our schema file and update our tests to match it. We'll start with using our schema as data validation code.

Creating a SchemaCase for Shared Test Code

Case templates are very useful when we identify a pattern for test files that would benefit from shared code. Our refactors on the basic schema tests created two helper functions, valid_params/1 and invalid_params/1, that would be good to move into a common place to be reused by all our schema tests. We'll create a case template called SchemaCase and move the helper functions there. Create a new file called testing_ecto/test/schema_case.ex and add the basic structure for a case template:

```
testing_ecto/test/schema_case.ex
defmodule TestingEcto.SchemaCase do
  use ExUnit.CaseTemplate

  using do
    quote do
      alias Ecto.Changeset
      import TestingEcto.SchemaCase
    end
  end

end
```

For now, it's pretty simple. We can alias Ecto.Changeset into the case template because all future schema tests will need it. We have import TestingEcto.SchemaCase included; so when we add the helper functions, anything that "uses" the template will get those functions. Our last step is to copy the two functions, valid_params/1 and invalid_params/1, into the file, below the "using" block. Just be sure to make both functions public (def instead of defp), as import only works with public functions. The case template is now ready to go, but we need to make sure it's compiled in our app when running tests. We'll also make one last refactor pass on our test file, making sure it uses the case template and no longer contains the code locally.

To make sure the case template is available in the application when it runs tests, let's modify our mix.exs file. Open it up and add elixirc_paths: elixirc_paths(Mix.env()), into the list in the project section:

```
testing_ecto/mix.exs
def project do
  [
    app: :testing_ecto,
    version: "0.1.0",
    elixir: "~> 1.10",
    start_permanent: Mix.env() == :prod,
    elixirc_paths: elixirc_paths(Mix.env()),
    deps: deps()
  ]
end
```

That's calling a function that doesn't exist yet, elixirc_paths/1, so we need to add that function as well. Above the deps section of your mix file, add the following function heads:

```
testing_ecto/mix.exs
Line 1  defp elixirc_paths(:test), do: ["lib", "test"]
     2  defp elixirc_paths(_), do: ["lib"]
```

The line that matters the most here is line 1, where we're telling the application to include all the files in the test directory when compiling in the test environment. This will make the SchemaCase file available in the :test environment while keeping it out of the :dev and :prod environments, or any other environments added later.

Now we just need to refactor the test file. Instead of changing the code in place, we'll make a copy of testing_ecto/test/schemas/user_basic_schema_2_test.exs, calling it testing_ecto/test/schemas/user_basic_schema_3_test.exs. Ignoring the tests, nested inside of the describe blocks, your file will look like the following code:

```
testing_ecto/test/schemas/user_basic_schema_3_test.exs
Line 1  defmodule TestingEcto.Schemas.UserBasicSchema3Test do
          use TestingEcto.SchemaCase
          alias TestingEcto.Schemas.UserBasicSchema

     5    @expected_fields_with_types [
            {:date_of_birth, :date},
            {:email, :string},
            {:favorite_number, :float},
            {:first_name, :string},
    10      {:last_name, :string},
            {:phone_number, :string}
          ]
          @optional [:favorite_number]

    15    describe "fields and types" do
          end

          describe "changeset/1" do
          end
    20  end
```

As before, make sure to rename your test module, upping the number to 3 (line 1) to avoid naming conflicts. Replace the two lines containing use ExUnit.Case and alias Ecto.Changeset with use TestingEcto.SchemaCase, as seen on line 2. Now, since SchemaCase has the valid_params/1 and invalid_params/1 functions, you can delete them from the file.

Run mix test test/schemas/user_basic_schema_3_test.exs to verify that all of your tests pass the same as before. We've now moved the code that we believe will be common between all our tests into a common place so that we only have to maintain one copy of the functions we've written. We'll add more common code to our case template later in this chapter.

Testing an Ecto Schema as a Data Validator

It's very common in web applications to do some basic validation of user input in the controller so that if easy-to-detect issues are present, the application doesn't spend time doing work (or calling the database) when there isn't a chance of success. The code that we have already written takes input and casts it to the appropriate value, returning errors for any data that can't be cast or for any required parameters that are missing. This is exactly the kind of basic validation that we're talking about. With some very minor changes, we will update our code to serve as a validator. After that, we will update our refactored tests to reflect the changes.

As mentioned, our code already does the work we want. The only issues we have now is that the interface isn't ideal. Our application code isn't going to want to receive a changeset when the code executes successfully. Ideally, when the input is valid, our validator will return a tuple with :ok and a struct with the fields and values. When it errors, we'll still return the changeset with errors, but inside of an error tuple. There's one other interface change we should make: renaming the function. Since we're no longer returning a changeset, we'll rename the one public function, changeset/1, to instead reflect what the code is doing. Make a copy of the schema file at the path lib/schemas/user_validator.ex. We'll show the updated file and then call out the changes that need to be made:

```
testing_ecto/lib/schemas/user_validator.ex
Line 1  defmodule TestingEcto.Schemas.UserValidator do
          use Ecto.Schema
          import Ecto.Changeset

    5     @optional_fields [:favorite_number]

          @primary_key false
          embedded_schema do
            field(:date_of_birth, :date)
   10       field(:email, :string)
            field(:favorite_number, :float)
            field(:first_name, :string)
            field(:last_name, :string)
            field(:phone_number, :string)
   15     end

          defp all_fields do
            __MODULE__.__schema__(:fields)
          end
   20
```

```
    def cast_and_validate(params) do
      %__MODULE__{}
      |> cast(params, all_fields())
      |> validate_required(all_fields() -- @optional_fields)
25    |> apply_changes_if_valid()
    end

    defp apply_changes_if_valid(%Ecto.Changeset{valid?: true} = changeset) do
      {:ok, Ecto.Changeset.apply_changes(changeset)}
30    end

    defp apply_changes_if_valid(%Ecto.Changeset{} = changeset) do
      {:error, changeset}
    end
35  end
```

The first change to make is to the module name, updating it to TestingEcto.Schemas.UserValidator, as seen on line 1. Hopefully this is self-explanatory, but it's just a reminder that our naming and file structure matches the contrived code for this book. We aren't recommending this file structure and definitely wouldn't recommend keeping validators and "normal" schemas in the same directory, since they are likely to be used in very different parts of the application.

Next, update the name of the public function on the file to cast_and_validate, as seen on line 21. The only thing left is to change the function to return tuples and possibly a struct instead of a changeset. Add the following two private function heads, as seen between lines 28 and 34. They're expecting an Ecto.Changeset struct and pattern matching off of the :valid? field in the changeset. You can see that each wraps the response in a tuple with the correct status (:ok or :error), and the success case calls Ecto.Changeset.apply_changes/1,[3] which will return a TestingEcto.Schemas.UserValidator struct with all the new values. Be careful, though, as Ecto.Changeset.apply_changes/1 will work even if the changeset isn't valid, which is why we've branched the code.

Now all that's left is to add our local apply_changes_if_valid/1 into the pipeline at the end of the newly renamed cast_and_validate/1. You can see it in our code on line 25. We now have a functional validator. We need to add tests.

We'll copy our updated test file, testing_ecto/test/schemas/user_basic_schema_3_test.exs, to a new location, testing_ecto/test/schemas/user_validator_test.exs. We'll be able to update the file without too much work. The first thing we need to do is update the name of the file under test. Every instance of UserBasicSchema in the file needs to be

---

3.   https://hexdocs.pm/ecto/3.4.4/Ecto.Changeset.html#//apple_ref/Function/apply_changes%2F1

replaced with UserValidator. If you're able to do a blanket find and replace, the top of your test file should end up looking like the following code:

```
testing_ecto/test/schemas/user_validator_test.exs
Line 1  defmodule TestingEcto.Schemas.UserValidatorTest do
2         use TestingEcto.SchemaCase
3         alias TestingEcto.Schemas.UserValidator
```

The module name (line 1) and the alias for your test subject (line 3) should match your code. Assuming you were able to easily replace all of the instances, the test should be able to compile, but running mix test will produce three failing tests because, while the test for "fields and types" exercises code through the reflection functions, the three tests in the "changeset/1" describe block all exercise a function that no longer exists. Let's update our test to address this next. Update the describe block and the first test in it to look like this:

```
Line 1  describe "cast_and_validate/1" do
          test "success: returns a valid changeset when given valid arguments" do
            valid_params = valid_params(@expected_fields_with_types)

5           {:ok, result} = UserValidator.cast_and_validate(valid_params)
            assert %UserValidator{} = result
            mutated = [:date_of_birth]

            for {field, _} <- @expected_fields_with_types, field not in mutated do
10            assert Map.get(result, field) == valid_params[Atom.to_string(field)]
            end

            expected_dob = Date.from_iso8601!(valid_params["date_of_birth"])
            assert result.date_of_birth == expected_dob
15        end
```

Change the describe description to be cast_and_validate/1 (line 1). Next, we need to update the line that exercises the code (line 5) in two ways. It should match to {:ok, result} and it should call UserValidator.cast_and_validate/1 to exercise the code. The following line (6) should be updated to assert that the result is the expected kind of struct, %UserValidator{}. Those two lines could've been combined, but we were facing line-length limitations. Feel free to add them together if that's your preferred style.

There are just two more places to update the test code. changes should be replaced with result at lines 10 and 14. The test should now be able to run and pass. Let's try it out by running it with mix test test/schemas/user_validator_test.exs: followed immediately by a line number from the middle of the test (for example, mix test test/schemas/user_validator_test.exs:39). This will run just the one test, skipping the tests that we already know don't work. This won't impact us here. The reason to use a line number from the middle of the test instead of the line the test starts on is so that, as you change your file, the line number you're using is more likely to continue to reference the same test. If you used the line number from the first line of the test, adding a single line of code in your file above breaks that reference. This is particularly useful if you have to add debugging code into the file, which might shift the start of your test to a later line number.

The test should pass, but you'll still see some warnings that tell you that you have an unused alias and that a private or undefined function is being called. Let's start to clear those up by updating the next test, the one focusing on errors for values that can't be cast.

The test should be updated to look like this:

```
Line 1  test "error: returns an error changeset when given un-castable values" do
          invalid_params = invalid_params(@expected_fields_with_types)

          assert {:error, %Changeset{errors: errors}} =
     5            UserValidator.cast_and_validate(invalid_params)

          for {field, _} <- @expected_fields_with_types do
            assert errors[field], "The field :#{field} is missing from errors."
            {_, meta} = errors[field]
    10
            assert meta[:validation] == :cast,
                   "The validation type, #{meta[:validation]}, is incorrect."
          end
        end
```

The only actual changes are on the line that exercises the code (4), but there are a few different things on that line. First, we need to update the pattern on the left of the = to wrap the changeset in a tuple with :error as the first element. Our test no longer cares if it's getting an invalid changeset back; instead, it only cares that if it gets an error tuple, the second element is a changeset with errors. So, we can remove the valid?: false from the pattern. Finally, update the function being called from changeset/1 to cast_and_validate/1. The test should run and pass just fine now.

The last test should take the same changes and then look like this:

```
test "error: returns error changeset when required fields are missing" do
  params = %{}

  assert {:error, %Changeset{errors: errors}} =
         UserValidator.cast_and_validate(params)

  for {field, _} <- @expected_fields_with_types, field not in @optional do
    assert errors[field], "The field :#{field} is missing from errors."
```

```
    {_, meta} = errors[field]
    assert meta[:validation] == :required,
           "The validation type, #{meta[:validation]}, is incorrect."
  end
end
```

All the tests should now be passing. You can see that the main concepts of our tests stay the same as when we were testing our basic schema. The tests just had to be updated to reflect the small changes in the UserValidator's interface.

Next we'll step back to the basic schema and modify it for interactions with the database. Then we'll discuss the ways to test a database schema.

Testing an Ecto Schema for Database Interactions

The most common use case for Ecto schemas is to enable easy interaction with a database. While we keep our schemas to a minimum of logic—just the schema definition and changeset function or functions—we still need to make some changes in order to use our schema with a database. We'll update the basic schema we wrote (skipping the changes we made for using it as a validator) and then update our tests. Once we've covered the schema aspects, we'll move on to cover testing queries that use the schema.

Adding a Database into Our Application

Before we can make the necessary changes, we need to make sure that we have a local running database. Given that every reader will have a different local setup, we're going to leverage Docker to reduce the chance issues due to local environment differences. We have to make the assumption that you already have or are able to set up Docker on your computer.[4] We've provided, with the testing_ecto application code, two files that you should copy into your application directory: testing_ecto/docker-compose.yml and testing_ecto/Makefile. Keep them at the root level of your local testing_ecto application.

The docker-compose.yml file has the specifications to start and run a Postgres container that matches the username and password used in this book. To make things easier, we've included a Makefile to give you simple commands to get up and running. Once the files are in place, open a new shell session in the same directory. This will allow us to jump between interacting with the database and the application more easily. Run make up to download the image and then create and start a running container with Postgres. You should see

---

4. https://docs.docker.com/get-started/

the image get downloaded (the first time you run it) and then confirmation that it's running. The Make command runs it in daemon mode, meaning that it's running in the background until you explicitly shut it down. Later, when you're ready to shut it down, running make down will take care of it. The only place where you might have trouble is if you're running another copy of Postgres on your computer. Our container will bind to port 5432, the default for Postgres. If you get errors over port collisions, you'll need to shut down your other running Postgres while working through the book examples.

Updating Our Application to Work with the Database

Now that we have a database, we need to set up our application to connect to it. The first thing is that we need to add in two new dependencies, {:ecto_sql, "~> 3.4"} and {:postgrex, "~> 0.15.0"}, into the deps section of your mix.exs file. Ecto SQL provides your application with the additional code needed to connect to a database, and Postgrex provides the adapter that Ecto SQL needs to be able to work specifically with a Postgres database. Run mix deps.get at the root directory of your testing_ecto application to pull down the new libraries.

In the testing_ecto codebase, you'll find that we've included a couple of very basic configuration files (testing_ecto/config/config.exs and testing_ecto/config/test.exs) and a very basic repo file (testing_ecto/lib/repo.ex). These are hard-coded with values that will work with the instance of Postgres created by the docker-compose file we provided. The only thing that might not be standard boilerplate is that we've added the option migration_timestamps: [type: :utc_datetime_usec] to our database configs. This will make our timestamps default to a UTC time zone, unless explicitly overridden, and include microseconds in their definition. We'll have to remember this for later. Copy those into your project.

We need to make sure that the TestingEcto.Repo application is started with our application so that we can interact with the database in later tests. Open up lib/testing_ecto/application.ex and we'll add our repo into the children:

testing_ecto/lib/testing_ecto/application.ex
```
Line 1  defmodule TestingEcto.Application do
   -      # See https://hexdocs.pm/elixir/Application.html
   -      # for more information on OTP Applications
   -      @moduledoc false
   5
   -      use Application
   -
   -      def start(_type, _args) do
   -        children = [
  10          TestingEcto.Repo
   -        ]
```

```
      opts = [strategy: :one_for_one, name: TestingEcto.Supervisor]
      Supervisor.start_link(children, opts)
15    end
    end
```

Since this isn't a real application but is just focused on testing the database, our list of children will just contain the one element, TestingEcto.Repo. Now, when we run our tests, we'll have a running repo application to allow us to interact with the database.

With database and repo running, plus the new libraries and the configuration files (config/config.exs and config/test.exs), your application should be ready to connect and interact with the database. Next, run MIX_ENV=test mix ecto.create from either shell session to create the test instance of the database, called testing_ecto_test. You should see the following output:

```
Generated testing_ecto app
The database for TestingEcto.Repo has been created
```

Whenever you're having your application make changes to your database structure, it's good practice to check that the expected changes are reflected in the database. In the second shell session, run make cli to connect to the Postgres cli client inside your Docker container. It verifies that your database was created correctly if you're able to connect using this command. Since we've only created the database, there isn't much for us to do now except to run \l to list the available databases. testing_ecto_test should be on the list. Now we need to add a table to the database to correlate with the schema that we're setting up. Back at the command line in the application directory, run mix ecto.gen.migration add_users_table. This will generate the nested directories and a file with a timestamp in the name, like in the following output (you'll have a different timestamp):

```
Generated testing_ecto app
* creating priv/repo/migrations
* creating priv/repo/migrations/20200518212741_add_users_table.exs
```

Open the file and you should see a migration file with an empty change/0 function. Let's add code to create a table to match our schema. Inside the change/0 function, add the code to make your file match the following:

testing_ecto/priv/repo/migrations/20200518212741_add_users_table.exs
```
Line 1  defmodule TestingEcto.Repo.Migrations.AddUsersTable do
          use Ecto.Migration

          def change do
5           create table(:users, primary_key: false) do
              add(:id, :uuid, primary_key: true)
```

```
      add(:date_of_birth, :date, null: false)
      add(:email, :string, null: false)
      add(:favorite_number, :float)
10    add(:first_name, :string, null: false)
      add(:last_name, :string, null: false)
      add(:phone_number, :string, null: false)

      timestamps()
15    end

    create(unique_index(:users, [:email]))
  end
end
```

There are a couple of details to call out here. The first is that we're telling the migration to skip giving the table an auto-incrementing primary_key at line 5 and then add a primary key on line 6. Our table will use UUIDs for the primary key. We'll need to remember this when we update our schema later. We also used the null: false option on all of our columns except favorite_number, which we left optional on our schema. The last thing to note in our change/0 is that with the addition of timestamps()(line 14), we'll be adding two fields that aren't currently on our schema, inserted_at and updated_at. These will also factor into the updates to our schema.

Below the table definition, we also create a unique constraint on the email column (line 17). We'll address this once we've started interacting with the database in our tests.

Now we need to run our migration to make sure that it works. We're going to focus on the test database here, so make sure to set the correct mix environment by running MIX_ENV=test mix ecto.migrate. This should produce successful feedback:

```
15:36:12.729 [info]  == Running 20200518212741
                TestingEcto.Repo.Migrations.AddUsersTable.change/0 forward

15:36:12.730 [info]  create table users

15:36:12.738 [info]  == Migrated 20200518212741 in 0.0s
```

Go back to your session logged into the Docker container, where the Postgres cli is open. You should now be able to run \dt to see the tables users and schema_migrations. Run \d users and verify that you see the following table definitions:

```
                          Table "public.users"
        Column       |            Type            | Collation | Nullable | Default
---------------------+----------------------------+-----------+----------+---------
 id                  | uuid                       |           | not null |
 date_of_birth       | date                       |           | not null |
 email               | character varying(255)     |           | not null |
 favorite_number     | double precision           |           |          |
 first_name          | character varying(255)     |           | not null |
 last_name           | character varying(255)     |           | not null |
 phone_number        | character varying(255)     |           | not null |
 inserted_at         | timestamp without time zone|           | not null |
 updated_at          | timestamp without time zone|           | not null |
Indexes:
    "users_pkey" PRIMARY KEY, btree (id)
```

Assuming your table matches ours, we're ready to move on.

Updating Our Schema to Work with the Database

We're now ready to update our schema to match this table. Technically we'll update a copy to the schema so that we can make changes without breaking our other test files. Copy testing_ecto/lib/schemas/user_basic_schema.ex to a new file called testing_ecto/lib/schemas/user_database_schema.ex. We'll copy the test file to match later.

For now, we're going to update the schema file to look like this:

testing_ecto/lib/schemas/user_database_schema.ex
```
Line 1  defmodule TestingEcto.Schemas.UserDatabaseSchema do
          use Ecto.Schema
          import Ecto.Changeset

     5    @timestamps_opts type: :utc_datetime_usec
          @primary_key {:id, :binary_id, autogenerate: true}
          @optional_fields [:id, :favorite_number]

          schema "users" do
    10      field(:date_of_birth, :date)
            field(:email, :string)
            field(:favorite_number, :float)
            field(:first_name, :string)
            field(:last_name, :string)
    15      field(:phone_number, :string)

            timestamps()
          end

    20    defp all_fields do
            __MODULE__.__schema__(:fields)
          end
```

```
     def changeset(params) do
25     %__MODULE__{}
       |> cast(params, all_fields())
       |> validate_required(all_fields() -- @optional_fields)
       |> unique_constraint(:email)
     end
30 end
```

First, change the module name in user_database_schema.ex to be TestingEc-to.Schemas.UserDatabaseSchema, like on line 1. We need to set some Ecto Schema options in the file (using module attributes) to make it compatible with the timestamp and primary key options we set in our migration. Add two options @timestamps_opts type: :utc_datetime_usec (line 5) and @primary_key {:id, :binary_id, autogen-erate: true} (line 6) to the file. These are options that could be set in a common schema template if this were a real application. If you recall, our basic schema had @primary_key false set right above the schema definition. Now that it's being updated to correspond to the database table, we'll need to remove that. By removing that, and by setting the option for the primary key to be a :binary_id, our schema now has an additional field, :id, of type :binary_id.

For now, our changeset function is still a generic changeset function and therefore would presumably be used for creating a new user. As a result, while :id might be needed for an update changeset, we'll need to make it an optional field for when it's used for create. Later we'll split this function into two more specific changeset functions, but we're keeping a simple one for now to keep the examples smaller. Notice that we updated the module attribute with optional fields to include :id (line 7).

At this point, our schema isn't designed to reference a database table because it uses embedded_schema and not schema. We can update that line of the definition to say schema "users" do (line 9) and the schema will now be set to reference our "users" table. We've strayed from the convention of having the module name match the table name because we're dealing with a bunch of different versions of the same file. Normally, we would've named our schema "User" and the table "users." At the bottom of the definition block, add timestamps(), like on line 17, to add :inserted_at and :updated_at to the schema.

We made the email field unique, so we need to update the changeset to take that into account, adding in the call to unique_constraint/2 on line 28. And that's it. Our schema file is now set up to reference a database table. Next, we'll update our tests to take the new fields into account. When that's done, we'll look at how to test the unique_constraint code.

Updating Our Tests to Include Database Fields

We have set up our schema, UserDatabaseSchema, to correspond with a database table, but that means that there are three new fields (:id, :inserted_at, and :updated_at). To make these changes, we'll make yet another copy of the last iteration of our basic schema test file, testing_ecto/test/schemas/user_basic_schema_3_test.exs. Make a copy of it, named testing_ecto/test/schemas/user_database_schema_test.exs. Let's update the test name to TestingEcto.Schemas.UserDatabaseSchemaTest and also replace all of our references to UserBasicSchema with UserDatabaseSchema, including the alias.

With the correct module names, your test file should be able to run. Run mix test --only schema_definition test/schemas/user_database_schema_test.exs and you should see some errors, because we added new fields, but the test's definition of the fields and types (stored in @expected_fields_with_types) hasn't been updated. The test that we should be looking at will have this output:

```
1) test fields and types it has the correct fields and types
                                (TestingEcto.Schemas.UserDatabaseSchemaTest)
   test/schemas/user_database_schema_test.exs:23
   Assertion with == failed
   code:  assert Enum.sort(actual_fields_with_types) ==
                                Enum.sort(@expected_fields_with_types)
   left:  [{:date_of_birth, :date}, {:favorite_number, :float},
          {:first_name, :string}, {:id, :binary_id},
          {:inserted_at, :utc_datetime_usec}, {:last_name, :string},
          {:phone_number, :string}, {:updated_at, :utc_datetime_usec}]
   right: [date_of_birth: :date, favorite_number: :float,
          first_name: :string, last_name: :string, phone_number: :string]
   stacktrace:
     test/schemas/user_database_schema_test.exs:30: (test)
```

We are familiar with this output and know what to do. We need to add :id, :inserted_at, and :updated_at into the test's schema definition. Update your @expected_fields_with_types to include the new fields:

```
testing_ecto/test/schemas/user_database_schema_test.exs
@expected_fields_with_types [
  {:id, :binary_id},
  {:date_of_birth, :date},
  {:email, :string},
  {:favorite_number, :float},
  {:first_name, :string},
  {:inserted_at, :utc_datetime_usec},
  {:last_name, :string},
  {:phone_number, :string},
  {:updated_at, :utc_datetime_usec}
]
```

After that, the individual test should pass, but what if we run the whole file? Running mix test test/schemas/user_database_schema_test.exs will now yield errors that we haven't seen yet. Those errors will be for the success test and the test on casting errors, and the output for both will look similar to the following:

```
 1) test changeset/1 success: returns a valid changeset when given valid
                          arguments (TestingEcto.Schemas.UserDatabaseSchemaTest)
     test/schemas/user_database_schema_test.exs:39
     ** (BadFunctionError) expected a function, got: nil
     code: valid_params = valid_params(@expected_fields_with_types)
     stacktrace:
       (testing_ecto 0.1.0) test/schema_case.ex:34:
                       anonymous fn/3 in TestingEcto.SchemaCase.valid_params/1
       (elixir 1.10.2) lib/enum.ex:2111:
                           Enum."-reduce/3-lists^foldl/2-0-"/3
       (testing_ecto 0.1.0) test/schema_case.ex:33:
                       TestingEcto.SchemaCase.valid_params/1
       test/schemas/user_database_schema_test.exs:40: (test)
```

The key to understanding these errors is line 4, where we see that the code was expecting a function but got nil instead. Combined with the top of the stacktrace (line 7), we can get a sense of what is breaking and where in the code it's happening. Our helper function, valid_params/1, is breaking because it doesn't have functions defined for our newly introduced data types, :binary_id and :utc_datetime_usec. The second test will fail for almost the same reason: invalid_params/1 is also missing those definitions.

We can take one of two approaches to address these failures: we can add just the types that we need or we can go through all of the Ecto primitive types and create functions to return valid and invalid data for each type.[5] It's rare that you'll ever need all of them and you may end up with custom Ecto types in your application.[6] Since we can't have a definitive list, it makes more sense to add new definitions as they're needed. The good news is that since the code is in the case template, we only need to add them once to make them available for any tests using the same template.

Open the SchemaCase file (testing_ecto/test/schema_case.ex) and update your two helper functions with the following new definitions:

```
testing_ecto/test/schema_case.ex
def valid_params(fields_with_types) do
  valid_value_by_type = %{
    date: fn -> to_string(Faker.Date.date_of_birth()) end,
    float: fn -> :rand.uniform() * 10 end,
```

---

5.   https://hexdocs.pm/ecto/Ecto.Schema.html#module-primitive-types

6.   https://hexdocs.pm/ecto/Ecto.Type.html

```
    string: fn -> Faker.Lorem.word() end,
    utc_datetime_usec: fn -> DateTime.utc_now() end,
    binary_id: fn -> Ecto.UUID.generate() end
  }

  for {field, type} <- fields_with_types, into: %{} do
    {Atom.to_string(field), valid_value_by_type[type].()}
  end
end

def invalid_params(fields_with_types) do
  invalid_value_by_type = %{
    date: fn -> Faker.Lorem.word() end,
    float: fn -> Faker.Lorem.word() end,
    string: fn -> DateTime.utc_now() end,
    utc_datetime_usec: fn -> Faker.Lorem.word() end,
    binary_id: fn -> 1 end
  }

  for {field, type} <- fields_with_types, into: %{} do
    {Atom.to_string(field), invalid_value_by_type[type].()}
  end
end
```

Now that we've updated those helper functions, there's one last test that isn't passing: the test for the required fields is complaining that there isn't an error for the :id field. Since it shouldn't be required, we just need to update our module attribute in test/schemas/user_database_schema_test.exs, @optional, to include :id:

```
@optional [:id, :favorite_number]
```

With our optional field updates, our schema is now set up to reflect our table, and our tests have been updated to match. We have a design issue, though, that we should acknowledge: our changeset function requires an ID to be passed in. This is because we have a single changeset function instead of specialized ones for different purposes, such as creating new users and updating an existing user. We'll address that soon, but for now, let's review what we've accomplished. We have a thoroughly tested user schema that's set up to work with the "users" table. We added new fields, and the tests let us know where to make updates. We're ready to start working against the database in our tests.

Testing Your Schema Through Database Calls

While we have a decent basic schema defined, we haven't covered a subset of the kinds of logic that you'll find in changeset functions—code that requires interaction with the database to verify that it works. The validations we've

tested so far have laid out a pattern for us that can be used with other validations beyond cast/3 and validate_required/2. Functions your code can call that can
be tested in similar ways include (but are not limited to) validate_inclusion/4, vali-
date_length/3, and validate_subset/4. A very common case where things are easier
to test with a database is a unique constraint on a column in your database.
In this section, we'll add a new field to our schema and table, including such
a constraint. We'll review why it makes sense to pull the database into testing
it, and then we'll update the tests to show how to exercise that constraint.

You'll recall that when we created our migration, we added a unique constraint
on the email field. We also updated our changeset/1 function to include logic
for this when we added unique_constraint/2. unique_constraint/2 is what we'll focus
on next. Before we test it, we should talk about what that function does.

The unique constraint is handled by the database, not by our changeset
function. So why are we calling unique_constraint/2 in our changeset function?
That function adds a "note" into the changeset to let Ecto know that if the
database returns an error for a unique constraint on the email field, instead
of raising the error, it should add an Ecto constraint error to the list of errors
on the changeset. If you were to inspect the changeset returned from changeset/1,
you won't see it because Ecto has a custom implementation for the Inspect
protocol.[7] There's a "hidden" section of the Changeset struct under the key
:constraints. If you were to dig into the value of that key on our returned
changeset, you would see the following code:

```
[
  %{
    constraint: "users_email_index",
    error_message: "has already been taken",
    error_type: :unique,
    field: :email,
    match: :exact,
    type: :unique
  }
]
```

This map is the "note" we mentioned in the previous paragraph. When Ecto
gets a unique_constraint error back from the database, it checks to see if the
changeset it was executing on has a matching constraint. If it does, it uses
the information in that map to generate an error. We can test that this logic
is in our function in one of two ways: test the return value on the changeset
or attempt to insert the changeset and test for the expected error. While the

---

7.   https://github.com/elixir-ecto/ecto/blob/87ce8e3223a1c8a92d40536cf56ac83c0270d711/lib/ecto/change-
     set.ex#L2935

first option has appeal for keeping our tests simple and keeping everything purely functional, it's going to be somewhat hard to understand what it's up to unless everyone maintaining that test understands why this is a valid way to test the unique constraint code.

"Philosophical purity" of the previous test aside, it's quite easy for us to use the second option, attempting to insert the data into the database, and the test will end up looking a good bit like our previous tests. Consistency makes things easier to maintain and easier to understand.

We'll add one more error test at the bottom of the describe block for "changeset/1" in the test file, test/schemas/user_database_schema_test.exs. Open up the file and add the following test:

```
Line 1  test "error: returns error changeset when an email address is reused" do
          {:ok, existing_user} =
            valid_params(@expected_fields_with_types)
            |> UserDatabaseSchema.changeset()
     5      |> TestingEcto.Repo.insert()

          changeset_with_repeated_email =
            valid_params(@expected_fields_with_types)
            |> Map.put("email", existing_user.email)
    10      |> UserDatabaseSchema.changeset()

          assert {:error, %Changeset{valid?: false, errors: errors}} =
                   TestingEcto.Repo.insert(changeset_with_repeated_email)

    15    assert errors[:email], "The field :email is missing from errors."
          {_, meta} = errors[:email]

          assert meta[:constraint] == :unique,
                 "The validation type, #{meta[:validation]}, is incorrect."
    20  end
```

Let's examine this test and see how it differs from all our previous testing. Our setup is creating an existing user in the database, actually calling TestingEcto.Repo.insert/1 at line 5. We need this insert because we're trying to trigger an error in the database for a unique constraint violation.

The second part of the setup is to create a changeset with valid params except for the email address, which we're overriding with the email address from the existing user (line 9). The exercise step of this test is not normal. The code under test, the changeset/1 function, has already been called. Instead, we're using a second insert call to the database to trigger the error we're looking for. You can see that at line 12: the pattern reflects that expected return value from the Repo.insert/1 and not that of our changeset/1.

We bind the errors to a variable, errors, and then the assertions look a lot like those from our previous tests. Because we only have one field that should reflect this error, we aren't using a list comprehension for the assertions. Also, it's worth pointing out that the meta data on our error is a :constraint and not a :validation like our previous tests.

This test was not written to either self-update or catch changes to the schema in the same way that our previous tests were. Our tests don't have a way of using reflection to know which fields should handle a unique constraint. The actual definition for that is in the database itself and not part of our schema definition. The reflection functions in Ecto.Schema are only available for the definition itself. This means that, while the basic functionality of our schema, the definition, and the cast and required validations can be fairly dynamic, when we want to update fields that have a unique constraint, we'll need to make sure to add them in. This test could be updated to use a list comprehension if we wanted to.

We should mention a couple of caveats about this test. The first is that the code to insert users into the database is leveraging our own application code, UserDatabaseSchema.changeset/1. In general, it's a good practice to avoid using your own application code in your setup steps because issues with your code that aren't relevant to that specific test can create numerous and misleading test failures. We'll present an alternative in the next chapter, using a helper module called a factory.

The second issue with this test is that it's missing an important stage of testing: teardown. Fortunately, each test doesn't need to keep track of what it needs to tear down. Ecto provides us a way.

Setting Up Sandbox Mode

Our database keeps state, and right now this test is leaving new rows in the database. In the short run, it's very unlikely to create a problem because we're using a new, random string every time we run the test. In the long run, having persistent data between test runs increases the likelihood of having test failures due to unforeseen data collisions. If the same random string did happen to be picked in different test runs, the test would fail on the first inserted user, which was supposed to be part of the setup.

Working against your database in tests is one of the most common places where leftover state changes can cause problems. We managed to avoid issues with our test on the unique constraint by using randomized data. But even with that, every successive test run is leaving one new row in the database.

Each test works best when operating in a known good environment because that's the only way they can guarantee that their own setup is complete and reliable. If a test can't assume a clean working environment, we need to write a lot more defensive code, checking the environment for existing data, instead of just making what's needed for the test and moving on. This approach both slows down writing the tests, because more code is needed, but it also slows down the tests themselves. While an extra database check or two isn't really an issue from a time standpoint, if you're writing enough tests, they'll add up. In an isolated test, we'd focus on just making sure the test cleaned up whatever it created. Fortunately, Ecto provides us a very nice solution so that each individual test doesn't have to track and clean up after itself: the Ecto Sandbox.[8]

The Ecto Sandbox provides two key values to our tests. The first is by managing the connection pool: when properly configured, concurrent tests can run without sharing state in the database. This means leveraging the speed boost of concurrent tests without the kind of defensive programming we're trying to avoid. It's a little bit complicated when setting it up, but it works well. The second value that the Ecto Sandbox provides is that each database connection is operating in a database transaction, and when a test is complete, the transaction is rolled back. This means that there are no changes to the state of the database when the tests are complete; in other words, the Ecto Sandbox gives us automated teardown for the changes in our database.

We're going to set up the Sandbox, choosing a mode that works well for the limited scope of unit tests. We'll discuss other modes, where the same Sandbox needs to be shared by multiple processes, in our chapter on testing Phoenix. In your case template file, testing_ecto/test/schema_case.ex, we'll add a setup block that will be used by all tests that use this case template. In that file, under the using block, above the valid_params/1 function, add a setup block that looks like this:

```
testing_ecto/test/schema_case.ex
setup _ do
  Ecto.Adapters.SQL.Sandbox.mode(TestingEcto.Repo, :manual)
end
```

Every test that uses this case template will now run this code before the test executes as part of the setup steps. This applies to the tests that don't cause any interactions with the database as well. Fortunately, this is a very fast,

---

8. https://hexdocs.pm/ecto_sql/Ecto.Adapters.SQL.Sandbox.html

lightweight call and it shouldn't impact your test suite's overall runtime significantly.

In order for the Sandbox to be available in our tests, we need to make sure that the configuration in config/test.exs sets TestingEcto.Repo to use the Sandbox. If you're using the file we provided with our copy of the application, you should be all set, but we'll call out the step to make sure you know how to set it up. In the Ecto part of your test config, you need to tell Ecto that your database connection pool will be using the Sandbox. It should have at least the following lines in it:

```
testing_ecto/config/test.exs
config :testing_ecto, TestingEcto.Repo,
  database: "testing_ecto_test",
  pool: Ecto.Adapters.SQL.Sandbox
```

Setting the Sandbox to :manual sets each test to be able to request its own sandbox connection. That connection will be the same connection throughout the life of the individual test. In other words, if our test setup inserts a record, that record will be present later, during calls to the database throughout the exercise phase. This probably feels like it's obvious, but it's actually not guaranteed with one of the other sandbox modes. The major limitation is that each sandbox instance is usable only in tests that utilize a single process. In our case, our test process is the only running process, as the code that's being exercised is all executed within the test process.

We need to update our test to explicitly request a connection from the Sandbox at the beginning of the test. This way, tests that don't utilize the database won't require any additional resources. In your test for the unique constraint errors, update your test so that your very first line reads Ecto.Adapters.SQL.Sandbox.checkout(TestingEcto.Repo). This tells the Sandbox to provide an isolated database connection associated with the process ID (PID) of the test.

That's all we need to do to make our tests not leave data in the database. Any future runs of this test will not leave data, but remember that we already ran the test at least once without the Sandbox. As a result, we should reset our test database before we move on. Shutting down the Docker container (running make down) will work because our docker-compose.yml doesn't mount a disk anywhere for persistence. Starting it back up, though, will require you to create and migrate your database again. The other option is to run the following commands in order: MIX_ENV=test mix ecto.drop, MIX_ENV=test mix ecto.create, and, finally MIX_ENV=test mix ecto.migrate. We have included a target in the Makefile to do all of this by running make reset.test from the command line. The good news is that now that we're using the Sandbox, we shouldn't need to do a reset like this again.

Wrapping Up

We've spent this chapter focusing on testing Ecto schemas. We used that topic as a way to visit case templates and helper functions, and we touched on the Ecto Sandbox. We also delved into building tests that either safely update themselves or let you know when your test file is out of sync with the schema definition, both of which reduce the work to maintain your test file.

In the next chapter, we'll learn about testing queries and leveraging the factory pattern to speed up writing tests and make robust setup easier.

CHAPTER 5

Testing Ecto Queries

Testing Ecto queries is fairly straightforward, especially if you're coming from testing database code in other languages. Some basic rules will help you make sure that your coverage is effective. In this chapter, we'll explore some additional tooling that can help make long-term ownership of your test suite easier, and then we'll write tests for Ecto queries. We'll build on concepts from the previous chapter, *Testing Ecto Schemas*. While it isn't strictly necessary to have read that chapter, without it you may miss some references to code or concepts we've already covered. We've provided complete examples of the previous chapter's code with the book, so when needed, you can use that for reference.

For this chapter, we're going to work with a schema called testing_ecto/lib/schemas/user.ex, which is provided in the copy of testing_ecto. It's an evolution of the schema we ended the last chapter with, with two notable changes: now that we're done changing the schema, we're calling it User and it has the changeset functions, create_changeset/1 and update_changeset/2, instead of a single, multi-use function. We've also included an updated test file, testing_ecto/test/schemas/user_test.exs. Copy both of those files into your local testing_ecto project. The test file assumes that you have a copy of testing_ecto/test/schema_case.ex as well, so if you skipped the work from the last chapter, you'll need to copy that over as well.

Next, we'll create a factory file to make the setup phase of our tests easier and more consistent. Then we'll create a new case template and use both the factory and the case template to test basic database query code.

Creating a Factory to Help with Setup

In testing, we create factories to give ourselves consistent, repeatable ways to provide data for our setup phase. One of the areas where this kind of tooling is the most useful is when interacting with the database.

When we write tests that interact with database tables, we need two sets of data that are either valid or invalid with regard to the table's definition. As our applications grow larger, we'll find that having a single source of setup data helps us keep the test suite maintainable. If we update our schema definition, that single source is often the only place (aside from the tests for the schema file itself) that'll need to be updated in your test suite.

It's totally possible to write a factory for your application entirely from scratch. When we were testing our Ecto schemas, we started to do that by creating a helper function called valid_params. It took a set of fields and types and returned a set of randomized parameters that met the minimum requirements of the schema's definition. That function has some notable limitations, however. It was written to be generic and therefore the data it returns isn't very specific to the exact field for which it's making the data. An example is that since the email field was a string, the function returned a single word string, not an email address. This isn't guaranteed to be an issue, but odd data can make the debugging of failed tests a little harder. Additionally, when we had a test that required the data to be inserted into the database, we had to write the code to do the insertion as well.

We can solve this by creating common code that handles the insert for you. While you can write your factory from scratch, we don't suggest it. If you go that route, you'll keep finding edge cases (like overrides on values or handling nested schemas) that require you to continue to update and upgrade your factory. Many people have worked to solve these problems, and we can build on their work. While there's no perfect solution, we have settled on using the ExMachina library from Thoughtbot as the basis for our factories.[1]

ExMachina brings a good bit of functionality out of the box, although it also has some notable quirks. We'll run through the basic use cases of ExMachina by incorporating it into our TestingEcto application, and then we'll show how you supplement your ExMachina-based factory with additional data functions. ExMachina was originally designed with producing data for Ecto schemas in mind. As a result, it works well for producing data for the schemas themselves, as well as providing a mechanism to insert data so that you don't have to write your own code.

1.　https://hex.pm/packages/ex_machina

To begin, we'll be working in the same project as the previous chapter. We need to add ExMachina as an application dependency. Open your mix file (testing_ecto/mix.exs) and insert {:ex_machina, "~> 2.4", only: :test}, into the list in the deps/0 private function. Run mix deps.get to pull the library code into your project. That's enough for us to start using the library.

Now let's add our own factory file. Create a new file for your factory at testing_ecto/test/factory.ex. Insert the following code and then we'll run through the notable parts:

```
testing_ecto/test/factory.ex
Line 1  defmodule TestingEcto.Factory do
          use ExMachina.Ecto, repo: TestingEcto.Repo
          alias TestingEcto.Schemas.User

5         def user_factory do
            %User{
              date_of_birth: to_string(Faker.Date.date_of_birth()),
              email: Faker.Internet.email(),
              favorite_number: :rand.uniform() * 10,
10            first_name: Faker.Name.first_name(),
              last_name: Faker.Name.last_name(),
              phone_number: Faker.Phone.EnUs.phone(),
            }
          end
15      end
```

Unless you need more than one factory file (which can be useful for separation of concerns as your application grows), sticking with the name Factory should be just fine. At line 2, our module is "using" ExMachina.Ecto and passing it the name of our application's repo, TestingEcto.Repo. This means that this factory will be usable specifically with that repo. In applications that connect to more than one database, you'll want to have multiple factories, naming each of them something more specific.

We've added a single factory function (line 5), following an ExMachina convention: the name of the schema followed by "_factory". ExMachina uses metaprogramming under the hood; and to make it work, this convention is a must. It ends up creating a slight disconnect when you actually use the factory function, which we'll call out later. For now, just know that any functions in the factory file that need to work with ExMachina will need to have "_factory" appended.

The function itself is pretty simple; it just returns a schema struct with pre-populated values. If we were to call this function by name, it would return a struct. That in itself is useful, but it isn't anything we need another library for. As long as you follow the naming convention, ExMachina offers a lot of helper functions, ones that we'll be using throughout the rest of this chapter. The different functionality it provides works in two phases. First it generates a data set from the factory defaults and any overrides passed in. When the data is ready, it performs the action from the function call, such as inserting a record or creating a string-keyed map. While the initial data set is based off the same struct, the return value and side effects are determined by the function you call. As we progress through this chapter, we'll use different ExMachina functions and explain them when we do.

As you develop your test suites, the factory might be a good place to add additional helper functions, like invalid_data/1 from the last chapter. Anything that's focused on data and is reusable across tests is a good candidate to move into the factory. The factory can then be pulled in directly or by using the case template that includes it.

Adding a DataCase to Help with Setup

When testing our Ecto schemas, we made a case template called SchemaCase. That was very specific to an exact kind of test. While the exercise of making that was useful, you'll likely find that a slightly higher-level case template can cover your needs for anything that's dealing with data as it's needed for database interactions. We're going to create a new case template that will look very similar and, if you took the time, would be able to replace the SchemaCase that we used in the schema tests. Create a new file called testing_ecto/test/data_case.ex and add the following code:

```
testing_ecto/test/data_case.ex
Line 1  defmodule TestingEcto.DataCase do
   -      use ExUnit.CaseTemplate
   -
   -      using do
   5        quote do
   -          alias Ecto.Changeset
   -          import TestingEcto.DataCase
   -          alias TestingEcto.{Factory, Repo}
   -        end
  10      end
   -
   -      setup _tags? do
   -        Ecto.Adapters.SQL.Sandbox.mode(TestingEcto.Repo, :manual)
   -      end
  15    end
```

Right now, using this file brings only two advantages over using ExUnit.Case. First, it provides the common sandbox setup, like our SchemaCase did in the last chapter. Second, it adds an alias for TestingEcto.Factory and TestingEcto.Repo on line 8. We'll need both of those for our query tests. As you build out a test suite, keep looking for helper functions that can be moved into common files to allow for reuse. A good rule of thumb is that if a function is focused on making data, it can go into a factory. If not, it might belong in a case template. If you find the same function is needed in multiple case templates, you may have a candidate for a module with helper functions that can be pulled into multiple case templates.

Now that we have a factory and a case template, we can start working on testing our query code.

Testing Create

We're going to start by looking at part of the logic file with our queries. The file, called Users, contains the basic CRUD actions, in this case called create/1, get/1, update/2, and delete/1. We've provided a file in the copy of testing_ecto included with the book. You're welcome to copy that over or type it in yourself. The file and the create/1 function look like this:

```
testing_ecto/lib/users/users.ex
defmodule TestingEcto.Users do
  @moduledoc false
  alias TestingEcto.Repo
  alias TestingEcto.Schemas.User

  def create(params) do
    params
    |> User.create_changeset()
    |> Repo.insert()
  end
end
```

It's pretty basic, as most CRUD queries are. As a result, testing it won't be very complicated, either. First we'll write a success path test. Open up a new file at testing_ecto/test/users/users_test.ex. In it, we'll set up a basic test file structure and then add a describe block for create/1 and our first test:

```
testing_ecto/test/users/users_test.exs
Line 1 defmodule TestingEcto.UsersTest do
   -   use TestingEcto.DataCase
   -   alias TestingEcto.Users
   -   alias TestingEcto.Schemas.User
   -
   5
   -   setup do
   -     Ecto.Adapters.SQL.Sandbox.checkout(TestingEcto.Repo)
   -   end
```

```
10   describe "create/1" do
       test "success: it inserts a user in the db and returns the user" do
         params = Factory.string_params_for(:user)
         now = DateTime.utc_now()

15       assert {:ok, %User{} = returned_user} = Users.create(params)

         user_from_db = Repo.get(User, returned_user.id)
         assert returned_user == user_from_db

20       mutated = ["date_of_birth"]

         for {param_field, expected} <- params,
             param_field not in mutated do
           schema_field = String.to_existing_atom(param_field)
25         actual = Map.get(user_from_db, schema_field)

           assert actual == expected,
                  "Values did not match for field: #{param_field}\nexpected: #{
                    inspect(expected)
30                 }\nactual: #{inspect(actual)}"
         end

         expected_dob = Date.from_iso8601!(params["date_of_birth"])
         assert user_from_db.date_of_birth == expected_dob
35
         assert user_from_db.inserted_at == user_from_db.updated_at
         assert DateTime.compare(now, user_from_db.inserted_at) == :lt
       end
40   end

   end
```

The first thing to note in this test file is that common setup block at line 7. Because this test file is for our queries, we can safely assume that every test will require a database connection. Since our case template, DataCase, is setting the Ecto Sandbox to :manual, we'll need to check out a connection for each test. Remember that at the end of the test, the connection will be released and the database transaction holding all of our interactions will be rolled back.

We see our first use of a factory function in the test itself, at line 12. We are calling string_params_for/2 (even though we're only passing one argument, there is a second, optional argument). Under the hood, this takes the atom being passed to it, in our case :user, and will call user_factory/0 in our factory. Even though our function, user_factory/0, returns a User schema, ExMachina will take the return value and convert it to a string-keyed map in order to provide "string_params". There's a similar function called params_for/2, which returns an atom-keyed map instead. We're requesting string params because that's the shape that most web-based input takes.

There's a general pattern that starts to play out in this test. When a test is exercising code that writes to the database, the test itself will need to read from the database during the assertion phase in order to verify the side effect(s). If a test is exercising code read from the database, the test will need to write directly to the database during the setup phase. Don't use your own application's code to do those reads and writes. On line 17, you'll see that our test is calling TestingEcto.Repo directly. You don't want your test to depend on your application code. If you do use application code and something changes in your code, breaking its functionality, your test suite will blow up with a lot of failing tests. Most of those will be misleading because they won't be tests that are focused on the failing code. One of our goals when designing tests is to make it so that if there is a failure, it's quick and easy to find where our code isn't behaving correctly.

On the line to exercise the code (line 15), we are asserting that the return value is an :ok tuple and binding the returned user to a variable. We typically strive to have a function do a single thing, focusing either on a return value or a side effect. Unfortunately, query code like this typically has both a significant return value (in our case the user that was inserted) as well as an important side effect (that data was inserted into the database). There are two common mistakes made when testing functions like these.

The first mistake is that people tend to only focus on the return value. If, under the hood, your code is as straightforward as this is, with the final call being to Repo.insert/1, it would be fine. The problem is that code can change over time, and testing only the return value doesn't guarantee what's arguably the most important responsibility of the function under test: inserting data into the database. Our test isn't only binding the return value but also then grabbing the data from the database. We're fairly safe to assume that the ID on the returned user is the same as that of the row in the database. At this point, we have both the return value from the exercise line and the data straight from the database. We compare them on line 18 to make sure they're identical (as they really should be). Once we know they're the same, we can pick either one to continue our testing. That leads us to the second common mistake.

It's incredibly common to see tests like this that make assertions on one or two of the values and then assume that the rest are good to go. This is unfortunate, because the point of the test is to make sure that the insertion code is correct. How can it prove that if it doesn't check all of the values? This is where a list comprehension comes in. We run through all the values that we're expecting and check that the same value is present in the database (and the returned User schema).

We have another layer of thoroughness in this test that we should discuss. We're checking that the two timestamps, :inserted_at and :updated_at, are the same, and we're checking that they're newer than the time the test started. Line 13 grabs a timestamp from before the test exercises the code, and then line 37 compares the timestamps to the pre-exercise time. Updating the values for the timestamps is the default behavior of the Ecto code. As long as your code is using Ecto.Repo's functions, this just happens. Additionally, the only built-in function to compare datetimes has a pretty awkward API. It's your call, but this might be a place where you can feel comfortable skipping a validation.

Aside from the assertions on the timestamps, the assertions in this test probably feel a whole lot like the assertions we made in the testing for the schema itself. While it's very similar, it's not the same, so don't skip out on one or the other. The schema tests are making sure that the schema's changeset function handles "correct" data, but it does nothing to cover whether or not that "correct" data is valid against the database table definition itself, whereas successfully inserting it does prove that. Why not skip the schema testing then? A schema changeset function can be used by multiple queries, sometimes even in different files. One of the nice things about having a well-tested schema is that when we test code that's using the schema, we don't need to write exhaustive tests for all of the error cases. The tests for the schema cover that. So, for testing a function like our create/1, we only need a single success test and a single error test. We'll write that error test next.

Add a new test into your existing describe block for a failure:

```
test "error: returns an error tuple when user can't be created" do
  missing_params = %{}

  assert {:error, %Changeset{valid?: false}} =
           Users.create(missing_params)
end
```

This test can be so simple because we've already tested the error cases thoroughly for the schema. Ecto has standardized the way that Repo errors and Changeset errors are handled. All our test is doing is making sure that if there is an error, the return value is shaped correctly: a tuple with :error as the first element and a changeset carrying errors as the second element. If any other functions use that same underlying changeset function on the schema, they can make the same assumptions, unless the function itself needs to change the behavior.

These two tests set up a pattern that will continue for the rest of the functions in this file: one success test and one error test. Let's test our next function and see it play out.

Testing Read

This next test is very simple. First, let's take a look at the code in our Users module. We used "Read" in the section header to keep it in line with CRUD, but you'll notice that we prefer to call our function get/1. This is entirely user preference.

```
testing_ecto/lib/users/users.ex
def get(user_id) do
  if user = Repo.get(User, user_id) do
    {:ok, user}
  else
    {:error, :not_found}
  end
end
```

Our function isn't a straight pass-through to the Ecto code. Instead, if the query returns a result, it wraps that result in a success (:ok) tuple, and if the user doesn't exist, it returns an error tuple. Our tests will be pretty straightforward as well. For success, we'll need to insert a user into the database before the exercise step. We'll assert on the shape of the return value and then make sure that the actual data matches what was inserted into the database prior. The error test will try to "get" a user for a nonexisting ID. Open up your test file, testing_ecto/test/users/users_test.ex, and add the following describe block:

```
Line 1  describe "get/1" do
   -      test "success: it returns a user when given a valid UUID" do
   -        existing_user = Factory.insert(:user)
   -
   5        assert {:ok, returned_user} = Users.get(existing_user.id)
   -
   -        assert returned_user == existing_user
   -      end
   -
   10     test "error: it returns an error tuple when a user doesn't exist" do
   -        assert {:error, :not_found} = Users.get(Ecto.UUID.generate())
   -      end
   -    end
```

These tests are pretty easy to understand. Because the function under test is reading from the database, our test code will have to insert data before the exercise step. We're using our factory to insert the data into the database at line 3. One of the many benefits of using a factory is that it provides an easy and consistent way to insert data into the database without relying on your own application code.

It's very important to note, though, that because it isn't using your application code, the inserted data won't be run through your changeset functions. If rules about the data are present in the changeset logic but aren't reflected in the database, you need to make sure that your factory function only returns valid data. That's testing a read function.

Testing Update

Testing update is a bit of a combination of the testing for the create and read functions. Let's first look at the function we're going to test:

```
testing_ecto/lib/users/users.ex
def update(%User{} = existing_user, update_params) do
  existing_user
  |> User.update_changeset(update_params)
  |> Repo.update()
end
```

You can see that, like create/1, this function is a very lightweight wrapper around calls to the schema's changeset function (update_changeset/2 in this case) and then to Repo.update/1. Testing it will be similar, but you'll need to insert an existing user to be updated by the code. Let's write our success test first:

```
Line 1  describe "update/2" do
          test "success: it updates database and returns the user" do
            existing_user = Factory.insert(:user)

     5      params =
              Factory.string_params_for(:user)
              |> Map.take(["first_name"])

            assert {:ok, returned_user} = Users.update(existing_user, params)
    10
            user_from_db = Repo.get(User, returned_user.id)
            assert returned_user == user_from_db

            expected_user_data =
    15        existing_user
              |> Map.from_struct()
              |> Map.drop([:__meta__, :updated_at])
              |> Map.put(:first_name, params["first_name"])
```

```
20      for {field, expected} <- expected_user_data do
          actual = Map.get(user_from_db, field)

          assert actual == expected,
                  "Values did not match for field: #{field}\nexpected: #{
25                   inspect(expected)
                  }\nactual: #{inspect(actual)}"
        end

        refute user_from_db.updated_at == existing_user.updated_at
30      assert %DateTime{} = user_from_db.updated_at
      end

  end
```

The test uses the factory to insert a user on line 3. On line 5, the test is creating a parameter map to pass in. It's using the factory to provide the data for consistency, but it's then using Map.take/2 to grab only a single key/value pair. This is to keep the test as simple and unlikely to become stale as possible. If the test updated every field allowed on the schema, the likelihood of the test becoming outdated with any changes to the schema is higher. By choosing a single field, and one that's less likely to change, this test will be easier to keep current. Additionally, the testing for update_changeset/2 does cover the logic around which fields can be updated, so we don't need to be robust in this test.

Our test needs to assert that all the original fields have the same value except :first_name (the updated field) and :updated_at (which will be handled separately). To do this, the easiest thing is to construct a map with the expected keys and values in it, and then compare that to the values pulled from the database. There are plenty of ways to do this, but we chose to start with the existing user because it carries almost all of the data we want.

At line 14, we transform that user's data into a map and then update the one value that changed. On line 17, the test drops two of the fields, meaning they won't be checked. :updated_at is dropped because it won't be the same between the two sets of data, and it doesn't need to be. :_meta_ is dropped, even though it'll be the same on both sets, because it's a hidden Ecto Schema field and not part of the concerns of the test. The test is focused on the data that exists in the database.

On line 29, we're making a very basic assertion to make sure that the value of the :updated_at field has been changed and that it's still the right shape of data, a DateTime struct. This ties back to our discussion of testing the timestamps when we were testing create/1. We are balancing between maintaining high coverage and reducing the work and maintenance involved in our assertions.

Let's add our error test next. Add a test under your success test, in the same update/2 describe block, that looks like this:

```
Line 1   test "error: returns an error tuple when user can't be updated" do
2          existing_user = Factory.insert(:user)
3          bad_params = %{"first_name" => DateTime.utc_now()}
4
5          assert {:error, %Changeset{}} = Users.update(existing_user, bad_params)
6
7          assert existing_user == Repo.get(User, existing_user.id)
8        end
```

This test is pretty easy to understand. On line 3, it's creating a parameter that can't be cast. This is the same kind of logic that we had in the helper function, invalid_params/1, called from our schema tests, by means of our SchemaCase file. This test isn't using that same case template. If you find yourself doing this sort of thing often in your query tests, it could be a good candidate for a function in either DataCase or in the factory, because it's focused on data.

A common mistake when testing a failed update, like this test is doing, is to miss checking that the data in the database hasn't changed. Given how little logic is in Users.update/2, it's very unlikely that anything would have changed, but it's very little effort on our part and it builds in safety from regressions. Line 7 shows a one-line assertion and call to the database to add that safety.

We've covered the major points of testing an update function. Let's finish with testing our logic to delete a user.

Testing Delete

Our last function, delete/1, is simple to test, as the code is a straight pass-through to Repo.delete/1. Let's look at the function:

```
testing_ecto/lib/users/users.ex
  def delete(%User{} = user) do
    Repo.delete(user)
  end
end
```

We'll only test the success path for this function because errors are incredibly unlikely. Additionally, writing a test that can force an error on delete is complicated and requires restructuring our code solely for testing. In this case, the payoff isn't there. When that's the case, we typically let our applications crash instead of trying to handle every possible failure. Let's write our final test and then review what it does:

```
describe "delete/1" do
  test "success: it deletes the user" do
    user = Factory.insert(:user)

    assert {:ok, _deleted_user} = Users.delete(user)

    refute Repo.get(User, user.id)
  end
end
```

Our test sets up by inserting a user. It then exercises the delete/1 function, asserting that it returns a success tuple. The last line is an assertion that the data is no longer in the database. In our case, we aren't even concerned about the return value, so we're dropping it. The most important thing is to just make sure that you have that last check on the database.

Wrapping Up

In this chapter, we covered the basic CRUD functions and how to test them. We looked at using a common setup source, a factory. We saw how to make thorough assertions on return values and the data in the database. While no two applications will have exactly the same functionality, these examples lay out the basics that you can build on to make sure your queries are covered by your tests.

Between Chapter 4, Testing Ecto Schemas, on page 101, and this chapter, we've discussed the main concerns you should keep in mind when testing your Ecto code. As you build bigger and more complicated query code, you just need to remember that your tests need to cover both the return values and the side effects. Failing to check the side effects (changes in the database) is one of the most common mistakes we see, and it's the most important part of testing your query code.

In the next chapter, we'll move on to testing a Phoenix application, building on all of the concepts we've laid out here and in the previous chapters.

CHAPTER 6

Testing Phoenix

While Elixir is flexible enough to be used in countless ways, most people writing Elixir will end up writing an application using the Phoenix framework at some point. The framework provides a lot of tooling to build a web server with relative ease and speed. Phoenix is rare among web frameworks, though, in that it doesn't have strong opinions on your application's architecture or file structure. It provides a standardized way of defining various web interfaces and connecting them to application code. This chapter will cover the different ways in which a Phoenix application can be tested, focusing on testing the application as a whole via the web and websocket interfaces.

While we'll cover testing Phoenix-specific patterns, it's really important to understand that for the most part, testing a Phoenix application will use everything we've already covered in the previous chapters: unit tests, integration tests, OTP tests, and Ecto tests (which really are just specific variations of unit and integration testing). We won't rehash those ideas here. As a result, this chapter isn't entirely stand-alone. If you aren't familiar with the basics of testing, this chapter won't be very helpful. Instead, we highly recommended that you read the preceding chapters first so you're familiar with the basics of unit testing, integration tests, testing OTP, and testing Ecto.

The Role of Phoenix in Your Application

What we think of as the Phoenix framework is really a combination of libraries: Ranch,[1] Cowboy,[2] Plug,[3] Phoenix,[4] and Ecto.[5] This combination provides a

---

1. https://github.com/ninenines/ranch
2. https://github.com/ninenines/cowboy
3. https://github.com/elixir-plug/plug
4. https://github.com/phoenixframework/phoenix
5. https://github.com/elixir-ecto/ecto

lot of tools to spin up web-server applications fairly easily, drawing on the history of many other frameworks, but it works very hard to not drive the design of your application. That ultimately means that a standard Phoenix application can be broken down into two main parts, the incoming web interface part (which includes Ranch, Cowboy, Plug, and Phoenix) and the rest of the application (mostly Elixir and Ecto code). In Phoenix lingo, that's YourAppWeb and YourApp. While Phoenix's generators and documentation nudge users to use the concept of contexts to organize their nonweb code, the truth is that you can write and organize the application however you want. As a result, testing the business logic of your application isn't Phoenix-specific in any way. It's going to look like the unit and integration testing in any Mix application.

Phoenix allows users to interact with it in several different ways: server-rendered HTML, JSON-based endpoints, and Phoenix Channels (web sockets). A new library, Phoenix LiveView, combines elements of server-rendered HTML and web sockets to provide interactive clients. It's not in the Phoenix core and so we won't cover it in this book. If you want to learn more about it and how to test it, check out *Programming Phoenix LiveView [TD21]*.

As part of testing these interfaces, we'll also rope in testing routes, plugs, and views. Code that calls out to other services while using the Internet to do so isn't included in this. This topic is covered under integration testing, and that code would normally live in the nonweb part of your application.

There's a lot of overlap between testing each kind of interface. To avoid very repetitious examples, we'll skip things we've already covered if there aren't any caveats. For example, if we cover testing plugs as part of testing a JSON API, we won't cover plugs in testing server-rendered HTML endpoints.

Plugs

The Phoenix library has been hugely helpful to the productivity of anyone wanting to write an Elixir-based web application, but it's useful to know that it owes a lot of its success to another library, Plug.[6] Plug is a basic specification and tooling set that allows users to create composable web applications. In this chapter, we'll mention "plugs" as a reference to middleware that you might be using in your application. Additionally, the Plug library provides some of the testing tools that we'll require. Don't worry, though: because Plug is a dependency of the Phoenix framework, if you're working in a Phoenix-based application, you already have Plug and its testing tools available to

---

6.   https://github.com/elixir-plug/plug

you. We'll refer to any modules, both those provided by Phoenix and those custom written, that match the interface defined by Plug as plugs.

How to Use the Provided Application

With this book, we've provided an application, called NotSkull, that will serve as the code samples for most of this chapter and the next. NotSkull is a working application, complete with tests.

The tests you'll write while working through this chapter will all be in new files. If you're having trouble, you'll find a complete test file that exists under the same name of the file we'll have you create, but with .bak.exs as the file extension instead of .exs.

Some of the functionality in the application is duplicated between interface types. For example, there are two controllers for users: one for server-rendered HTML and the other for a JSON-based API. There isn't complete feature parity, though, as the JSON-based code was just added to provide samples for the book.

Like in the Testing Ecto Schemas chapter, the sample code provides a Makefile to help get your database up and running. It's important to note that while the application code and tests are good, the database setup is insufficient for a real application. It's important to use stronger security practices than our sample application provides. Don't use our database setup in a real application.

This chapter will only cover a fraction of the code and tests written in the application, but the application has been tested using the same concepts as those presented throughout this book. Feel free to use the examples as a starting point for your own testing.

Testing JSON-Based APIs

We're going to start by looking at testing a JSON-based API. This is a very common use case for Phoenix and it's the least complex of the interfaces we'll test. This will allow us to focus on some concepts that will apply across all of the interface types we'll cover, without getting too lost in the specifics of the interface itself.

What Controller Tests Need to Cover

We strive to keep our controllers as small as possible, with as little branching logic as possible. This accomplishes two goals: it keeps our business logic out of the web part of our application, and it keeps the number of test cases needed to a minimum. Controller tests are some of our most expensive (in terms of running time) since they often require the most setup. Ideally, we have as few of them as possible while still leaving our application with solid coverage.

The logic for most controller actions can be tested with two tests: a happy path test and an error case test. There will always be exceptions to this, but it should be your starting goal.

Beyond testing the logic in the actions themselves, you may need to include tests to verify that certain plugs are included in your application's call stack. In this section, we'll test a JSON-based endpoint, with a happy path and an error case, and we'll test for the presence of a plug.

Before we start writing tests, let's look at the code we'll test and how it fits into the application.

Familiarizing Ourselves with the User Controller

Our application is a simple game. It's a pared-down version of a classic game called Skull and Roses. In our version, players simply take turns guessing if the other players have presented a skull or a rose. Our focus starts when players register in the application as users. Users are then able to create a new game or edit their own profile settings. While the application has HTML-rendered controller actions for user registration and profile updates, the JSON-based API provides this same functionality. We'll focus on testing the edit endpoint, meaning that our test will start with a registered user. Let's take a look at the controller code called when a user hits the update endpoint to change their own profile:

testing_phoenix/not_skull/lib/not_skull_web/controllers/json_api/user_controller.ex

```
Line 1  defmodule NotSkullWeb.JsonApi.UserController do
    -     @moduledoc false
    -
    -     use NotSkullWeb, :controller
    5
    -     alias NotSkull.Accounts
    -
    -     def update(conn, params) do
    -       with {:ok, user} <- Accounts.get_user_by_id(params["id"]),
   10           {:ok, updated_user} <- Accounts.update_user(user, params) do
    -         conn
    -         |> put_status(200)
    -         |> json(user_map_from_struct(updated_user))
    -       else
   15         {:error, error_changeset} ->
    -           conn
```

```
              |> put_status(422)
              |> json(errors_from_changset(error_changeset))
      end
   end

   defp user_map_from_struct(user) do
      user
      |> Map.from_struct()
      |> Map.drop([:__struct__, :__meta__])
   end

   defp errors_from_changset(changeset) do
      serializable_errors =
         for {field, {message, _}} <- changeset.errors,
            do: %{"field" => to_string(field), "message" => message}

      %{errors: serializable_errors}
   end
```

The start of the file looks like any other controller file. The update function is a standard controller action, accepting a Plug.Conn and a map of params. There's a two-condition with statement (line 9) that'll either execute the code in the provided block if successful (line 11) or in the error handling (line 16) if something goes wrong.

Only an existing user can call this endpoint. They must be logged in and they can only try to edit their own information. To enforce this, the application has a minimal implementation of JSON Web Tokens (JWT).[7] Calling the endpoint to update the user will require a signed JWT, gained by logging in through the login controller. The encoded JWT contains the user's ID, allowing the application to verify that a user is logged in. This decode and validation logic exists in a custom plug (found in lib/not_skull_web/plugs/validate_jwt.ex), which is why it isn't seen in this file. There's another plug that makes sure that the user ID in the JWT matches the user ID in the path.

Both of these plugs are unit-tested, which is possible because plugs are purely functional. While we aren't covering the testing of the plugs used in this chapter, they are tested in the application. The code under test, as well as tests for verifying the JWT, can be found at lib/not_skull_web/plugs/validate_jwt.ex and test/not_skull_web/plugs/validate_jwt_test.exs, respectively. The code under test can be found in lib/not_skull_web/plugs/match_jwt_user_id.ex, and the tests are in test/not_skull_web/plugs/match_jwt_user_id_test.exs. Aside from needing to conform to the standards for plug callbacks (plugs must have a call/2 function that takes

---

7.   https://jwt.io/

a Plug.Conn and parameters), you can see that the tests are structured like they would be for any purely functional code, only focusing on return values.

While we won't spend more time on the testing of the plugs, we will need to write tests to make sure they're utilized for this endpoint. After we've written some tests around the logic in the controller itself, we can learn how to test for the presence of plugs.

Let's starting writing tests.

Testing the Update Endpoint

In the included repo, NotSkull, create a new test file at test/not_skull_web/controllers/json_api/user_controller_test.exs. We've added nesting under json_api to avoid conflicting with the tests for the user controller that we used for the server-rendered HTML endpoint.

The following code will add a basic structure and setup block to the file you created:

```
testing_phoenix/not_skull/test/not_skull_web/controllers/json_api/user_controller_test.bak.exs
Line 1  defmodule NotSkullWeb.JsonApi.UserControllerTest do
          use NotSkullWeb.ConnCase, async: false

          alias NotSkull.Accounts.User
   5
          describe "PUT /api/users/:id" do
            setup context do
              {:ok, user} = Factory.insert(:user)

  10          conn_with_token =
                put_req_header(
                  context.conn,
                  "authorization",
                  "Bearer " <> sign_jwt(user.id)
  15            )

              Map.merge(context, %{user: user, conn_with_token: conn_with_token})
            end
          end
  20  end
```

When starting a new Phoenix project, the generators will create a few different ExUnit test cases. One of them, ConnCase, or specifically NotSkull.ConnCase in our app, will be used as the test case for all the HTTP-based interfaces. It's pulled in, as seen on line 2, by "using" the module. This makes a number of helpers available, making it easier for us to build and manipulate conns, or Plug.Conn structs. These helpers are a main extra component when testing web interfaces. Additionally, using the test case also imports our own custom functions, defined in NotSkullWeb.ConnCase itself. This allows us to create functions that we need more than once, across different tests, and to make them available in the tests that need them.

The string passed to describe breaks our pattern of using a function name and arity because, as a controller test, the exercise will hit an endpoint instead of calling a specific function. As a result, we've named the describe block after the HTTP action and path: "PUT /api/users/:id".

Leveraging the ConnCase

Our tests will use a common setup block, as most of them need two things: a user to exist in the database and a signed JWT for that user. It's good to default to having your setup in each test so that the test reads without having to look elsewhere. If you have multiple tests that need the same setup, though, it can be useful to move that common code into a single place, in this case the setup block. The JWT is included as a header in the Conn, as seen on line 10. The actual JWT is created by a function defined in NotSkull-Web.ConnCase (called on line 14), as we need to share some of its logic with the other controller test file, for the login controller. While diving into how the JWT is created isn't terribly helpful, adding things to request headers with put_req_header (line 11) is a very common thing to do in tests like these. That function comes from Plug.Conn and is imported via NotSkullWeb.ConnCase.

Unlike most of the tests we've written in previous chapters, our setup block accepts a context. This context comes from the test case. The generated file has a function that looks like this:

```
testing_phoenix/not_skull/test/support/conn_case.ex
Line 1  setup tags do
          Mox.verify_on_exit!()

          :ok = Ecto.Adapters.SQL.Sandbox.checkout(NotSkull.Repo)
     5
          unless tags[:async] do
            Ecto.Adapters.SQL.Sandbox.mode(NotSkull.Repo, {:shared, self()})
          end

    10    {:ok, conn: Phoenix.ConnTest.build_conn()}
        end
```

The first behavior worth noting is that it sets the sandbox mode to :shared (line 7). This setting is important because it impacts how your tests can be run. Shared mode allows any process to access the same database transaction, behaving like a database would when running in production. Our interface

(API) tests are integration-style, and there's a good chance that many processes will want to access the same data, for example the user we seeded in the database. You'll notice that there's a conditional (unless) wrapped around the line setting the mode. Remember the async: false from the use line of our test file? This code evaluates the value passed for async. This unless block makes it so that any test using NotSkullWeb.ConnCase will default the sandbox mode to shared mode unless it's overridden with async: true. We added async: false to our test file because being explicit is always good.

Also in that function is a call to the library Mox, on line 2, which we discussed in Chapter 2, Integration and End-to-End Tests, on page 35. This is a good reminder that the setup block in a test case will be shared by all tests that use that file (unless specifically overridden). In this case, setting Mox to a specific mode doesn't hurt the tests that don't use Mox, so while it doesn't pertain to the tests we're looking at, it's not a problem to have it there, either.

The setup block returns a new Plug.Conn because it's assumed that all the tests using the file will need it.

Defining an Error Test

It's common to have your success tests before your error tests, but that doesn't mean you have to write them in that order. In our case, we're going to start with the simplest test for this endpoint: our error case.

Add the following test inside of the describe block you already created:

```
testing_phoenix/not_skull/test/not_skull_web/controllers/json_api/user_controller_test.bak.exs
Line 1  test "error: does not update, returns errors when given invalid attributes",
  -           %{
  -             conn_with_token: conn_with_token,
  -             user: existing_user
  5           } do
  -      conn =
  -        put(conn_with_token, "/api/users/#{existing_user.id}", %{name: ""})
  -
  -      assert body = json_response(conn, 422)
  10
  -      user_from_db = Repo.get(User, existing_user.id)
  -      assert user_from_db == existing_user
  -
  -      actual_errors = body["errors"]
  15     refute Enum.empty?(actual_errors)
  -
  -      expected_error_keys = ["field", "message"]
  -
  -      for error <- actual_errors do
  20       assert_unordered_lists_are_equal(
```

```
        actual: Map.keys(error),
        expected: expected_error_keys
      )
    end
25  end
```

As mentioned before, the test accepts a context from the setup block, in this case giving it a user and a Plug.Conn that contains a header with a JWT for that user (line 3). Because the setup is done before the test, the very first line of the test body is the call to exercise (line 7). It's using the function put/3, which it has imported from Phoenix.ConnTest by "using" NotSkullWeb.ConnCase. Similar functions are available for each of the HTTP action types, some of which we'll use later. In this case, the function takes a Plug.Conn (we're passing the one with the JWT), the path for the endpoint, and a PUT body. The return value from all of them is an updated Plug.Conn that contains the response data.

Line 9 uses json_response/2 to do two things: it checks that the HTTP status code on the returned Plug.Conn matches the code that's passed as the second argument (we're expecting a 422 in this case). If those values match, it parses the body field of the Plug.Conn from JSON into an Elixir map. While normally it's not great to do two things at once, especially two unrelated things like an assertion and a transformation, this function has been around for years and has never caused any issues. When it fails, it provides errors that make it clear if it's failing because of the status code or because it can't parse the body to JSON.

The rest of the test is fairly straightforward. It checks that, because this is an error case, the data in the database hasn't been changed as a result of the HTTP call (line 12). This is an assertion that's often overlooked in error cases but needs to be there. Because the input was invalid, nothing should have been changed in the database. This is an extra check on top of the assertions on the return value. Unlike in most unit tests, endpoint tests, because they're inherently integration tests, almost always includes assertions for the code under test's return value *and* assertions on its side effects.

Speaking of return values, the test also verifies that the response body has errors that are maps with the keys "field" and "message" (line 19). The test does NOT check for specific errors, just that they are shaped correctly. We've already written tests to make sure that the correct error is handed back from our database code. This test is just focused on the controller and making sure that it calls out to the right code and can properly handle an error. Since our application standardizes the way we handle errors, we only need one somewhat generic test to confirm that our controller can handle any error correctly.

We are going to add three more tests, but we won't dive as deeply into what's happening in each of them, as they build on the basic structure that we just wrote.

Testing the Happy Path

Our next test will be our happy path. In the same describe block, add this test, ideally before the error case that we just reviewed:

testing_phoenix/not_skull/test/not_skull_web/controllers/json_api/user_controller_test.bak.exs

```
Line 1  test "success: updates db returns record with good params", %{
          conn_with_token: conn_with_token,
          user: existing_user
        } do
5         new_name = "#{existing_user.name}-updated"

          conn =
            put(conn_with_token, "/api/users/#{existing_user.id}", %{
              name: new_name
10          })

          assert parsed_return = json_response(conn, 200)

          user_from_db = Repo.get(User, existing_user.id)
15
          assert_values_for(
            expected: %{existing_user | name: new_name},
            actual: user_from_db,
            fields: fields_for(User) -- [:updated_at]
20        )

          assert DateTime.to_unix(user_from_db.updated_at, :microsecond) >
                   DateTime.to_unix(existing_user.updated_at, :microsecond)

25        # checking that the updated record is what is returned from endpoint
          assert_values_for(
            expected: user_from_db,
            actual: {parsed_return, :string_keys},
            fields: fields_for(User),
30          opts: [convert_dates: true]
          )
        end
```

The test is structured very similarly to the error test we wrote before it. The common elements are these:

- It accepts a context with a Plug.Conn that contains a valid JWT.

- It calls the endpoint using put/3, a helper from the Phoenix library.

- It uses json_response/2 to assert on the HTTP response code and to deserialize the JSON response.

- It makes assertions on the return value.

- It makes assertions on the side effects.

In this case, it differs from the error case at the assertions. Because it's a happy path test, we should see that the HTTP response code was a 200. The return value should be a serialized version of the updated record.

The assertions on the return value and the side effect are very related here. Assuming the code under test is working correctly, the return value should be the same information that's in the row in the database: the updated user. We also want to assert that the return value is the original record updated with the new params, in this case just the new name. But it's important to lock down that the only values that changed are the ones that were passed in through the endpoint. To assert that the values are correct for both the return value and the data in the database (the side effect), we'll turn to a custom helper function, called assert_values_for/1.

Our Custom Test Helpers

All of the code for the helper function is provided in code/testing_phoenix/not_skull/test/support/assertion_helpers.ex, and you have access to it in the tests you are writing via use NotSkullWeb.ConnCase. It's more useful here to discuss *what* it does and *why* it does it than how. The function accepts two pieces of data for which Enumerable is implemented. It also takes a list of field names to check against. Assuming atom-based keys, but allowing for the option of string keys, it iterates through and checks that every field named has the same value in both the *expected* and the *actual* data. It also accepts an option to convert between Elixir *DateTime* structs and ISO 8601 strings. The *why* of this function is simple: most engineers don't explicitly test all of the data available in their tests because writing assertions on every field is tedious. By creating an easy-to-use, easy-to-reason-around, thorough helper function, we're attempting to eliminate this bad habit.

The first use of assert_values_for/1 is on line 16, where we define the expected to be the existing user's values updated with the new name (from the parameters passed in the exercise call). A second helper function called fields_for/1 is used on line 19. It returns a list of all the fields for whatever you pass it. In our case, we're giving it the User struct. Because it's a list, we can easily remove any fields we want to skip by using Elixir low-level list subtraction, Kernel.--/2. In our case, we're removing :updated_at from the list of values to check because it'll have changed and we don't have a way to know the new value from inside our test. We've tested enough of the fields to have confidence that our code called the correct function(s) under the hood. Because we emphasize thoroughness, though, we've added one last assertion to cover :updated_at as well, at line 22. Our code is calling out to thoroughly tested code, so this assertion could be considered optional.

Our second use of assert_values_for/1 is on line 26, where we're checking the data in the response. By already asserting that the data in the database is correct, we can now treat it as our expected data. Because the returned data and the data from the database have the same source, they should have identical values, except where the formatting has changed due to serialization to JSON; the keys and datetimes will be strings. assert_values_for/1 provides options so that we don't need to do any conversions in our test—the helper function can handle them.

Our test has now checked every value relevant to this scenario. The controller code is sending the params to the right place, causing the right side effects, and it's rendering all the data as expected. We've completed a happy path test and tested that our controller handles errors correctly. This constitutes the minimum basic coverage you'll want on any interface for your application. As mentioned earlier, though, two plugs should be called when hitting the update endpoint. Let's take a look at how to test that these calls happen.

Testing for the Presence of Plugs

While any basic plugs that you write should be unit-tested, we need to add tests to our test suite to assert that they're called on every endpoint that's in a pipeline that includes them. While every Plug is different, in our use case, both are run before the controller in the call stack. The existing happy path test we wrote covers when things are right. We only need to test for when things aren't right. That means that testing multiple endpoints for the presence of the same plug(s) will start to look a little repetitive because the setup, if it exists, and the assertions will be nearly identical. Often only the endpoint will change. We'll add two tests to assert the presence of our two plugs.

In the router (code/testing_phoenix/not_skull/lib/not_skull_web/router.ex), our update endpoint is in a pipeline that contains our two custom plugs: ValidateJWT and MatchJWTUserId. Let's take a look at each, understanding what it does and then adding a test to make sure it's present.

The first Plug, ValidateJWT, decodes the JWT and makes sure that it's valid. If it is valid, the Plug takes the user's ID from the JWT and adds it into the incoming params. If the Plug doesn't detect a valid JWT, it halts the call stack, returning an HTTP status code of 401 ("Unauthenticated") and a simple JSON response with a descriptive error.

Add the following new test in the same describe block, "PUT /api/users/:id", after your error test:

```
testing_phoenix/not_skull/test/not_skull_web/controllers/json_api/user_controller_test.bak.exs
Line 1 test "auth error: returns 401 when valid jwt isn't in headers", %{
         conn: conn,
         user: existing_user
       } do
   5     conn =
           put(conn, "/api/users/#{existing_user.id}", %{
             name: "#{existing_user.name}-updated"
           })

  10     assert body = json_response(conn, 401)

         assert %{
                 "errors" => [
                   %{"message" => "Invalid token.", "field" => "token"}
  15               ]
                } == body

         user_from_db = Repo.get(User, existing_user.id)

  20     assert_values_for(
           expected: existing_user,
           actual: user_from_db,
           fields: fields_for(User)
         )
  25 end
```

We already have the code in setup that makes sure that we have a correctly signed JWT; but in this case, we don't want that, so our test uses the original Plug.Conn provided to it by the setup block in NotSkullWeb.ConnCase. You can see that it's taking that from the context on line 2. It would also be OK to add a header with an incorrectly encoded JWT. Both will have the same result when decoded in our Plug. We chose the option with a little less work.

The exercise looks like the exercise step in the rest of our tests in this describe block, as seen on line 6. We're using a valid set of params because even though that data should never have made it to the underlying update and changeset functionality, our test is treating our code like a black box. As a result, the implementation may change, but we need our tests to lock down the outside behavior. In this case, if the JWT isn't valid, we should not only get an error response, which we've tested, but the data in the database should also not be changed. We'll address that assertion shortly.

Our test asserts that the response body is a correctly formatted error, as you can see on line 12. When previously testing errors, we went to lengths to not assume we knew all of the errors but instead to just make sure the errors we expected were present. That requires a list comprehension and some work around being able to match. In this case, we're testing a plug that should only be run if all code executed before it was successful. If the preceding code fails, no other code should run. As a result, the error is the only one that should be present, so we can cut a corner by making a comparison against the whole response body.

The last part of this test is fairly standard. Because the call was unauthenticated, there should have been no side effect. As we mentioned a few paragraphs above, we need to make sure that the data in the database hasn't changed. On line 18, we grab the row from the database and then use assert_values_for/1 to make sure it's identical to our record from before the call, the data bound to the variable existing_user.

Our Plug test calls the endpoint that's expected to have the plug. It intentionally fails the check in the plug, short-circuiting the call stack and forcing a return value. The test then makes assertions on both the return value and the data in the database (checking against side effects). This is very similar to our other tests on the same endpoint.

Our last test for this endpoint is our second Plug test. This time, it's a basic plug to make sure that the user making the request is the same user whose record is being updated. Open the same test file (test/not_skull_web/controllers/json_api/user_controller_test.exs) and add this last test at the bottom of the same describe block ("PUT /api/users/:id"):

testing_phoenix/not_skull/test/not_skull_web/controllers/json_api/user_controller_test.bak.exs

```
test "auth error: returns 403 when path and jwt user ids don't match",
    %{
      conn_with_token: conn_with_token,
      user: existing_user
    } do
    conn =
      put(conn_with_token, "/api/users/#{Factory.uuid()}", %{
        name: "#{existing_user.name}-updated"
      })
  assert body = json_response(conn, 403)
  assert %{
          "errors" => [
```

```
                   %{
                     "message" => "You are not authorized for that action.",
                     "field" => "token"
                   }
                 ]
               } == body

      user_from_db = Repo.get(User, existing_user.id)

      assert_values_for(
        expected: existing_user,
        actual: user_from_db,
        fields: fields_for(User)
        )
    end
  end
end
```

The test itself is structured like our other Plug test. The differences are that it uses the Plug.Conn with the valid token (JWT) and that the user ID in the URL is different from what's encoded in the token. The assertions are similar, checking the status code (this time a 403), checking the error(s) in the response body, and finally asserting that there were no side effects.

By running through these tests, we've laid out a basic structure that will be used or built on in our tests for the other kinds of application interfaces. Let's look at server-rendered HTML endpoints next.

Testing Server-Rendered HTML Applications

Testing server-rendered HTML endpoints is very similar to testing JSON endpoints, but the response is an HTML document instead of JSON. We'll write tests for the user controller that handles the server-rendered HTML endpoints. Let's start by looking at the controller code that we'll be testing:

```
testing_phoenix/not_skull/lib/not_skull_web/controllers/user_controller.ex
defmodule NotSkullWeb.UserController do
  use NotSkullWeb, :controller

  alias NotSkull.Accounts
  alias NotSkull.Accounts.User
  alias NotSkull.ExternalServices.Email
  def new(conn, _params) do
    user = User.create_changeset(%{})
    render(conn, "new.html", changeset: user)
  end

  def create(conn, %{"user" => user_params}) do
    case Accounts.create_user(user_params) do
      {:ok, user} ->
        Email.send_welcome(user)
```

```
    conn
    |> put_session(:user_id, user.id)
    |> put_flash(:info, "Your account was created successfully!")
    |> redirect(to: Routes.user_path(conn, :show, user))

  {:error, %Ecto.Changeset{} = changeset} ->
    render(conn, "new.html", changeset: changeset)
    end
  end

end
```

This code is a controller that, under the hood, calls to the same context module as the JSON controller we've already tested. Our testing will focus on the two endpoints that call the new and create controller actions. new renders the HTML form for adding a user, while create will accept the parameters for a new user and, assuming good data, create a user with that data. We'll dive into the details of each before we write the tests.

Testing New

To begin, in the provided application, create a new test file at test/not_skull_web/controllers/user_controller_test.exs and add in the following file structure:

testing_phoenix/not_skull/test/not_skull_web/controllers/user_controller_test.bak.exs
```
defmodule NotSkullWeb.UserControllerTest do
  use NotSkullWeb.ConnCase, async: false

  alias NotSkull.Accounts.User
end
```

This code should look like a very similar version of our test for the JSON API endpoints. We use the exact same test case, NotSkullWeb.ConnCase and alias NotSkull.Accounts.User. We aren't including any setup because the first endpoint we'll test, to render the form, requires no setup. Additionally, because there's no branching logic in the controller or the code that it's calling, we'll only need a happy path test. In your file, add this describe block and test:

testing_phoenix/not_skull/test/not_skull_web/controllers/user_controller_test.bak.exs
```
Line 1  describe "GET /users/new" do
     2    test "success: it renders the form", %{conn: conn} do
     3      conn = get(conn, Routes.user_path(conn, :new))
     4
     5      assert response = html_response(conn, 200)
     6
     7      assert response =~ "Create a new account"
     8    end
     9  end
```

There's a lot in common with our JSON API endpoint testing. Line 1 shows us using the HTTP action and URL path to describe the block of tests. We accept the Plug.Conn from the testing context on line 2. Line 3 does have a difference that's worth mentioning. Instead of passing our controller test's helper function, get/2, a path, we're passing the result of Routes.user_path(conn, :new). This helper is provided by the Phoenix framework. It's your choice whether or not to use it instead of the path. It can make maintenance a little easier in situations when there are small shifts in the path, but it leaves a level of obfuscation about which endpoint it's calling. If you don't have an opinion, use the path like we did in the test for the JSON API, not the helper.

Line 5 shows us using a slightly different helper function, html_response/2, which is provided by Phoenix, just as json_response/2 was. They work very similarly, first asserting the HTTP status code; but instead of a decoded Elixir map, this function returns the raw HTML as a string. That leads us to our last assertion, on line 7, which uses the fuzzy match operator, Kernel.=~/2, to make sure that the string "Create a new account" is present in the HTML response. This test assumes that if that exact string is in the HTML, the whole form must have been returned. Given that we've spent most of this book encouraging very comprehensive test coverage, this may feel a little light. It is. Phoenix, out of the box, doesn't provide a way to verify a whole HTML payload.

Later, when we cover the error case, we'll provide a more explicit approach, but this is a fine time for us to remind you that even if your tests are well designed and passing, you should still run your code on your computer and verify with your own eyes that your application is behaving correctly. In this case, that means running your server, mix phx.server, and hitting the endpoint, http://localhost:4000/users/new. You should see the form rendered. Even if we had every aspect of this endpoint locked down in tests, you should still always just make sure your code behaves as intended by manually exercising it.

Testing the Happy Path for Create

Now that we've covered testing the new endpoint, which renders the form to create a user, let's take a look at the create endpoint. This is the endpoint hit by the form rendered by our previous endpoint, for new. Let's take a second look at the code and discuss what we'll need to test:

```
def create(conn, %{"user" => user_params}) do
  case Accounts.create_user(user_params) do
    {:ok, user} ->
      Email.send_welcome(user)

      conn
      |> put_session(:user_id, user.id)
```

```
        |> put_flash(:info, "Your account was created successfully!")
        |> redirect(to: Routes.user_path(conn, :show, user))

      {:error, %Ecto.Changeset{} = changeset} ->
        render(conn, "new.html", changeset: changeset)
    end
  end
end
```

There's branching logic in this function, depending on the success of Accounts.create_user(user_params). As a result, we know that we'll need at least two tests, a happy path test and an error test. There are four new code elements that we haven't tested before: sending email (an outside call as a side effect), setting values in the session, setting the flash, and redirecting a call. Let's write our happy path test first, since it's where we'll cover these. Open up your test file and add a new describe block and test as follows:

```
Line 1  describe "POST /users" do
  -       test "success: creates_user, redirects to show page when user is created",
  -            %{conn: conn} do
  -         params = Factory.atom_params(:user)
  5
  -         expect_email_to(params.email)
  -
  -         conn = post(conn, Routes.user_path(conn, :create), user: params)
  -
  10        assert %{id: id} = redirected_params(conn)
  -         assert redirected_to(conn) == Routes.user_path(conn, :show, id)
  -
  -         assert %{"user_id" => ^id} = get_session(conn)
  -         assert get_flash(conn, :info) =~ "success"
  15
  -         user_from_db = Repo.get(User, id)
  -
  -         fields_to_check = Map.keys(params) -- [:password]
  -
  20        assert_values_for(
  -           expected: params,
  -           actual: user_from_db,
  -           fields: fields_to_check
  -         )
  25
  -         assert user_from_db.password
  -       end
  -     end
```

Like our previous tests, this one inherits a Plug.Conn from the test setup. On line 4, we're getting valid parameters from our factory. Line 6 calls out to a custom helper function, expect_email_to/1, that sets up an expectation that we'll attempt to send email. When we're done reviewing this test, we'll circle back and look at the code of that helper function. For now, we can assume from the name that it creates an expectation that an email will be sent to the address from our params. If that doesn't happen, we'll expect a test failure.

After the exercise line, which uses the Phoenix-provided post/3 in conjunction with Routes.user_path/2, we can see that we aren't parsing the response as HTML. This is because, on successful user creation, the controller should return a redirect instead of a page. We need the ID of the newly created user so that we can make sure the redirect is to the expected path and to find the user in the database. Phoenix provides a helper function, redirected_params/1, to give us the parameters used in the redirect. Our test is using that function on line 10 to get that ID.

Now that we know the ID of the new user, we can assert that the server's response to a successful creation is a redirect to the "show" endpoint, as shown on line 11. We can presume that endpoint is also tested on its own, so our test can be scoped to just the interactions in the controller action to create a user.

We're about to show one of our first, and likely only, violations of the testing black box we discussed in Chapter 1, Unit Tests, on page 1. Part of the behavior of signing up in the application is to set the new user's ID in the server session so that subsequent calls to the API will have it available without requiring login credentials with every call. If we were writing tests that exercised an entire flow through multiple API calls, we would be leveraging the session, and the subsequent calls would fail without that ID set in the session. But we're testing this endpoint in isolation. We still need to make sure that the code is setting that ID. Line 13 makes sure that the ID from our redirected_params/1 is set in the session with the key "user_id".

Because the response was a redirect, the only user-facing element for us to check is that the flash is set correctly. Line 14 shows how to use get_flash/2 to retrieve the contents of a specific key (:info in our case) from the flash. We then assert that the message is what we expected.

The last part of the test is to validate the side effect, namely the creation of the new user. We use assert_values_for/1 to check that all of our params, except :password, made it into the database. The value for :password can't be checked directly because it won't be the same value but a hashed value instead. We can't predict what the value will be. We can, though, assert that a password value has been set. After that, we can feel confident that our code called the intended context function and that the context function is tested well enough that we don't need to write a more explicit assertion in our controller test.

Testing Side Effects—Calls to a Third Party

Earlier, we said we would look at the helper function that asserted that an email was sent out. Let's take a look at that code, which is already included in the sample application. It's defined in NotSkullWeb.ConnCase and is called expect_mail_to/1. Here is the code:

```
Line 1  def expect_email_to(expected_email_address) do
          Mox.expect(HttpClientMock, :request, fn method,
                                                  url,
                                                  _headers,
     5                                            json_body,
                                                  _opts ->
            assert method == :post
            assert url == "https://api.sendgrid.com/v3/mail/send"

    10      decoded_body = Jason.decode!(json_body)

            assert %{
                     "personalizations" => [
                       %{
    15                   "to" => [
                           %{"email" => ^expected_email_address}
                         ]
                       }
                     ]
    20             } = decoded_body
          end)
        end
```

As can be seen on line 2, the function is a wrapper around a pre-defined Mox call. The name is specific enough to tell us *what* it's doing without us having to worry about the *how*. That can be useful, as a single, descriptive function call in our test can leave it more readable than dropping an entire Mox function setup inside a test. And, of course, it makes it reusable.

Notice that we don't pin the arguments in the anonymous function that we pass to Mox.expect/3. Instead, we have assertions inside the anonymous function. That's because when there's more than one required value, pinning the value throws a FunctionClauseError on failure, which doesn't highlight which value didn't match. Having each value in a separate assertion will provide immediate, clear feedback as to which value is incorrect. That doesn't mean you can't pin values if you need to. You can see that on line 16. We're still able to use a pinned value with a pattern match, but it's happening inside the anonymous function and not in the function head.

Our test helper makes sure that the specifics to sending an email out to a customer are there, but it doesn't go so far as to assert on the content of that email. It's your decision whether you find additional assertions to be helpful there. The module to send email will need to be unit-tested on its own. We could make our helper function less generic, taking in a string as an argument and making sure that string was in the email body. We chose not to, though, as this test just needs to make sure that the email is sent, leaving the explicit testing to unit tests. Additionally, any email your application sends should be manually tested to make sure that it renders correctly. As a result, getting more explicit in the endpoint test is redundant.

Testing the Error Case for Create

We complete our coverage of this endpoint and controller action by testing a failure case. Inside the same describe block, and under our previous test, add this:

```
Line 1  test "error: does not insert, redirects to 'new' page w/invalid attributes",
          %{
            conn: conn
          } do
     5  flunk_if_email_is_sent()

        expected_user_count = Repo.all(User) |> Enum.count()
        conn = post(conn, Routes.user_path(conn, :create), user: %{})

    10  assert html = html_response(conn, 200)

        parsed_html = Floki.parse_document!(html)
        for field <- ["name", "email", "password"] do
          # using <> so that the first #(indicating an id) is easy to read
    15    field_as_id = "#" <> "#{field}-error"
          span = Floki.find(parsed_html, field_as_id)
          assert Floki.text(span) == "can't be blank"
        end

    20  assert Repo.all(User) |> Enum.count() == expected_user_count,
              "There should have been no records inserted during this test."
      end
```

The test leverages a new custom helper function called flunk_if_email_is_sent/0, on line 5, that's defined in NotSkull.ConnCase, right next to our other helper function. Like before, we'll visit that code after we've discussed the rest of this test.

Because our test is a failure case, it needs to make sure that no new users were created as a side effect. On line 7, the test is getting the pre-exercise count of users in the database. This allows us to assert at the end of the test (line 20) that the count didn't change. While not bulletproof, this gives us reasonably high confidence that nothing has changed. We don't assert that the count is zero, which it probably will be because of the sandbox, because the test isn't actually concerned that there's no data in the database. It's only concerned that there isn't *new* data as the result of exercising the code under test. This way, if a new feature is added and the common setup is updated to include adding a user for a different test, our test will still pass and provide us the same confidence that no new users have been added. This reduces the required maintenance for our test suite. It's always worth looking for opportunities to make your tests low maintenance.

A big difference between this test and our happy path test is that we're using a different method to make assertions on the values returned in the HTML. On line 13, we have a list comprehension that goes through the three known field names in the signup form. Because our test is posting empty parameters, the rendered HTML should include a warning about each field being blank. In the code block passed to the list comprehension, we're using a newer library called Floki.[8] Floki gives you the ability to search HTML for specific selectors, in our three cases, #name-error, #email-error, and #password-error. Calling Floki.text/1 and passing that element will return the text, as seen on line 17, allowing us to make an assertion on the value.

Modified Boilerplate

 When Phoenix generates a new project, the application has a generated ErrorHelpers module that includes a function, error_tag/2, that indirectly creates the HTML for form errors. It doesn't normally allow a CSS ID to be passed in. Our sample code has modified that function to allow for an optional ID. You can see the modified function, error_tag/3, in the included application in the file, not_skull/test/support/assertion_helpers.ex. This function is generated and not part of the Phoenix library, specifically to allow this kind of customization specific to your needs.

Using Floki, and making sure our HTML is structured and includes CSS IDs for the dynamic elements of the page, allows us to be very specific that the view code is working correctly. We can now be certain that our application is not only rendering the correct view but that the information in that view is correct. We have effectively tested the return value from our endpoint.

Let's finish this test exploration with a look at the helper function, flunk_if_email_is_sent/0. Like expect_mail_to/1, this function is a wrapper around some Mox functionality, as seen here:

---

8. https://hex.pm/packages/floki

```
def flunk_if_email_is_sent do
  Mox.stub(HttpClientMock, :request, fn _, _, _, _, _ ->
    flunk("An email should not have been sent.")
  end)
end
```

If *any* email is sent for any reason during the execution of our test, the test will fail. We chose to use Mox.stub/3 instead of Mox.expect/4 with an expectation of zero calls because this allows us, by adding in ExUnit's flunk/1, to write a customized error message. This is just a test style preference. Using the alternative would work just as well, but the error message if it failed would be a little more vague about what happened.

In this test, we made assertions on the return value from the endpoint by using Floki to assert on the dynamic information in the HTML. Our test also covered side effects, specifically that no new users were created and that no email was sent. We can feel confident that our test is protecting us from regressions.

With these examples, we covered the concerns of controller testing that are specific to server-rendered HTML endpoints. You may come up with edge cases that aren't covered here. When you do, try to remember to move most branching logic out of a controller and into small files that can be individually tested. This will allow you to keep your larger, more expensive tests (i.e., controller tests) limited in scope. Controller tests should just focus on making sure "none of your wires are crossed." In other words, controller tests make sure that all of the code you tested in unit tests interacts correctly as a whole application.

One last interface is included with the core of the Phoenix library, Phoenix Channels. Let's look at how to test those.

Testing Phoenix Channels

Phoenix Channels are an abstraction of web sockets that put a certain amount of framework code on top of a somewhat open transfer protocol. They provide enough opinion on how to use web sockets that it's easier to get going, and there's a well-written and well-supported Phoenix JavaScript package that makes building JavaScript clients relatively easy.[9] Fortunately for us, Phoenix also includes plenty of test helpers (called Phoenix.ChannelTest, and pulled in by way of a generated ChannelCase module) to make testing Channels code fairly straightforward as well.

---

9.   https://www.npmjs.com/package/phoenix

Unlike JSON-based APIs and server-rendered HTML, it seems useful here to talk a little more about the actual use cases of Channels, to set the context of the code we'll test. Phoenix Channels are often used in conjunction with a fully developed front-end JavaScript client. The application included with this book uses a very small spattering of JavaScript to modify a server-rendered HTML view. In either scenario, the server-side Channel code is the concern of this book. We won't focus on testing the JavaScript.

This section won't exhaustively show every way to test Phoenix Channel code, but it will cover enough to make it clear how testing Channels works. It'll also dive into some of the nuances that the test tooling provided with the library specific to testing Phoenix Channels.

Testing the UserSocket

When a Phoenix Project is generated, it comes with a boilerplate UserSocket module. We've added some authentication code to our UserSocket module so that it looks like the following code:

```
testing_phoenix/not_skull/lib/not_skull_web/channels/user_socket.ex
defmodule NotSkullWeb.UserSocket do
  use Phoenix.Socket
  alias NotSkull.{Accounts, JWTUtility}
  require Logger

  channel "lobby:*", NotSkullWeb.LobbyChannel

  @impl true
  def connect(%{"token" => token}, socket, _connect_info) do
    jwt = URI.decode_www_form(token)

    with {:ok, user_id} <- JWTUtility.user_id_from_jwt(jwt),
         {:ok, _valid_user} <- Accounts.get_user_by_id(user_id) do
      socket = assign(socket, :user_id, user_id)
      {:ok, socket}
    else
      something_else ->
        Logger.warn(inspect(something_else))
        :error
    end
  end

  def connect(_, _socket, _connect_info), do: :error

  @impl true
  def id(socket), do: "user_socket:#{socket.assigns.user_id}"
end
```

The biggest changes from the boilerplate are on lines 12, 13, and 14. On line 12, we're validating the JWT and getting the associated user ID. On 13, we're making sure that the user ID is actually in our system's database. Your authentication choices may vary, but it's important to make sure that you have authentication on your user socket. If those two checks are successful, the function will return a socket with the user ID from the JWT set in the assigns under the key :user_id.

Our test for the happy path will need to check that the user ID has been added to the assigns as well as the socket ID, determined by the id/1 function at line 26. Normally, we wouldn't cover the behavior of two public functions within a single test, but the way Channels are implemented, we have to verify that the ID function behaves within the test for connect/3 and that the function wouldn't be called at any other time. With two possible places where this code path could fail, we'll need to make sure that we have tests for both of those code paths as well.

Avoid Logging Tokens

This isn't testing-related, but it's important to call out if you are using a pattern similar to the one we have in our sample code. The JWT authentication token is being passed as a query parameter. Even if your application is using an encrypted protocol, it's very common for the requests to be logged, unencrypted, server-side. Make sure that your logging isn't including the query params because logging an unencrypted, unexpired JWT can open up a hole in your security. Anyone that can access your logging could then impersonate the user whose JWT was logged.

To start testing this code, create a file called test/not_skull_web/channels/user_socket_test.exs with the following test structure:

testing_phoenix/not_skull/test/not_skull_web/channels/user_socket_test.bak.exs
```
defmodule NotSkullWeb.UserSocketTest do
  use NotSkullWeb.ChannelCase
  alias NotSkullWeb.UserSocket

  describe "connect/3" do
  end
end
```

This file is structured like all our other tests. The most notable callout is line 2, where we're using NotSkullWeb.ChannelCase. This is a new test case, very similar to our others, but it imports Phoenix.ChannelTest, the Channel-specific tooling we mentioned earlier. It also has one line, @endpoint NotSkullWeb.Endpoint, that

we'll discuss after we've written some tests. Add your first test, a happy path
to check that a socket will be returned when called with a valid JWT, by
adding the following code inside the describe block:

```
test "success: allows connection when passed a valid JWT for a real user" do
  {:ok, existing_user} = Factory.insert(:user)
  jwt = sign_jwt(existing_user.id)

  assert {:ok, socket} = connect(UserSocket, %{token: jwt})
  assert socket.assigns.user_id == existing_user.id
  assert socket.id == "user_socket:#{existing_user.id}"
end
```

This test uses the first of the test helpers provided by Phoenix.ChannelTest (via
our ChannelCase module), called Phoenix.ChannelTest.connect/3 on line 5. It's important
to understand that this isn't directly calling connect/3 on our module under
test. Calling that function would require it to be called with the module name
as aliased, UserSocket.connect(UserSocket, %{token: jwt}). UserSocket.connect/3 doesn't
have any optional params, whereas Phoenix.ChannelTest.connect/3 does, which is
how our test can call with it just passing two parameters.

This is one of the noticeable nuances of testing Channels. The boilerplate
code that was set up when the application was generated includes a line in
the ChannelCase module that reads @endpoint NotSkullWeb.Endpoint. This line is setting
a module attribute used by the Phoenix.ChannelTest.connect/3 macro. You can look
at the source code to get a better understanding of how it works.[10] This macro
accepts the name of the socket module, NotSkullWeb.UserSocket in our case, and
parameters. It calls functions in NotSkullWeb.UserSocket that were added by macros
when "using" Phoenix.Socket, and eventually calls the connect/3 function defined in
our NotSkullWeb.UserSocket file, passing in the params from the test and a Socket
struct. The main takeaway is just to understand that the call to connect/3 on line
5 is effectively a call to the function connect/3 in your module under test.

As this is a happy path test, the return value from the code will be a tuple
with :ok and the Socket struct, which we'll refer to as the socket. The code under
test doesn't have side effects, so all that needs to happen now is to make sure
that the returned socket has the correct information. The first assertion is
that the user ID was placed in the assigns in the socket. That's covered on line
6. As we mentioned earlier, our code will also have assigned an ID to the
socket. This ID is a string that'll be used when the user needs to send a tar-
geted message instead of a broadcast to everyone subscribed to the channel.

---

10. https://github.com/phoenixframework/phoenix/blob/c8883af5582a38496e4b7e45e05d3a4d759a6caa/lib/phoenix/
    test/channel_test.ex#L269

The string returned from id/1 needs to be specific to the UserSocket but also include the user's ID. Our assertion on line 7 checks that. This is, in a roundabout way, checking the other public function in our module under test, id/1, which, like connect/3 is part of the implementation required when "using" Phoenix.Socket.

Our happy path test covers the return value when valid parameters are passed in. Now we need to write error tests for the two ways that things can go wrong. Inside of the same code block, add the following test:

```
@tag capture_log: true
test "error: returns :error for an invalid JWT" do
  assert :error = connect(UserSocket, %{token: "bad_token"})
end
```

This first check in the code under test is to verify that there is a good JWT. All our test needs to do is to pass in a known bad value for the token. In our case, "bad_token" will suffice, and it makes it clear from reading the test what we're doing to cause the failure. The contract from our function is that the return value in this situation should just be the atom :error. Our test is capturing the logs so that our test output isn't marred with the expected logging from the code.

The error case for a valid JWT that contains an invalid user ID isn't much more complex. Within the same describe block, add this last test:

```
@tag capture_log: true
test "error: returns :error if user doesn't exist" do
  jwt = sign_jwt(Factory.uuid())

  assert :error = connect(UserSocket, %{token: jwt})
end
```

This test is using our JWT helper to create a valid JWT with a bad user ID in it. We can guarantee that the user ID will be bad by creating a new UUID specifically for this payload. There is no way that it exists in the database. Just like the previous test, we're able to combine our assertion that :error is returned in the same line that we exercise the code under test. Also like the previous test, the logs are captured since we expect error logging from our code.

With these three tests, we've now covered every code path possible when calling connect/3. The UserSocket module will be used to connect to our server for the Channel that we do have, the LobbyChannel, but also to any other Channels that we would need in the future. We have the connection code covered. Next, let's look at the code in the LobbyChannel and learn the nuances of testing it.

Testing a Channel

The Phoenix Channel example we've provided in the NotSkull sample app, LobbyChannel, has pretty limited functionality. As we test it, we won't exhaustively show how to use all of the test macros included in Phoenix.ChannelTest, but we'll cover enough so that you'll understand how to use all of them. Let's take a look at the file:

```
testing_phoenix/not_skull/lib/not_skull_web/channels/lobby_channel.ex
Line 1  defmodule NotSkullWeb.LobbyChannel do
  -       use NotSkullWeb, :channel

  -       alias NotSkull.GameEngine.Game

  5
  -       @impl true
  -       def join("lobby:lobby", _payload, socket) do
  -         {:ok, socket}
  -       end

  10
  -       @spec broadcast_new_game(Game.t()) :: :ok | :error
  -       def broadcast_new_game(%Game{current_phase: :joining} = game) do
  -         NotSkullWeb.Endpoint.broadcast!("lobby:lobby", "new_game_created", %{
  -           game_id: game.id
  15          })
  -       end

  -       def broadcast_new_game(_) do
  -         :error
  20      end
  -     end
```

This file provides just two functions, join/3 and broadcast_new_game/1. join/3, found on line 7, is a required callback for the Channel framework and simply returns a socket, assuming it's been called with valid parameters. As a result, we'll cover this functionality in our test as part of our setup. On line 13 is broadcast_new_game/1, which will broadcast a map containing the ID of a new game to any client connected to the Channel.

There's one more clause for broadcast_new_game/1 that returns an error if either something other than a %Game{} struct is passed in or if the value of the game struct's current_state is something other than :joining. We'll need a happy path test and error tests for each state that falls into the error clause. Create a new test file at test/not_skull_web/channels/lobby_channel_test.exs and populate it with the following code for the test file:

```
Line 1  defmodule NotSkullWeb.LobbyChannelTest do
          use NotSkullWeb.ChannelCase
          alias NotSkullWeb.{LobbyChannel, UserSocket}

     5    describe "broadcast_new_game/1" do
            setup do
              user_id = Factory.uuid()

              {:ok, _, socket} =
    10          UserSocket
                |> socket("user_socket:#{user_id}", %{user_id: user_id})
                |> subscribe_and_join(LobbyChannel, "lobby:lobby")

              %{socket: socket}
    15      end
          end
        end
```

Typical tests for a Phoenix Channel will start with the assumption that the user has already connected to the websocket, through the code in the UserSocket, and has joined the Phoenix Channel under test. Phoenix.ChannelTest provides two test functions that we can use in the setup block to meet those conditions.

The first test function is socket/3, which we're calling on line 11. It takes, as arguments, the module name of the socket you want to connect to, which in our case is UserSocket, the ID that the individual socket would have, and the values that should be expected in the assigns. The second two arguments require an explicit knowledge of what the UserSocket code does. The ID passed in should be the same ID that's generated by UserSocket.id/1, and the assigns need to match whatever would be put in there from UserSocket.connect/3. While this isn't ideal, you'll find that the UserSocket code is typically very low churn. As a result, it's rare that you'll ever need to touch them again after you set these values in your setup.

Once the socket is created, we'll need to have that socket join the actual Phoenix Channel itself and subscribe to events that come from the Channel. The function called subscribe_and_join/3, called on line 12, provides exactly that means. The arguments it requires are the socket that was created by the previous function, socket/3, the module name for the Phoenix Channel, Lobby-Channel in our case, and the topic for the correct join/3 function for the module under test (LobbyChannel). We mentioned earlier that we wouldn't be testing join/3 directly but that it would be covered in our setup. This is a response to the way the test functions were built. If you wanted to have more logic in your LobbyChannel.join/3, it would be good to create a describe block for join/3 and use one of the three Phoenix.ChannelTest.join functions (three different arities, depending on what you need) for your exercise step. In our case, there's only one way that the function can respond, so it would be overtesting to focus on it.

It's important to understand "what" has been subscribed to the Channel after we've made this call. When subscribe_and_join/3 is called, the test process itself is what's subscribed. That means that the test process's mailbox is where messages from the Channel will arrive. There are test helpers, which we are about to describe, that abstract the need to check the mailbox directly, but it's useful to understand what's happening behind the scenes.

This leads us to writing tests for the other function in the Channel, broadcast_new_game/1. Under the hood, this function uses NotSkullWeb.Endpoint.broadcast!/3, which is an imported function from Phoenix.Endpoint. Let's add the following test after the setup in our file and look at how to test the output:

```
Line 1   test "success: returns :ok, sends broadcast when passed an open game" do
     2     open_game = Factory.struct_for(:game, %{current_phase: :joining})
     3
     4     assert :ok = LobbyChannel.broadcast_new_game(open_game)
     5
     6     assert_broadcast("new_game_created", broadcast_payload)
     7     assert broadcast_payload == %{game_id: open_game.id}
     8
     9     assert Jason.encode!(broadcast_payload)
    10   end
```

The first thing to note about this test is that on line 1, it isn't accepting the test context, %{socket: socket}, from the setup. Our test doesn't actually need the socket because the test process itself is subscribed to the Channel. The setup returns the socket to make it available in case we want to add more functionality, and therefore more tests, to our application.

Our function under test never hits that database, so the data that we pass in doesn't need to be there. On line 2, we create a new game, passing in the only override that's important to the function we're testing, which sets the game's current_phase to :joining. Then we exercise the function on line 4, asserting that the return value is :ok, which happens to be the return value of NotSkull-Web.Endpoint.broadcast!/3. The code under test is just passing that response back to the test code.

The main behavior of the function under test isn't the return value but a side effect. Unlike other places, though, where we need a test double to verify that a side effect happened, the side effect here is that a message should've been sent to the mailbox of the test process. If any other processes were also subscribed to the same Channel, they would've received the broadcast as well.

On line 6, our test calls assert_broadcast/2. That function takes as arguments the expected event name, "new_game_created", and a pattern, for which we've passed an unbound variable. It's common here to pin a pattern instead, but we wanted to capture the whole payload for later assertions.

We do assert that the payload is what we were expecting on line 7. The last assertion of our test is one that takes a little bit of understanding. As you recall, the test process is subscribed directly to the Channel. Our test is intended to be focused on the interaction that a client application would have if a JavaScript client were subscribed to the same Channel. There's a functional difference between the interactions that client would have and that our test has. When the socket/2 helper function was called, it created a socket that skipped going through the real connection process in order to provide convenience.

If you were to look at the data in the socket that was returned, you would find a key called :serializer with a value of Phoenix.ChannelTest.NoopSerializer. This "no operation" serializer doesn't change the values it sends to the test process in any way. If our test process was intended to represent another Elixir process running inside of our application, this would be great. In our case, though, we're focused on what would come to a JavaScript client. Sockets for a JavaScript client would have a different serializer. In our application's case, it would be the JSON serializer library, Jason. The test tools don't allow you to override this value, but one extra step in our tests can help us make sure that this difference doesn't cause us problems when trying to run our application.

On line 9, we're trying to find the lightest-weight way of testing that our application won't have issues by simply making sure that the event payload *can* be serialized. We're stopping at testing the values after serialization because we should have a solid idea of what they'll look like and we don't want to test the Jason library itself. This one extra step is very relevant when dealing with return values that aren't inherently serializable to JSON, for example an Ecto schema struct. This'll help make sure that the code in your Channel takes care of the necessary conversion of data before the Phoenix Channel framework tries to serialize the data.

The two biggest takeaways from this test should be that assert_broadcast takes a pattern and that your payloads won't be serialized. These lessons also apply to assert_push/3 and assert_reply/4, which are the two most common test helpers that we aren't covering. It will help to demystify testing Phoenix Channels, as well as build a foundation for robust coverage, if you remember that the test process itself is subscribed to the Channel and that the Phoenix.Channel-Test.NoopSerializer is always used.

Wrapping Up

In this chapter, we covered testing controllers and Phoenix Channels as the interfaces to our Phoenix-based web application. Controller tests are used in applications that serve JSON-based API endpoints as well as server-rendered HTML endpoints. Channel tests cover the interactions over web sockets. You should now be familiar with using the most common test-helper functions provided by Phoenix, Plug, and ChannelTest. You should also understand the how and why of making sure your tests cover both return values and side effects.

In the next chapter, we'll introduce you to property-based testing. We'll show you tooling that will help you lock down the behavior of your code where it's most likely to have large variation in its input.

CHAPTER 7

Property-Based Testing

Even the best-designed unit tests are limited to the number of inputs you can throw at your code and that you can come up with. You can use some sort of enum wrapper around a test or try to come up with edge cases, but you're still limited to the inputs that you can actually type out, often leaving out problematic inputs because, well, you never thought of them.

In this chapter, you're going to learn about a new testing technique called *property-based testing*. Property-based testing introduces *randomness* into your tests by generating random inputs to feed to your code. This increases your confidence in the code and can lead to discovering pesky bugs by generating weird edge cases. Property-based testing also forces you to think differently about the accepted inputs and the properties of your code, often helping with the design and implementation.

The goal of this chapter is to introduce you to the basics of property-based testing and when and how to integrate it into your test suite. You'll also learn about a particular tool called stream_data,[1] a fairly common property-based testing framework for Elixir written by one of the authors of this book (Andrea), but the concepts and ideas discussed here apply to most frameworks you'll find in the wild.

Let's start the chapter with an anecdote that we think captures the power and usefulness of property-based testing.

---

1. https://github.com/whatyouhide/stream_data

Property-Based Testing in Practice in the Elixir Standard Library

A while ago, an issue was opened in the Elixir language repository reporting a problem with String.replace/3.[2] String.replace/3 is a function that takes a subject string, a pattern string, and a replacement string. The job of the function is to replace the pattern string with the replacement string in the subject string. The issue reported that the function failed when given an empty string "" as the pattern string (the second argument). In other terms, replacing the empty string in any string with something else wouldn't work. It was soon pointed out that the behavior of an empty string as the pattern string is tricky to define: on one hand, you would think that the empty string is not contained in any string, so you should never replace it and the code below should fail or return the subject string unchanged:

```
String.replace(any_string, "", "some other string")
```

On the other hand, what if you try to use the empty string as the pattern string but also as the subject string? That is, what if you replace the empty string in the empty string?

```
String.replace("", "", "x")
```

Intuitively, you should get "x", right? To settle this discussion, the Elixir core team ended up coming up with a *property* of String.replace/3. A property of a piece of code is something that "holds" (stays true) regardless of the input given to that code. In this case, a property of String.replace/3 could be something that's true regardless of the subject string and the string to replace. Ignore the check all syntax here, which we'll cover later on in the chapter, and just focus on the semantics.

```
check all subject <- string(:printable),
          replacement <- string(:printable) do
  assert String.replace(subject, subject, replacement) == replacement
end
```

The property states that *for any random string* as subject string and *for any random string* as replacement string, if you use the same string as the subject string and the pattern string, then String.replace/3 should return the replacement. As soon as tests were run to check this property, the empty string was found to make the property not true. Since the Elixir team was confident that String.replace/3 should have had this property, it meant that the implementation

---

2.   https://github.com/elixir-lang/elixir/pull/6559

of String.replace/3 was effectively wrong. String.replace/3 was fixed to handle the empty pattern string in a way that would make the property hold.

```
iex> String.replace("ELIXIR", "", ".")
".E.L.I.X.I.R."
```

```
iex> String.replace("ELIXIR", "", "")
"ELIXIR"
```

This story about the replacement string is just an example of a property used in the real world to drive the design of a piece of code and verify that it behaves as expected. However, it shows the power of thinking about code in terms of properties and generating random data to verify those properties when testing. In the rest of the chapter, we're going to learn more about the techniques and tools around property-based testing. We'll start by looking at the tests we've written so far and how they fit in from the perspective of property-based testing.

Example-Based Tests

When writing tests, we usually write something that we could call *example-based* tests. In this section, we'll have a new look at them from the perspective of the inputs that we feed to our code. We'll define terminology to identify example-based tests, which will help us later compare them to property-based tests.

Let's start with an example. Let's say we want to test that the Enum.sort/1 function correctly sorts lists. We could call the following an example-based test because it verifies that the code we want to test (Enum.sort/1 in this case) works by giving a few examples of how it should work:

```
property_based_testing/sorting/test/example_based_sort_test.exs
defmodule ExampleBasedSortTest do
  use ExUnit.Case

  test "Enum.sort/1 sorts lists" do
    assert Enum.sort([]) == []
    assert Enum.sort([1, 2, 3]) == [1, 2, 3]
    assert Enum.sort([2, 1, 3]) == [1, 2, 3]
  end
end
```

In this example, we're verifying that sorting an empty list returns an empty list, that sorting an ordered list leaves it unchanged, and that sorting an unsorted list returns the sorted version of that list. We chose three examples that we thought would cover a representative sample of all the possible inputs to Enum.sort/1. This works, but you can see that there are a lot more inputs we could test, such as negative numbers, lists with duplicates in them, and so on.

Sometimes, we try to test more inputs and simplify the test at the same time by extracting the inputs and corresponding expected outputs and then running the test on those inputs and outputs:

```
property_based_testing/sorting/test/tabular_sort_test.exs
defmodule TabularSortTest do
  use ExUnit.Case

  test "Enum.sort/1 sorts lists" do
    inputs_and_outputs = [
      {[], []},
      {[1, 2, 3], [1, 2, 3]},
      {[2, 1, 3], [1, 2, 3]},
      {[2, 1, 2], [1, 2, 2]},
      {[0, -1, -2], [-2, -1, 0]}
    ]

    for {input, expected_output} <- inputs_and_outputs do
      assert Enum.sort(input) == expected_output
    end
  end
end
```

When using this kind of approach, tests look like *assertion tables*. An assertion table is a table of inputs and outputs, and the tests assert that running the code on the input of each row of the table results in the output on that same row. For this reason, an alternative name for example-based tests is *tabular tests*.

This kind of test has many benefits. First of all, tests like these are easy to write since we know how our code works, and it's usually straightforward to come up with inputs for the code we're testing. Another benefit of these tests is that, since we're specifying all inputs, we can choose to test corner cases that we suspect might be problematic for our code. In our trivial sorting example, we know that the empty list is a corner case because it's a peculiar list, so we can just go ahead and test our code on it every time we run the test.

However, these tests have some downsides as well. Testing the same known inputs on every test run means that it's hard to discover unknown corner cases because, well, they're unknown. At the same time, it's hard to discover inputs that our code doesn't support or that it should support because we're the ones writing the examples in the test. Let's see how we can improve the situation.

Introducing Randomness and Property-Based Testing

We can solve some of the problems that example-based tests suffer from by introducing a bit of chaos in our tests. Using randomness to generate inputs will allow us to test a wider range of inputs against our code and potentially create inputs that trigger edge cases.

In our sorting example, what we really want to test is that the output of Enum.sort/1 is a sorted version of the input. For any random input, we can think of a few properties that the output will always retain. For example, the output list always has the same length as the input list. Another property is that the output list is always sorted, which is something that we can check in a pretty straightforward way by checking that each element is smaller than or equal to the following one. Now that we've thought of these properties, we could change our test so that we generate random lists and test these properties on the output of our code instead of checking *what* the output is. Let's see how to do that:

```
property_based_testing/sorting/test/randomized_sort_test.exs
Line 1  defmodule RandomizedSortTest do
          use ExUnit.Case

          test "Enum.sort/1 sorts lists" do
     5      for _ <- 1..10 do
              random_list = random_list()
              sorted_list = Enum.sort(random_list)

              assert length(random_list) == length(sorted_list)
    10        assert sorted?(sorted_list)
            end
          end

          defp random_list do
    15      Stream.repeatedly(fn -> Enum.random(-100..100) end)
            |> Enum.take(_length = Enum.random(0..10))
          end

          defp sorted?([first, second | rest]),
    20      do: first <= second and sorted?([second | rest])

          defp sorted?(_other), do: true
        end
```

The random_list/0 function creates an infinite stream of random numbers between -100 and 100 and then picks a random number of elements from the stream using Enum.take/2. The number of elements we pick from the stream is the length of the random list, which we keep between 0 and 10 elements. The sorted?/1 function checks that the first two elements of the list are sorted and then recursively checks the rest of the list until it arrives at an empty or one-element list, which is always sorted. On line 9, we check our first property, that the sorted list has the same number of elements as the input list. On line 10, we check the second property, that the sorted list is sorted.

This approach to testing has a few benefits. One of the most obvious is that it can potentially test on a lot more inputs than example-based testing can. In our example, if we want to change the number of tested lists to a hundred or a thousand, we can just change the right end of the range on line 5. However, the usefulness of testing on many inputs is limited unless the inputs vary.

The Role of Randomness

This is where randomness comes into play. By having a lot of inputs generated at random, our hope is to cover a decent part of the possible inputs to our code and at the same time cover a good *variety* of inputs. Essentially, we want a good sample of inputs that represents the *input space*, which is the set of all possible inputs. In our example, we're still covering a tiny part of our input space (all lists of numbers), but covering the whole input space is often unfeasible. Random generation gives us a nice compromise, especially considering that every time the tests are run, possibly different lists are generated. Generating random elements also helps us to uncover potential corner cases that we didn't anticipate.

You might be asking yourself how much randomness is *enough*, that is, how many inputs you need to generate or how many times you need to run these tests to have confidence that they cover enough of the input space. In many cases, the input space is infinite or too vast to cover, but only you will know how far to push it based on the specific use case.

The test we wrote for Enum.sort/1 is an example of a kind of test called *property-based tests*. They are called that because of the method we used to come up with this kind of test: we think of *properties* that our code holds regardless of the input we feed to it, provided the input is valid.

The benefits of property-based testing don't end with what we've just discussed. Coming up with valid inputs and properties is a huge part of property-based testing, but it's also a helpful design tool. If you have to write down in clear terms what the valid inputs of your code are, you could end up expanding or shrinking the space of valid inputs. Coming up with properties, instead, forces you to think about what your code should do regardless of the specific input you feed to it, which might help with the design or implementation of the code. In the list-sorting example, the functionality is trivial, so it's hard to see the design benefits of property-based testing; but in more complex contexts, it can be useful to think about these things.

Property-based testing is rarely done in a hand-rolled way like we did in our example, as there's a plethora of frameworks (for all kinds of programming languages) that facilitate the implementation of property-based tests. Usually, property-based testing frameworks provide powerful ways of generating data and an infrastructure for verifying properties against that generated data. There's also one important feature that makes using a property-based testing framework a clear advantage over rolling out your own randomness-based tests: frameworks *simplify* the randomly generated inputs when a failure occurs, and they present error messages that tend to be significantly easier to understand and address than if you handwrite tests with random data like we did.

For Elixir, the property-based testing framework we're going to use from now on is called stream_data.[3]

Why Use stream_data?

The Elixir and Erlang ecosystems have good support for property-based testing through well-established libraries such as Quviq's QuickCheck and PropEr for Erlang,[a] [b] and PropCheck,[c] Quixir,[d] and stream_data for Elixir.

However, we're biased toward stream_data since Andrea wrote the original library, which means we know it well and are comfortable with it. In any case, the property-based testing concepts we're going to illustrate work well with all libraries.

We feel like having some context on why stream_data was created in the first place, even if other property-based testing frameworks were already available, could be helpful to readers. One reason was that originally the plan was to include stream_data in the Elixir standard library, which meant having to write something from scratch to make sure licensing wasn't a problem and that the Elixir core team would be able to maintain the code. The team later realized that stream_data worked well enough as a library and so it didn't end up in Elixir itself. Another reason was that all existing property-based testing frameworks would only generate random data in the context of property-based testing, without taking advantage of Elixir streams to make data generation a general-purpose tool.

---

a. http://www.quviq.com/products/erlang-quickcheck/
b. https://github.com/proper-testing/proper
c. https://github.com/alfert/propcheck
d. https://github.com/pragdave/quixir

---

3. https://github.com/whatyouhide/stream_data

Introducing stream_data

stream_data is a property-based testing framework for Elixir. It provides two main functionalities, data generation and a framework for writing and running properties. The data generation aspect of the library is usable outside of property-based testing as a standalone feature, but it's the backbone of the whole framework and is also used extensively when writing properties.

To follow along in the next few sections, create a new Mix project with $ mix new sorting and then add :stream_data as a dependency in your mix.exs file:

property_based_testing/sorting/mix.exs
```
defp deps do
  [{:stream_data, ">= 0.0.0", only: [:dev, :test]}]
end
```

Now, run $ mix deps.get to fetch the dependency. As you can see in the code, we've only added :stream_data in the :test environment since we'll only be using the library when testing.

Before diving into the framework, let's rewrite the RandomizedSortTest test we hand-rolled earlier to use the tools that stream_data provides:

property_based_testing/sorting/test/randomized_sort_stream_data_test.exs
```
Line 1  defmodule FirstStreamDataPropertySortTest do
          use ExUnit.Case
          use ExUnitProperties

     5    property "Enum.sort/1 sorts lists" do
            check all list <- list_of(integer()) do
              sorted_list = Enum.sort(list)

              assert length(list) == length(sorted_list)
    10        assert sorted?(sorted_list)
            end
          end

          defp sorted?([first, second | rest]),
    15      do: first <= second and sorted?([second | rest])

          defp sorted?(_other), do: true
        end
```

Don't worry about the new things you see in this test. We'll cover all of them in this chapter. The goal here is to show you what stream_data looks like. For now, run mix test in the project where you added this file and see the beautiful green dots.

As it turns out, the underlying shape of the test is quite similar to Randomized-SortTest. Instead of using the test macro to define a test, we use property (on line 5). Then we use a new construct, check all, on line 6. This replaces the for comprehension we had. On the same line, we have list <- list_of(integer()). That's exactly one of the most important features of a property-based framework: *data generators*. Here stream_data takes care of generating random data (with cool characteristics we'll see later) for you. Now that we have an idea of what a stream_data test looks like, let's move on to dissecting its components in a more detailed way.

In the next sections, we're going to start exploring from the data generation aspect of stream_data and then move on to designing and running properties. To follow along, run iex -S mix to fire up an IEx session from the root of the project that includes stream_data as a dependency.

You might be wondering why we won't illustrate these concepts on one of the applications we developed in the previous chapters (such as Soggy Waffle). Well, the reason is that we would have to bend those applications in weird ways to be able to show these ideas effectively. Instead, we decided to use simple, small, and self-contained examples so that we can focus on property-based testing concepts and tools.

Data Generation

One of the design goals of stream_data is to provide a set of tools for data generation that could also work outside of property-based testing. For example, generating random data can be useful when seeding databases with fake data.

At the core of data generation are *generators*. A generator is a data structure that contains logic that stream_data uses to generate data. Essentially, a generator is like a function that we can call to generate random terms. Let's start with a simple instance of a generator, StreamData.integer/0. This generator produces random integers. We can use all the stream_data generators as Elixir streams since they implement the Enumerable protocol.

```
iex> StreamData.integer() |> Enum.take(5)
[-1, 2, -3, 0, 2]
```

stream_data generators are infinite streams of random data, so we only had to take a few items out of the stream using Enum.take/2 in this example. If we had called Enum.to_list/1 passing the generator as the argument, we would've waited forever.

stream_data comes equipped with a few generators for simple data types, like the ones for integers or booleans, plus a bunch of ways to *combine* generators. For example, there's no built-in generator for non-negative integers (positive integers plus zero), but we can easily build one using StreamData.map/2 to map the abs/1 function over the StreamData.integer/0 generator. This is similar to how Enum.map/2 maps a function over an enumerable.

```
non_negative_integer = StreamData.map(StreamData.integer(), &abs/1)
```

Wait, why are we using StreamData.map/2 instead of Stream.map/2, given that generators are Elixir streams? Stream.map/2 would work in the context of generating data for purposes that lie outside of property-based testing, such as seeding a database with random data:

```
non_negative_integer = Stream.map(StreamData.integer(), &abs/1)
```

In general, all functions that operate on streams (such as many functions found in the Enum and Stream standard-library modules) work on stream_data generators. However, you should only use those functions in the context of data generation and not in property-based tests. When using generators in property-based tests, using Stream functions instead of StreamData ones will render the generators unusable. In the example above, Stream.map/2 would return a plain stream of non-negative integers, while StreamData.map/2 would return a stream of non-negative integers that also provides specific functionality for property-based testing. We'll learn more about this a little later, when we talk about *shrinking* the generated data.

Mapping is just one of the ways to combine generators. There's also filtering as well as a few ways to create more complex data types based off simpler generators. An example is StreamData.list_of/1, which takes a generator and returns a new generator that produces lists of elements produced by the generator we passed to it. For example, to generate lists of integers we can use the StreamData.list_of(StreamData.integer()) generator.

```
iex> StreamData.list_of(StreamData.integer()) |> Enum.take(3)
[[1], [], [1, -2]]
```

The Basic Tool for Composing Generators: Binding

While there are a few ways to compose generators, like StreamData.map/2, it's important to know about StreamData.bind/2. bind/2 is a powerful function, and other ways of combining generators can usually be built on top of it. It's the basic tool you can reach for when you need to combine two generators together. bind/2 takes a generator and a function: the function will be invoked with each element produced by the generator and should return a new generator.

Let's make this easier with an example. Say we have a generator that produces random email domains (like gmail.com or icloud.com). We want to generate random emails that have a random alphanumeric username followed by a random domain produced by our domain generator:

```
property_based_testing/misc/random_email_generator.exs
Line 1  domains = ["gmail.com", "yahoo.com", "icloud.com"]
     2  random_domain_generator = StreamData.member_of(domains)
     3  username_generator = StreamData.string(:alphanumeric, min_length: 1)
     4
     5  random_email_generator =
     6    StreamData.bind(random_domain_generator, fn domain ->
     7      StreamData.map(username_generator, fn username ->
     8        "#{username}@#{domain}"
     9      end)
    10    end)
```

In the first couple of lines, we can see our random domain generator, which uses StreamData.member_of/1 to produce elements taken at random from the given list. On line 3, we have our username generator, which produces alphanumeric strings. Then we have our bind/2 call. We bind on the value produced by the random domain generator, which is passed to the function we give to bind/2. That function should return a new generator. On line 9, we start with the username generator and map a function that concatenates an @ plus the domain to the values that the username generator produces. The result of the StreamData.map/2 call is a generator. When random_email_generator needs to produce a random email, it will first create a random domain, then use the generator returned by the anonymous function passed to bind/2 to produce a random email.

bind/2 is powerful because it lets us create complex generators by combining simpler generators. We'll see that it's heavily used in the context of property-based testing. bind/2 is also necessary in cases such as this one: we wouldn't otherwise be able to take two generators and combine them together.

Next, let's look at how generators can control the complexity of generated data through generation size.

Generation Size

If you take a few elements out of a generator like StreamData.integer/0, you'll notice that those integers are *simple*, that is, they are small integers centered around zero. Now, try to take a few elements out of integer/0 but after discarding a lot of elements:

```
iex> StreamData.integer() |> Stream.drop(100) |> Enum.take(5)
[43, -96, 45, -17, 40]
```

As you can see, the integers produced by the generator are now more complex—as in, they're bigger. This suggests that generators produce increasingly more complex terms the more terms they generate. In the case of streaming terms out of a generator, that's exactly what happens. However, the mechanism behind this is more generic. In order to have a generator generate a term, we need to pass a size to the generator that we refer to as the *generation size*. The generation size is a positive integer. Generators use the generation size as a measure of the complexity of the generated terms. Some generators will need to be tweaked to your use case so that they generate the "right" data, so to use most property-based testing frameworks effectively (including stream_data), it's worth spending just a moment understanding generation size better.

Let's look at how integer/0 uses generation size. With a generation size of n, integer/0 will produce an integer between -n and n. Other generators may use the generation size differently: for example, binary/1 uses it to determine the length of the generated binary. Composite generators (such as list_of/1) will pass the generation size down to the inner generators. For example, list_of(integer()) will use the generation size to determine both the length of the generated list as well as the "complexity" of the integers in that list.

You might be wondering how the generation size is passed to a generator when we want to produce an element out of that generator. There's no way to directly pass the generation size because generation is hidden from the user, either by stream_data when using generators in property-based testing or by the implementation of the Enumerable protocol. This is a design decision in the library itself.

When using generators as streams, the implementation of the Enumerable protocol doesn't allow for extra information to be passed alongside functions (which would allow passing the generation size). In fact, when generators are used as streams they start generating with a size of 1 and increase by one every time a term is generated. This means that if we use Enum.take(generator, 5) to take five elements out of a generator, the fifth element will be produced with a generation size of 5. While there's no way to *directly* pass the generation size when producing elements, there are a few indirect ways to manipulate it. These effectively "wrap" the generator so that it can carry the generation size information around.

stream_data provides a few functions that change how a generator treats the generation size passed to it.

The simplest of these functions is StreamData.resize/2. This function takes a generator and an integer representing a new generation size and returns a new generator. The new generator will always use the given generation size, ignoring the generation size we pass to it. This is useful when you want a generator with a fixed complexity.

```
iex> StreamData.integer() |> StreamData.resize(50) |> Enum.take(5)
[28, 25, -44, 10, 41]
```

If you want to apply some modifications to the generation size, you're looking for the StreamData.scale/2 function. It takes a generator and a function that takes a size and returns a new size, and then it returns a new generator. The new generator uses the generation size returned by the passed function. (That was a mouthful.) Essentially, it modifies the generation size of a generator in a dynamic way, based on the original generation size.

Scaling is especially useful in a couple of scenarios. The first one is when you want to increase or decrease the *speed* at which the generation size progresses. For example, it might be a good idea to reduce the growth of the generation size for a complex and deeply nested generator. To do that, we can scale the generation size with mathematic functions like square roots:

```
iex> generator = StreamData.list_of(StreamData.string(:ascii))
iex> scaled_generator =
...>    StreamData.scale(generator, fn size ->
...>      round(:math.sqrt(size))
...>    end)
iex> scaled_generator |> Stream.drop(50) |> Enum.take(3)
[[""], ["#HdJ", "'x>", "3y](I", "D", "FFe?"], ["", "", "+,"]]
```

As you can see, even after fifty dropped elements we're still generating small lists with small strings in them.

The other use case for scaling is having a *cap* on the generation size.

```
capped_integer =
StreamData.scale(StreamData.integer(), fn size -> min(size, _cap = 20) end)
```

In this example, the capped_integer generator will use the given generation size up to the cap, which is 20, and then we'll keep using 20 for larger generation sizes. After all, resize/2 is just a particular version of scale/2, where the function passed to scale/2 ignores the given generation size and always returns a fixed size.

The last size-related function provided by stream_data is StreamData.sized/1. It constructs a generator starting with only the generation size. This function is useful if we want to determine the generator to use based on the generation size. For example, we might want a generator that generates only integers up to a given generation size, and then it starts generating floats as well:

```
property_based_testing/misc/sized_generator.exs
StreamData.sized(fn size ->
  if size < 20 do
    StreamData.integer()
  else
    StreamData.one_of([StreamData.integer(), StreamData.float()])
  end
end)
```

It's important to understand the purpose of the generation size and to know about the functions we mentioned so that we can generate better data for our use cases. The generation size is used both when treating generators as streams, as well as when generators are used in the context of property-based testing.

Let's make one last practical example of how controlling generation size can be useful in the real world. We'll start from our random_email_generator generator that we discussed earlier. In that generator, we were using a fixed list of domains (such as "gmail.com") for our emails:

```
property_based_testing/misc/random_email_generator.exs
domains = ["gmail.com", "yahoo.com", "icloud.com"]
random_domain_generator = StreamData.member_of(domains)
```

We could have a "smarter" domain generator that does the following:

1. Picks one of the most common domains for small generation sizes (effectively *starting* generation with those known domains), and

2. Uses the string/2 generator to generate random domains after a certain generation size (keeping them small by scaling the generator).

This example might look a bit convoluted, but it's not far from what a good email domain generator might look like in real code. Note that we're forcing domains to end with .com: this is just to keep the generator contained and to avoid having to use StreamData.bind/2 to combine random domain names with random TLDs (such as .com, .org, .net, and so on):

```
property_based_testing/misc/random_email_domain_generator.exs
common_domains = ["gmail.com", "yahoo.com", "icloud.com"]

random_email_domain_generator =
  StreamData.sized(fn
    size when size <= 5 ->
      StreamData.member_of(common_domains)

    _size ->
      StreamData.string([?a..?z], min_length: 1)
      |> StreamData.scale(fn size -> trunc(:math.log(size)) end)
      |> StreamData.map(fn string -> string <> ".com" end)
  end)
```

Now that we're familiar with generators, let's have a look at the tools that stream_data provides to write properties. In the next sections, we'll start by writing some properties using the stream_data library. Then we'll look at a few design patterns that can make writing properties a bit easier.

Writing Properties

As we saw in our initial examples, part of property-based testing is generating data and the other part is coming up with properties. In this and the next sections, we're going to focus on the latter.

The first thing to do when coming up with properties is to figure out what is the *shape* of valid inputs that our code works with. "Shape" is not a technical term or a definition: we're using it to describe the space of possible values that the input can be, such as all strings or all lists of integers. Figuring out the shape of valid inputs is where generators come into play in the context of property-based testing. If our code works with lists of integers, and therefore the shape of valid inputs is "lists of integers," we can use the StreamData.list_of(StreamData.integer()) generator to produce a sample of the possible values of that shape. You create and combine generators that output valid data in the shape accepted by your code.

After figuring out the valid inputs that our code accepts, we need to come up with properties that our code holds regardless of the input, provided that the input is valid.

Once we have generators to produce inputs of our desired shape and properties that hold for all of those inputs, it's the job of the property-based testing framework to provide the infrastructure for generating data and verifying the properties. stream_data comes bundled with tools and a DSL that let you do exactly that. You know about stream_data generators by now, so the missing piece is using those generators to produce inputs and test properties against those inputs. Let's start with rewriting our properties for the Enum.sort/1 function using the tools provided by stream_data in order to have a look at what stream _data in action looks like. Then we'll examine the snippet in more detail.

property_based_testing/sorting/test/first_property_sort_test.exs
```
Line 1  defmodule FirstPropertySortTest do
          use ExUnit.Case
          use ExUnitProperties

     5    property "Enum.sort/1 sorts lists" do
            check all list <- list_of(integer()) do
              sorted_list = Enum.sort(list)

              assert length(list) == length(sorted_list)
    10        assert sorted?(sorted_list)
            end
          end

          defp sorted?([first, second | rest]),
    15        do: first <= second and sorted?([second | rest])

          defp sorted?(_other), do: true
        end
```

The first thing we need in order to use the property-based testing tools that stream_data provides is the use ExUnitProperties call on line 3. This will import all the generator functions (like list_of/1 or integer/0) as well as make the stream _data DSL available. The DSL is made up of the StreamData.check/2 macro that we used on line 6. This macro resembles the syntax of for comprehensions, with clauses (<-) that have a generator on the right side and a generic pattern on the left side (in our case, that pattern is a simple variable). With this syntax, stream_data will take care of generating an element out of the generator, matching it on the left side of the <- clause, then running the contents of the do/end body. If the assertions don't fail, then stream_data will repeat the process.

By default, check all runs the assertions one hundred times, but that's configurable in a number of different ways. Sometimes, you'll have generators that take more time to generate complex values or you'll need to use many generators for a single property. In those cases, it might help to lower the number of check all runs.

Running our SortTest case is the same as running any test case. If we were in a Mix project, we would use mix test. The only difference in the output is that properties will be reported as properties instead of tests.

```
> mix test

..

1 property, 1 test, 0 failures
```

Don't worry about the "1 test" part of the output. That's coming from the dummy test that mix new generates when scaffolding the project.

The check all macro is important to understand in order to take advantage of many stream_data features. Let's look at it more closely.

The Check All Macro

check all supports multiple <- clauses. It also supports simple assignments (with =) as well as expressions that are used as *filters*, similar to what for supports. To show a more complex use of check all, let's write an example of a test that first generates a list, filters out empty lists, generates an element taken out of that list, and finally checks that the in operator always returns true for the two generated terms:

property_based_testing/misc/check_all_clauses.exs
```
check all list <- list_of(term()),
         list != [],
         member <- member_of(list) do
  assert member in list
end
```

Given the example here, it might be a little easier to understand why Stream-Data.bind/2, which we learned about earlier, is so important. Generating a list and then generating a random element out of that list is essentially a call to bind/2.

check all also supports options passed in after the <- clauses. You can find a comprehensive list of options in the documentation for check all, but an important one to know about is :max_runs. :max_runs lets you configure the maximum number of times that check all should generate all inputs and check that the property holds. By default, check all runs one hundred times, but it can be useful to decrease the number of runs for slower properties or to increase it to cover more of the input space. Here's an example of how to decrease the maximum number of runs for slower properties:

```
# This is executed only 10 times.
check all value <- some_generator(), max_runs: 10 do
  slow_code(value)
end
```

> ## The Reason for "Check All"
>
> A common question about stream_data is why check all is written as two words instead of one (check_all). The reason is that check all needs to trick the Elixir compiler in order to work. Elixir supports macros, which are functions executed at compile time that take code as Abstract Syntax Tree (AST, a representation of the code as data) and return AST. Elixir doesn't allow macros with a variable number of arguments since the arity of functions and macros must be fixed. The AST for <- clauses is the AST for the application of the :<- operator to the left side and right side. This means that every <- clause would be an argument to a possible check_all macro. However, we want the number of clauses to be variable, so that wouldn't work. The trick we use is that the compiler will parse the code and then call the check/2 macro with the AST for the call to all(clause1, ...). The all function doesn't exist, but this isn't known yet at parsing time, so the AST is happily passed to check/2, which can then manipulate it as desired. for and with, two built-in constructs in Elixir that use the same syntax, can avoid this trick because they're *special forms* that are handled directly at the language level. With this trick we can have a syntax that looks like for and with, but without having to change the compiler or the runtime of Elixir. Awesome, right?

stream_data also provides a syntax similar to check all to create generators. We'll look at that in the next section.

The Gen All Macro

Writing new generators by composing other generators with functions like bind/2 works fine, but for complex generators the syntax can become a bit convoluted. For this reason, stream_data provides a gen all macro. This macro looks exactly like check all, but it creates a generator instead. The values produced by the generator are whatever is returned from the block passed to gen all. Let's see an example of how to use this macro to generate an email, starting from a random alphanumeric username and a random domain chosen from a list of domains.

```
property_based_testing/misc/email_generator_gen_all.exs
domains = ["gmail.com", "yahoo.com", "icloud.com", "hotmail.com"]

email_generator =
  gen all username <- string(:alphanumeric),
          domain <- member_of(domains) do
    username <> "@" <> domain
  end
```

As you can see, the <- clauses are used to take values out of generators, exactly like in check all. The generated value is the content of the do/end block, in our case the concatenated strings that make up the email.

gen all supports all the clauses supported by check all, like filtering clauses and assignment (=) clauses.

Now that we've written a few properties, let's see how property-based testing frameworks handle failures in the properties.

Shrinking

In this section, we'll look at what happens when a property-based test fails. As we mentioned at the beginning of the chapter, property-based testing frameworks such as stream_data help you in those cases by *shrinking* the input that caused the test to fail and coming up with a simpler input that still causes the failure. Shrinking plays a fundamental role in the usefulness of property-based testing, and it's important to understand how it works in order to take full advantage of the testing framework.

What a Property Failure Looks Like

We've seen how property-based testing helps us write robust tests, in part by covering a larger space of inputs to feed to our code. However, we haven't discussed what happens when the tests find an error in the code. To see what happens in that case, let's come up with a sorting function that we know won't work well. The simplest one that comes to mind is the identity function, which is a function that takes one argument and returns that argument unchanged. This is a terrible sorting function because, well, it doesn't do anything to the input list. However, this "sort" function still holds at least one of the two properties we've been testing: the length of the sorted list is the same as the length of the input list. That makes sense, since it's the same list. However, the identity function definitely doesn't hold the property of the output list being sorted. Let's write this up in a property and see what happens when it fails:

```
property_based_testing/sorting/test/bad_sort_test.exs
```

```
Line 1  defmodule BadSortTest do
          use ExUnit.Case
          use ExUnitProperties

     5    property "bad_sort/1 sorts lists" do
            check all list <- list_of(integer()) do
              IO.inspect(list)
              sorted_list = bad_sort(list)

    10        assert length(list) == length(sorted_list)
              assert sorted?(sorted_list)
            end
          end
```

```
15    defp bad_sort(list), do: list

      defp sorted?([first, second | rest]),
        do: first <= second and sorted?([second | rest])

20    defp sorted?(_other), do: true
   end
```

When we run this test, it fails as expected, thanks to how we implemented the sorting function on line 15 (as the identity function). Let's take a look at what a property failure looks like:

```
> mix test

  1) property bad_sort/1 sorts lists (BadSortTest)
     test/bad_sort_test.exs:5
     Failed with generated values (after 3 successful runs):

         * Clause:    list <- list_of(integer())
           Generated: [1, 0]

     Expected truthy, got false
     code: assert sorted?(sorted_list)
     arguments:

         # 1
         [1, 0]

     stacktrace: «stacktrace»

Finished in 0.04 seconds
1 property, 1 failure
```

That looks a little bit different than our usual ExUnit tests. stream_data adds the information in the highlighted lines to regular ExUnit errors. This section includes information about the generated data. The first line tells us how many terms stream_data generated before finding the failure. In this case, it successfully generated three lists before finding one that would fail. After that, stream_data reports the values that were generated for each clause in the check all (we have only one clause here). This is more useful when there are many clauses since it helps retrace the steps of what pieces of data were generated.

We expected that our bad sorting function would fail for any list that wasn't already sorted. That's exactly what happened: as soon as we got a simple not-sorted list, [1, 0], the test failed. On second thought, isn't it a bit suspicious that the list that caused the failure is the simplest possible list that causes this particular failure? This suspicion would be confirmed by running the property again. If we run the property a few times, [1, 0] is going to be the failing list most of the time. Alternative results might look similar: for example, [0, -1] or [2, 1]. To better understand what's going on, we could print the generated list right as the first line in the do/end block of the check all.

```
> mix test
[]
[-1]
[1, 2]
[1, 1, 0]
➤ [1, 0]
➤ [0]
➤ [1]
«rest of the test result»
```

Let's make sense of these generated lists. The first one is [], which is a sorted list, so our test passes. Same goes for [-1] and [1, 2]. Then, our generator spits out [1, 1, 0], which makes our test fail. Why wasn't that the list shown in the test failure?

The reason is that property-based testing frameworks like stream_data perform a process, called *shrinking*, on the terms that cause a property to fail. Shrinking consists of *simplifying* the generated terms so that they keep causing the test to fail but make them simpler to understand. In our example, we can see the shrinking process in action in the highlighted lines. [1, 1, 0] is first reduced to [1, 0] by removing the first element. [1, 0] still fails, so stream _data tries to shrink it even more by taking more elements out. It tries [0] and [1], but those are sorted lists, so our properties hold and we have to take a step back to [1, 0]. 0 and 1 are the simplest possible integers from the perspective of stream_data, so the framework doesn't try to simplify their values. This means that the simplest list to cause the failure was found.

It might be hard to see the value of shrinking in such a simple example. However, imagine you are generating complex data and feeding them to complex code. In those cases, shrinking is fundamental since it can make it much easier to understand what aspect of the generated data is causing the failure. However, it's important to understand that the shrinking process is heuristic, which means that it doesn't always find the *simplest* possible term that causes a failure. Exploring the many possibilities of simpler data takes time, so stream _data will go ahead and try a few ways of shrinking the generated data. After a while, however (a hundred tries by default), it'll stop and report the simplest term it could come up with. This is why this same test might conclude that the simplest list that causes a failure would be [0, -1], [2, 1], or similar, and why you might see slightly different results when running the test.

Shrinking and Generators

Remember how, when talking about data generators, we said that even if they're Elixir streams, you should use StreamData functions to manipulate them? Well, the reason for that is shrinking—stream_data generators produce terms that carry their own shrinking logic with them. For example, the integer/0 generator produces integers that know how to "shrink themselves." When you compose generators through StreamData functions, the composition carries over to the shrinking logic as well. This is one of the most valuable reasons to use a property-based testing framework in the first place over rolling out your own randomness-based tests. Let's look at a quick example. Let's take our friend bind/2 and use it to generate a tuple with two elements: a list and a random element from that list:

```
bind(list_of(term()), fn list ->
  tuple({constant(list), member_of(list)})
end)
```

We're using constant/1 to turn a simple term into a generator, and we're using tuple/1 to return a generator of tuples. When shrinking, the term generated by the inner tuple generator is shrunk first, but then the initial list generated by list_of(term()) is shrunk and used to produce a new tuple generator in the anonymous function. This behavior might seem complex, but most of the time the user doesn't need to care that this is happening behind the scenes when composing generators. Even so, stream_data documents how every generator shrinks and how every composition function affects the shrinking.

Strategies for Designing Properties

Up until now, we've only looked at property-based testing in simple scenarios, where it's easy to come up with good properties that give us confidence in our code. However, one of the biggest challenges of property-based testing in less-straightforward situations is coming up with good properties. Right at the beginning of this chapter, we saw how the Elixir team used property-based testing in a real-world scenario and how they came up with a property that helped test code *and* drive its behavior.

In this section, we'll discuss ways to make it easier to design properties for your own code. We'll start by showing you some design patterns that you can recognize and apply to your code. Then we'll quickly cover some common pitfalls made when coming up with properties.

Design Patterns

Let's dive into a few patterns that can help with the design of properties. These patterns can help you with the difficult task of designing efficient, accurate, and useful properties to test your code. The examples and ideas we're going to discuss aren't specific to stream_data because they apply to property-based testing in general, regardless of the framework.

Circular Code

This pattern can be applied any time you have two pieces of code where the first piece does something and the second "undoes" it. This is where the name *circular code* comes from. A common example of this kind of code is encoding and decoding. Take the JSON protocol. If you write a JSON encoder/decoder, it's likely that it'll provide a function to encode a term into JSON and a function to decode the term from JSON. When you spot circular code, it's usually straightforward to design a property for it that verifies that the code is indeed circular. Let's see an example for this imaginary JSON library:

```
property_based_testing/misc/circular_property.exs
property "encoding + decoding is circular" do
  check all term <- term() do
    assert term == (term |> JSON.encode() |> JSON.decode())
  end
end
```

This property could detect cases where the encoding loses information, resulting in decoding to something different from what was encoded.

Oracle Model

Most of the time we tend to write code from scratch, but sometimes we need to rewrite an existing piece of functionality. For example, sometimes we need to rewrite something in a different language or rewrite some code to make it more performant. In these scenarios, we can refer to the existing system as the *oracle*. When we have an oracle and we're writing a system that has the same functionality as the oracle, we can take advantage of property-based testing by testing that our system behaves like the oracle.

Let's have a look at a concrete example. Imagine we wanted to write the function for sorting lists that we tested throughout this whole chapter. Erlang already provides a function for sorting lists, :lists.sort/1, but we want to write an implementation in pure Elixir. We choose to go with the quicksort algorithm. Let's write this algorithm down in a ListSort.quicksort/1 function:

```
property_based_testing/sorting/lib/list_sort.ex
defmodule ListSort do
  def quicksort([head | rest]) do
    {smaller_elements, larger_elements} =
      Enum.split_with(rest, &(&1 <= head))

    quicksort(smaller_elements) ++ [head] ++ quicksort(larger_elements)
  end

  def quicksort([]), do: []
end
```

Now we want to check whether our pure-Elixir quicksort implementation works. What better way than to check against an implementation that already exists and that we can assume works correctly, like :lists.sort/1? The property for this is straightforward, as it's just a matter of generating random lists and asserting that sorting them through our quicksort implementation yields the same results as using :lists.sort/1. Basically, :lists.sort/1 is our oracle. Let's see this property in action.

```
property_based_testing/sorting/test/list_sort_test.exs
defmodule ListSortTest do
  use ExUnit.Case
  use ExUnitProperties

  property "quicksort/1 correctly sorts lists" do
    check all list <- list_of(term()) do
      assert ListSort.quicksort(list) == :lists.sort(list)
    end
  end
end
```

In our simple example, the oracle is just a small pure function, but this pattern can be useful even when the oracle is an entire system.

Smoke Testing

Smoke testing refers to the practice of testing that code doesn't behave in unexpected ways rather than testing for the exact behavior of the code. The idea is to run tests that only verify that nothing major is severely broken. For example, our list-sorting function should always either return a list or fail with a FunctionClauseError in case the argument is not a list, but it should never fail with any other error or return anything other than a list. If that would be the case, it would mean that something is very wrong. The list-sorting example is a bit too simple to understand the benefits of smoke testing. But when the system under test is complex, then a smoke test can be significantly faster to write and to run, thus providing a lot of value. When it's hard to generate precise data for your code and it's hard to find accurate properties to ensure that code works correctly, property-based testing can still help with smoke testing. Let's take a look at our list-sorting example:

```elixir
property_based_testing/sorting/test/list_sort_smoke_test.exs
defmodule ListSortSmokeTest do
  use ExUnit.Case
  use ExUnitProperties

  property "quicksort/1 returns a list or fails with FunctionClauseError" do
    check all term <- term() do
      try do
        ListSort.quicksort(term)
      rescue
        FunctionClauseError ->
          :ok

        other ->
          raise "raised unexpected exception: #{inspect(other)}"
      else
        term ->
          assert is_list(term)
      end
    end
  end
end
```

As we mentioned, this example is contrived because we saw that it's easy to come up with properties to test a list-sorting function. However, when the system under test gets more complex, this pattern becomes useful. For example, let's imagine we have an HTTP API. To write property-based tests that cover the interaction with the API, we would need complex generators capable of generating valid API calls with valid paths, headers, and bodies. We'd also need to be able to come up with properties of responses to those calls. Quite often, this is hard to do. However, we know that by design our API can return responses with a status code of 200 if everything went well, 400 if there was an error with the request, or 404 if the URL was not found.

Without knowing anything else about our system, we can write a property that generates random HTTP requests (with random paths, headers, and bodies), sends them to our API, and then asserts that the API returns only one of the expected codes. We're not interested in whether the response returned by the API is the correct response to the request that we sent; we only care about the API not blowing up with something unexpected. We're just asserting that nothing is majorly broken. Let's see what this property could look like in pseudocode:

```
property_based_testing/misc/api_smoke_test.exs
property "API only returns a response with status of 200, 400, or 404" do
  host = "myapi.example.com"

  check all method <- http_method_generator(),
            path <- path_generator(),
            headers <- headers_generator(),
            body <- binary() do
    response = send_http_request(host, method, path, headers, body)
    assert response.status in [200, 400, 404]
  end
end
```

This pattern is powerful. It tests a broad range of inputs to our system using a small amount of code, with the chance of finding inputs that our system blows up on, and it doesn't require us to come up with good properties.

Avoiding Reimplementing Your Logic to Test It

A problem that often arises for novice users of property-based testing (and possibly testing in general) is the feeling of having to reimplement the logic of a piece of code in order to test it. In our examples, we didn't suffer too much from this problem, but we could see it creeping up when we had to implement a sorted?/1 function to test if a list was sorted. That function is simpler than a function that actually sorts the list. But we can imagine cases where, in order to check that our logic is correct, we have to reimplement a lot of the original logic in the properties.

Sometimes rewriting a working implementation can be a useful technique. The trick is to not just rewrite the same implementation but to focus on writing an implementation that makes us more confident that the logic works at the expense of something else, like performance. If we write an inefficient version of our code that we're confident works correctly, we can use that as the oracle for the code we're trying to test.

Are Properties Enough?

Are properties enough to ensure that your code works and behaves correctly? Sometimes, yes. Most times, no. A property verifies *invariants* of your code, that is, properties of your code that stay the same regardless of the input. Sometimes, the wrong code can maintain the same invariants that you're testing. Let's see an example. Imagine we have a property that asserts that when we concatenate two strings, then we can use String.contains?/2 to verify that the concatenated string contains both the original strings:

```
property_based_testing/misc/property_and_example_test.exs
property "concatenation of a and b contains both" do
  check all left <- string(),
            right <- string(),
            concatenated = left <> right do
    assert String.contains?(concatenate, left)
    assert String.contains?(concatenate, right)
  end
end
```

This is a good property for String.contains?/2 to hold. However, if this is the only kind of testing that we're doing on String.contains?/2, it means we can implement String.contains?/2 as a function that always returns true.

```
def contains?(_string, _substring), do: true
```

This obviously wrong implementation still passes our property. For this reason, it's important that we still have unit or integration tests that actually verify that our code works as we expect for some given inputs. Having tests alongside properties is also useful for testing known corner cases of our code, because those problematic inputs might not always be produced by the generators. In the String.contains?/2 example, we'd probably have a test like the one below alongside our property:

```
property_based_testing/misc/property_and_example_test.exs
test "String.contains?/2 works on known inputs" do
  assert String.contains?("foobar", "foo")
  assert String.contains?("foobar", "bar")
  assert String.contains?("foobar", "ob")
  refute String.contains?("foobar", "baz")
end
```

This test makes the dummy implementation that always returns true fail right away. The combination of properties and example-based tests is powerful: the properties assert that our code holds invariants, while example-based tests verify that our code works for a few known (and corner) cases. This can give us a high confidence in the correctness of the code.

In general, property-based testing is not a tool that can usually *replace* example-based testing. Instead, it's a tool that can complement example-based testing. When it makes sense and when coming up with properties isn't too hard, then property-based testing can make it easy to test a large number of inputs and corner cases in a concise way.

Stateful Property-Based Testing

Until now, we've mostly looked at property-based testing in the context of testing pure, stateless functions that take an input and return an output. However, property-based testing is also useful for testing stateful systems. A *stateful system* is a system that, well, carries state. For example, a database is a stateful system.

In our examples so far, we only used property-based testing to generate some data and then feed it to a piece of code and assert on the result of that. With stateful systems, things change: we now have to deal with setting a state and only executing some operations when the system is in a given state. Let's see how we can use property-based testing for something like that.

Modeling the Stateful System

We know how to generate random data through our property-based testing framework. We can take advantage of this knowledge to generate random *commands* that we can issue on our stateful system. For example, if our stateful system is a database, we can generate random commands to issue against this system. However, if the commands are random, how do we assert on their effects on the system? Enter the *system model*. The whole idea behind property-based testing of a stateful system revolves around the idea of modeling the real system with a model that represents that system from the perspective we're interested in. Once we have this model, we can execute the commands we generated on the real system and on the model and then verify that the effects of the commands match. This sounds complex, so let's break it down with an example.

Let's imagine we wrote a key-value store where we can write values stored under unique keys and retrieve those values using the corresponding keys.

```
iex> kv_store = KVStore.new()
iex> KVStore.set(kv_store, "key1", "some value")
iex> KVStore.get(kv_store, "key1")
"some value"
iex> KVStore.delete(kv_store, "key1")
iex> KVStore.get(kv_store, "key1")
nil
```

This is a stateful system where the state is the set of key-value pairs stored in the key-value store created with KVStore.new/0. One thing we could test about this system is that retrieving an existing key always returns the last value set for that key or a null value if the last operation was to delete the value, no matter how many times we set or delete that key. How can we model our key-value store in order to test this property? We can start with a simple two-element tuple {key, value} that stores the key we're interested in and its current value (or nil if the key hasn't been set yet). Let's use pseudocode to see how we could generate a command assuming we've already generated a random key called random_key:

property_based_testing/misc/stateful_testing.exs
```
def command do
  one_of([
    command(:set, [random_key, term()]),
    command(:delete, [random_key])
  ])
end
```

For every possible command that we can issue on the stateful system, we need to define what happens to our model. Let's continue with pseudocode:

property_based_testing/misc/stateful_testing.exs
```
def set({key, _old_value}, key, new_value) do
  {key, new_value}
end

def delete({key, _value}, key) do
  {key, nil}
end
```

Now we also need to define a get command to retrieve the current value for the key in our model:

property_based_testing/misc/stateful_testing.exs
```
def get({key, value}, key) do
  value
end
```

We have our commands reflected in the model. Now comes the fun part. We generate a random list of commands. Then, we execute those commands one by one both on the model and on the real system. Finally, we verify that the value stored in our model is the same as the value stored under our key in the stateful system.

The reason we're being generic and not showing working code in these examples is that stream_data still doesn't provide tools for working with stateful testing (even if it's coming up in the future).

The Benefits of Stateful Property-Based Testing

Even if stream_data doesn't support stateful property-based testing yet, we still wanted to mention it and go over the basic concepts behind it since it's a powerful and useful tool. All of the benefits of property-based testing that we've discussed in this chapter apply to stateful property-based testing as well.

An especially useful behavior of stateful property-based testing is that the random lists of commands that we generate is shrunk in case of failure. This means that when a property fails, the framework will present us a small list of commands with small inputs that cause the failure. This can turn out to be invaluable. A great testimony of this is Google's leveldb, where as mentioned in Joseph Wayne Norton's slides,[4] property-based testing uncovered a sequence of 17 calls and then 31 calls that would generate ghost keys in the database. Those were *shrunk* sequences of commands! Reproducing those bugs would have been a nightmare for a human.

Wrapping Up

We saw how property-based testing is a powerful tool that can help strengthen your test suite and increase confidence in your code by testing it against randomly generated inputs. You learned to use the stream_data library both for data generation as well as for property-based testing. Then, we looked at some patterns that can help when designing properties. Finally, we had a quick look at stateful property-based testing. An important thing to remember is that property-based testing is not a silver bullet and it doesn't replace other kinds of testing, but it can be a great addition to your test suite.

This is the last chapter of the book. You made it! You're now a skilled tester of Elixir code. We hope you'll have fun (or at least productive times) with the things you learned. Happy testing!

---

4. http://htmlpreview.github.io/?https://raw.github.com/strangeloop/lambdajam2013/master/slides/Norton-QuickCheck.html

When To Randomize Test Data

Many of the test examples in this book show the use of randomized test data. This is a topic where experienced software developers have differing opinions. We're adding this appendix to help you understand when it's safe to use randomized data and to give you enough background to help you decide if you'll take that approach.

When setting up data for a test, the values can fall into two categories: essential data and incidental data. Explaining the difference is easier if we start with incidental data. Data is incidental if it should have no impact on the behavior of your code under test. In *Unit Tests*, we used this example:

when_to_randomize_data/soggy_waffle.ex
```
Line 1  defmodule SoggyWaffle do
          alias SoggyWaffle.WeatherAPI

          def rain?(city, datetime, weather_fn \\ &WeatherAPI.get_forecast/1) do
     5      with {:ok, response} <- weather_fn.(city) do
              {:ok, weather_data} =
                SoggyWaffle.WeatherAPI.ResponseParser.parse_response(response)

              SoggyWaffle.Weather.imminent_rain?(weather_data, datetime)
    10      end
          end
        end
```

As a reminder, in this example, our test is passing in a test double. The behavior of the code under test is largely to pass data that it's received to other functions. The first time it does this is on line 5, where it passes the city name it was provided to the test double it was also provided. In this case, the value bound to the city variable won't affect the way that the code behaves in any way. In fact, the important part of the behavior here is that no matter the value bound to that variable, it'll always pass that to the test double.

Let's take a look at the test to better understand how this all works together.

```elixir
when_to_randomize_data/soggy_waffle_test.exs
test "success: gets forecasts, returns true for imminent rain" do
  now = DateTime.utc_now()
  future_unix = DateTime.to_unix(now) + 1
  expected_city = Enum.random(["Denver", "Los Angeles", "New York"])
  test_pid = self()

  weather_fn_double = fn city ->
    send(test_pid, {:get_forecast_called, city})
    # «build return data»
    {:ok, %{"list" => data}}
  end

  assert SoggyWaffle.rain?(expected_city, now, weather_fn_double)

  assert_received(
    {:get_forecast_called, ^expected_city},
    "get_forecast was never called"
  )
end
end
```

The first line of code executed when the test double is called is send(test_pid, {:get_forecast_called, city}) (seen on line 8). This code sends the value bound to that variable back to the test process itself. At the end of the test, on line 16, the code uses assert_received to verify that the value the code under test passed to the test double was the same value the test originally sent when exercising the code.

Our test uses a naive way to randomize the data, using Enum.random/1 to choose the value passed in and expected to be passed to the double. In an application with more complete data generators, like Factory.city_name/0 or something similar, the data set might be larger, but the effect will be the same: the city name itself is incidental, but the same value must be passed along by the code under test.

Randomizing the incidental data in this test makes sure that the code under test isn't changing that data. Our tests should focus on the outside contracts of the code under test (keeping our black box), and in this case that means input data and data sent to another function or process.

Understanding incidental test data will help us define essential test data. In our previous example, we don't need to test all the possible input values. If a specific set of city names would work while others wouldn't, the data would no longer be considered incidental but instead would be essential. We would need to test that every valid city name did work while names not in that list did not.

An example of this in the book is from Chapter 1, Unit Tests, on page 1, where we used a list comprehension to assert on every valid response value that we knew of from the weather API we were calling:

```
when_to_randomize_data/response_parser_test.exs
defmodule SoggyWaffle.WeatherAPI.ResponseParserTest do
  use ExUnit.Case
  alias SoggyWaffle.WeatherAPI.ResponseParser

  # weather codes come from: https://openweathermap.org/weather-condition
  @thunderstorm_ids {
    "thunderstorm",
    [200, 201, 202, 210, 211, 212, 221, 230, 231, 232]
  }
  @drizzle_ids {"drizzle", [300, 301, 302, 310, 311, 312, 313, 314, 321]}
  @rain_ids {"rain", [500, 501, 502, 503, 504, 511, 520, 521, 522, 531]}

  for {condition, ids} <- [@thunderstorm_ids, @drizzle_ids, @rain_ids] do
    test "success: recognizes #{condition} as a rainy condition" do
      now_unix = DateTime.utc_now() |> DateTime.to_unix()

      for id <- unquote(ids) do
        record = %{"dt" => now_unix, "weather" => [%{"id" => id}]}

        assert {:ok, [weather_struct]} =
                 ResponseParser.parse_response(%{"list" => [record]})

        assert weather_struct.rain? == true
      end
    end
  end
end
```

The code under test, ResponseParser.parse_response/1, will behave differently depending on the response it's passed. If we're to prevent regressions, each valid weather condition ID must be tested. In the test, these IDs are essential data.

This may all feel like a lead into property-based testing, but it's important to understand the difference. When you can know all of the valid values, you can test explicitly for them, treating them as essential data. When you can't know them all but you can define rules about them, you can look to property-based testing.

We promised to empower you to make a decision about whether you should randomize your incidental test data or not. First, we'll discuss reasons to do it and then follow up with the arguments often made against it.

Randomizing your incidental data has a couple of benefits. If you're reading an existing test and you see that data is being randomized, it can be a very quick indicator that the data is incidental. This will help you to reason about behavior of the code under test from the test itself.

If you write your code before your tests, it's entirely possible to accidentally have hard-coded values present. Normally your tests would help you find this mistake; but if you just wrote the code, that hard-coded value might be fresh in your memory and you could use the same value in your test. This will result in a false sense of security that your code under test is behaving correctly, though it's actually quite broken. This is another case where randomized data would help.

Randomizing your incidental test data has potential risks as well. People who are opposed to randomizing often cite examples where the random values actually cause issues that can be hard to replicate. An example that we've seen is a test that selected a random time zone for a timestamp in the test, with the code under test converting between time zones. As it turned out, our test would occasionally pick a time zone that was offset from UTC by half an hour. The code under test couldn't handle anything that wasn't offset by complete hours. Given that the application only needed to serve time zones that were offset by whole hours, it could be viewed that the random failures were an issue with the test and not the code.

The problem was that it took some debugging time to understand why the test was failing in the first place. Fortunately, ExUnit provides the ability to pass the seed for randomization to the test run. If the seed reported in the output of a failed test run is 654321, you can replicate the test run by passing the flag --seed 654321 when you run mix test. Combined with some additional test output (IO.inspect/1 calls), we were able to identify the problem. But if we'd written the test with a known valid value in the first place, we never would've lost time on this issue, and our code still would've operated as intended.

Remember that if you're ever intentionally trying to find values that will break your code, property-based testing is the correct solution. Randomizing your test inputs finds specific value dependencies in your code, but it won't help you guarantee that your code works for a wide variety of inputs in a single test run.

Having good failure output from your tests and being able to pass a random seed can help reduce issues like this, but the more asynchronous your test runs are, the more likely that you can't replicate a previous test run exactly.

Whether you prefer to randomize your incidental data is up to you. But either way, understanding the difference between essential and incidental data will help you design your tests in a thoughtful and intentional way.

Test Life Cycle

Once you get familiar with ExUnit as the tool you use to write Elixir tests, you'll probably want to have a deeper understanding of the exact life cycle of a test and of your whole test suite. In this appendix, we'll look at how ExUnit executes your test suite, including setup, running tests, and teardown. We'll also learn about how tests, setup callbacks, and teardown callbacks relate to *processes*, that is, what the "process architecture" of an ExUnit test suite is.

This knowledge isn't only useful to improve your understanding of ExUnit as a tool. At some point, you'll likely need to come up with unconventional strategies in order to test particular pieces of code (for a number of possible reasons). In those cases, it's important to know which process your test code is running on, which steps in the testing suite are blocking and which are asynchronous, and which test processes are linked between each other.

The Life Cycle of an ExUnit Suite

When you run mix test, Mix is essentially compiling your project, loading all the files ending in _test.exs from the test directory of your project and then running test/test_helper.exs. Mix is taking care of *starting the ExUnit suite* for you. However, there's no magic involved.

What Mix executes is a single call to ExUnit.start/1 that Mix itself includes in all test/test_helper.exs files, which typically look like the snippet below:

```
ExUnit.start()
```

The documentation for ExUnit.start/1 does a good job at summing up the role of this function:[1]

> Starts ExUnit and automatically runs tests right before the VM terminates.

---

1.   https://hexdocs.pm/ex_unit/ExUnit.html#start/1

ExUnit.start/1 relies on System.at_exit/1 to actually run the whole test suite right before shutting down the virtual machine. This gives you a chance to load everything you need and compile every *test case module* before running any tests. That's all Mix is doing when you run mix test.

If you want to run the test suite "on demand" and not before shutting down the VM, you can use ExUnit.run/0. It's what ExUnit.start/1 also uses under the hood, after all. However, you'll need to somehow start the :ex_unit application before running ExUnit.run/0. A common way of doing this is to call ExUnit.start/1 with the autorun: false option, which tells ExUnit to *not* run the test suite before shutting down the VM. A possible example of manually running the test suite is included below:

```
ExUnit.start(autorun: false)

IO.puts("About to run the test suite!")

result = ExUnit.run()

IO.puts("The test suite finished running.")
IO.puts("The result is: #{inspect(result)}")
```

To run some code *after* your ExUnit suite finishes running, you can use the ExUnit.after_suite/1 callback available since Elixir 1.8. Before Elixir 1.8, you would've used System.at_exit/1 directly, but ExUnit.after_suite/1 gives you handy additional information about the results of the suite itself. ExUnit.after_suite/1 takes a callback function and runs that function when the suite finishes executing. The callback function must take one argument, a map that contains non-negative integers representing the numbers of different categories of tests in the suite.

```
%{
  excluded: 2,
  failures: 1,
  skipped: 0,
  total: 84
}
```

You can call ExUnit.after_suite/1 as many times as you want. All callbacks that you register will be executed, in reverse order to how you registered them, at the end of the test suite. All the callbacks are executed *sequentially* in the same process that calls ExUnit.run/0. If you use ExUnit.start/1, all the callbacks are going to be executed in the separate process that System.at_exit/1 creates to execute its callback.

ExUnit.after_suite/1 is useful for different things, but we found it most useful for any sort of teardown or notification. You can use some Internet of Things magic to make a smart light in your house turn red if there are any failures in the suite. You can use it to delete all the temporary directories you set up in your tests. Your imagination is the limit.

We looked at code and callbacks related to the ExUnit suite as a whole. Let's move on and learn how *cases* are executed.

Test Cases

Every module whose name ends with a trailing Test and that contains a call to use ExUnit is considered a *test case*. A test case is essentially a collection of setup callbacks and tests.

The most important thing to know here is that test cases can be executed either concurrently or sequentially in relation to other test cases. All the test cases that use the async: true option in use ExUnit are executed concurrently. Then, the rest of the test cases are executed sequentially (in the order they were defined), by default in random order.

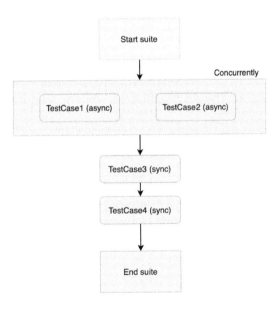

As we mentioned, a test case by itself doesn't contain any logic. It's only a container for setup callbacks and tests. The execution of a test case goes like this:

1. All setup_all callbacks are executed.
2. All tests are executed with their test-specific setup and teardown callbacks.

Let's start from setup_all. All setup_all callbacks are executed in the order they're defined in the test case, and they're executed in the *same process*. Essentially, before running any tests, the test case spawns a process, runs all the setup_all callbacks in that process, and then starts running tests.

After the setup_all callbacks, the test case runs tests. Tests inside a single test case are *always run sequentially*, by default in random order (unless a suite seed is provided). If you're curious as to why single tests are not run in parallel, the reason is performance: in most cases, single tests are quick enough that the overhead of executing them in parallel and each in its own process is bigger than the time it takes to run the tests.

The only thing left to understand is the life cycle of single tests.

Executing Tests

When executing a single test, the test case does roughly this:

1. Runs all the setup callbacks in the order they were defined.
2. Runs the test body.
3. Runs all the on_exit callbacks in the order they were registered.

Let's look at each of these steps separately.

The first thing a test case does when running a test is spawn a new process to run that test in. All the setup callbacks are run sequentially *inside that process*.

After the setup callbacks are executed, the test case runs the body of the test itself inside the test process.

Once the test body exits (by finishing or by exiting explicitly, for example through an exception), it's time to run the on_exit callbacks. A new process is spawned for the purpose of running all on_exit callbacks. All on_exit callbacks are executed *in that process*, one after the other (that is, sequentially). on_exit callbacks are not executed in the test process because, after all, the test process just exited so it's not alive anymore.

An Example and a Drawing

In this short section, we'll provide a very artificial example of a test case with some tests, setup callbacks, and teardown callbacks in it. We'll also provide a visual representation of the processes involved in running this test case, as well as the output of running the test case. You can run this file yourself and see the results by calling elixir test_case_example.exs.

test_lifecycle/test_case_example.exs

```elixir
# We use an empty list of formatters so that ExUnit doesn't
# output anything on the standard output.
ExUnit.start(autorun: false, formatters: [])

defmodule TestCaseExampleTest do
  use ExUnit.Case

  setup_all do
    IO.puts("setup_all #1 in process: #{inspect(self())}")
  end

  setup_all do
    IO.puts("setup_all callback #2 in process: #{inspect(self())}")
  end

  setup do
    IO.puts("setup callback #1 in process: #{inspect(self())}")
  end

  setup do
    IO.puts("setup callback #2 in process: #{inspect(self())}")
  end

  test "#1" do
    on_exit(fn ->
      IO.puts(
        "on_exit callback #1 (test #1) in process: #{inspect(self())}"
      )
    end)

    on_exit(fn ->
      IO.puts(
        "on_exit callback #2 (test #1) in process: #{inspect(self())}"
      )
    end)

    IO.puts("test #1 in process: #{inspect(self())}")
  end

  test "#2" do
    IO.puts("test #2 in process: #{inspect(self())}")
  end
end

result = ExUnit.run()

IO.puts("The return value of ExUnit.run/0 is:")
IO.inspect(result)
```

The output is below.

```
setup_all #1 in process: #PID<0.109.0>
setup_all callback #2 in process: #PID<0.109.0>
setup callback #1 in process: #PID<0.110.0>
setup callback #2 in process: #PID<0.110.0>
```

```
test #2 in process: #PID<0.110.0>
setup callback #1 in process: #PID<0.111.0>
setup callback #2 in process: #PID<0.111.0>
test #1 in process: #PID<0.111.0>
on_exit callback #2 (test #1) in process: #PID<0.112.0>
on_exit callback #1 (test #1) in process: #PID<0.112.0>
The return value of ExUnit.run/0 is:
%{excluded: 0, failures: 0, skipped: 0, total: 2}
```

Maybe the visual representation below also helps:

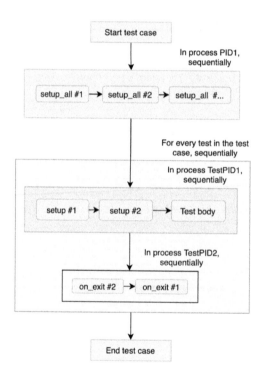

We hope that this appendix helps when you're dealing with trickier tests or if you just want to understand the exact life cycle of a whole ExUnit suite, down to the test cases and the single tests within them.

Test Coverage

When writing tests, it's useful to be able to *measure* the impact of your tests. You want to know that the tests you're writing are exercising your code. Moreover, you want to know that the codebase has as few "blind spots" as possible, meaning code that's never executed when running tests. Code could be run by different levels of testing: unit tests, integration tests, and end-to-end tests. Usually, many parts of the codebase are exercised by more than one level of testing, as it's common that higher levels of testing (like end-to-end testing) cover large parts of the codebase.

The most commonly used metric to measure how much code your tests are exercising is *test coverage*, which is the subject of this appendix. It's a *percentage* that measures the relative amount of code in your codebase that's run by tests. For example, a test coverage of 60% means that six out of every ten lines of your code are executed *at least once* during the test suite, but four are not executed at all. Test coverage support is usually part of the language's test tooling, either as a built-in functionality or as an additional tool. Measuring coverage is a language-specific problem and, as you can imagine, requires deep language integration in order to find out what lines of source code are being executed during a test suite.

Elixir and Erlang provide built-in support for test coverage. Mix and ExUnit ship with test coverage functionalities, providing a default built-in test coverage tool as well as support for external test coverage tools. In this appendix, we're going to talk about the default test coverage tool as well as a third-party tool that integrates with Coveralls.[1] We're gonna end the appendix looking at the shortcomings of test coverage tools that are specific to Elixir.

---

1. https://coveralls.io

Built-In Test Coverage

ExUnit provides a built-in test coverage tool. You can use it right out of the gate in a Mix project via the --cover flag passed to mix test.

Let's use the code we wrote for Chapter 1, Unit Tests, on page 1, to try things out. Open up the unit_tests/soggy_waffle directory in your terminal and run mix test --cover:

```
> mix test --cover
Cover compiling modules ...
...............

Finished in 1.8 seconds
15 tests, 0 failures

Randomized with seed 384102

Generating cover results ...

| Percentage  | Module                                      |
|-------------|---------------------------------------------|
| 0.00%       | SoggyWaffle.SmsApi                          |
| 75.00%      | SoggyWaffle                                 |
| 85.71%      | SoggyWaffle.Weather                         |
| 100.00%     | SoggyWaffle.WeatherAPI                      |
| 100.00%     | SoggyWaffle.WeatherAPI.ResponseParser       |
| ----------- | --------------------------                  |
| 85.00%      | Total                                       |

Generated HTML coverage results in "cover" directory
```

As seen in the output above, we get a list of the modules contained in our Mix project. Each module is listed alongside a percentage: that's our code coverage ratio right there. A result of 100% means that every single line in a module is executed *at least once* during our test run. A result of 0% means that none of the code in that module has been executed during the test run.

The built-in code coverage tool also generates a bunch of HTML report files (by default in the cover directory). Let's open the HTML file for the SoggyWaffle.Weather module, you can see what it looks like in the figure on page 229.

Reading this report is straightforward. The lines highlighted in green are the ones that've been executed during the test run. Each of the green lines has a number to the left that shows how many times the line has been executed. The lines highlighted in red are the ones that *have not been executed* during the test run. All the other lines are lines that don't account for any coverage for various reasons. For example, function definitions aren't counted toward code coverage and neither are lines that contain multiline expressions.

`cover/Elixir.SoggyWaffle.Weather.html`

```
1          defmodule SoggyWaffle.Weather do
2            @type t :: %__MODULE__{}
3
4      4     defstruct [:datetime, :rain?]
5
6            @spec imminent_rain?([t()], DateTime.t()) :: boolean()
7  :-(       def imminent_rain?(weather_data, now \\ DateTime.utc_now()) do
8      5       Enum.any?(weather_data, fn
9                %__MODULE__{rain?: true} = weather ->
10     6           in_next_4_hours?(now, weather.datetime)
11
12               _ ->
13                 false
14             end)
15          end
16
17          defp in_next_4_hours?(now, weather_datetime) do
18     6       four_hours_from_now =
19               DateTime.add(now, _4_hours_in_seconds = 4 * 60 * 60)
20
21     6       DateTime.compare(weather_datetime, now) in [:gt, :eq] and
22     5         DateTime.compare(weather_datetime, four_hours_from_now) in [:lt, :eq]
23          end
24        end
```

Code coverage reports like the HTML ones generated by mix test --cover are fundamental in order to spot and address potential problems. Knowing only the coverage percentage of a module is useful to have an idea of which modules might need more attention, but a detailed line-by-line report allows us to know exactly what tests we might be missing in order to increase the coverage of our code.

A few aspects of the coverage can be configured through a handful of options to return from the project/0 function of a mix.exs file. An option that's often useful is the :ignore_modules option. In our example above, the SoggyWaffle.SmsApi module has 0% coverage because it's the "real" implementation of the HTTP API that reaches out to an external system, and we don't have any *integration tests* or *end-to-end tests* executing it. Let's pretend we don't want to write such tests and that we don't want to count this particular module toward the total coverage. We can include it in the list of ignored modules in mix.exs:

```
defmodule SoggyWaffle.MixProject do
  use Mix.Project

  def project do
    [
      app: :soggy_waffle,
```

```
        version: "0.1.0",
        elixir: "~> 1.9",
        start_permanent: Mix.env() == :prod,
        deps: deps(),
        test_coverage: [ignore_modules: [SoggyWaffle.SmsApi]]
      ]
    end
```

≪rest of mix.exs contents≫

We can see this in action when running mix test --cover again:

```
> mix test --cover
Cover compiling modules ...
. . . . . . . . . . . . . .

Finished in 1.6 seconds
15 tests, 0 failures

Randomized with seed 969266

Generating cover results ...

| Percentage  | Module                               |
|-------------|--------------------------------------|
| 75.00%      | SoggyWaffle                          |
| 85.71%      | SoggyWaffle.Weather                  |
| 100.00%     | SoggyWaffle.WeatherAPI               |
| 100.00%     | SoggyWaffle.WeatherAPI.ResponseParser |
| ----------- | ------------------------- |
| 89.47%      | Total                                |

Generated HTML coverage results in "cover" directory
```

The SoggyWaffle.SmsApi module isn't present anymore in the report, and the total code coverage went up a few percentage points.

Coveralls and the Excoveralls Library

The built-in test coverage tool provides a useful set of functionalities out of the box: percentage summaries and line-by-line HTML visual reports. However, many of us might want a more "complete" package, with additional functionality, such as hosting for those HTML reports, CI-friendly integrations, and insights into test coverage history of a given project.

A common service that provides such features is Coveralls.[2] This service allows you to "post" test coverage results on their platform and then browse projects, see insights, browse file-by-file and line-by-line reports, and more. The service is free for open-source projects and has a paid option for businesses.

---

2.   https://coveralls.io

The Excoveralls library integrates Elixir projects with Coveralls and allows reporting of test coverage to Coveralls.[3] To try it out, let's add it as a dependency in our mix.exs file and set it as the test coverage tool via the :tool option under :test_coverage:

```
defmodule SoggyWaffle.MixProject do
  use Mix.Project

  def project do
    [
      app: :soggy_waffle,
      version: "0.1.0",
      elixir: "~> 1.9",
      start_permanent: Mix.env() == :prod,
      deps: deps(),
      test_coverage: [tool: [ExCoveralls]],
    ]
  end

  defp deps do
    [
      {:excoveralls, "~> 0.13.0", only: :test}
      «rest of the dependencies»
    ]
  end

  «rest of mix.exs contents»
```

Now, running mix test --cover will use Excoveralls as its "coverage tool" instead of the built-in tool:

```
mix test --cover
Compiling 5 files (.ex)
Generated soggy_waffle app
..............

Finished in 1.5 seconds
15 tests, 0 failures

Randomized with seed 131302
----------------
COV    FILE                                        LINES RELEVANT  MISSED
100.0% lib/soggy_waffle.ex                            11      3        0
100.0% lib/soggy_waffle/weather.ex                    24      5        0
100.0% lib/soggy_waffle/weather_api.ex                20      4        0
100.0% lib/soggy_waffle/weather_api/response_pa       30      4        0
[TOTAL]  100.0%
```

This looks very similar to what we saw with the built-in tool. The coverage percentages are different because this tool calculates code coverage differently,

---

3.   https://github.com/parroty/excoveralls

but the report style is alike. If you want HTML reports as well, you can run MIX_ENV=test mix coveralls.html instead. Excoveralls also provides other output formats, such as JSON (MIX_ENV=test mix coveralls.json) and XML (MIX_ENV=test mix coveralls.xml), which allow developers to integrate the output of test coverage runs in different systems and platforms programmatically.

As far as integrations go, Excoveralls provides a few ways to post coverage results to Coveralls. You can post to Coveralls from common CI platforms, such as CircleCI[4] (mix coveralls.circle) or Semaphore[5] (mix coveralls.semaphore). Additionally, Excoveralls allows you to post to any Coveralls-compatible host via mix coveralls.post. For example, OpenCov[6] is a solid self-hosted coverage platform compatible with the Coveralls API.

We briefly looked at what test coverage is, why it's useful, and how it can be used for Elixir projects. Test coverage is just one possible tool to increase confidence in your test suite, but it's not necessarily a guarantee that your test suite is solid and well written. However, it can be useful to spot areas of your code that aren't well tested or, at the other end of the spectrum, areas of your code that are "hot paths" and are executed many times during testing. In our experience, a sky-high test coverage (somewhere around 95% and above) doesn't necessarily translate to a healthy and functioning codebase. Once the code coverage is high enough, striving to increase it might start to have diminishing returns. On the other hand, a low coverage (for example, somewhere around 40% or 50%) can point to an undertested codebase that might need some work. In general, the usefulness of test coverage varies from project to project, but it's a useful tool to have in our testing tool belt.

---

4.   https://circleci.com
5.   https://semaphoreci.com
6.   https://github.com/danhper/opencov

Bibliography

[TD21]   Bruce A. Tate and Sophie DeBenedetto. *Programming Phoenix LiveView*.
          The Pragmatic Bookshelf, Raleigh, NC, 2021.

Index

Thank you!

How did you enjoy this book? Please let us know. Take a moment and email us at support@pragprog.com with your feedback. Tell us your story and you could win free ebooks. Please use the subject line "Book Feedback."

Ready for your next great Pragmatic Bookshelf book? Come on over to https://pragprog.com and use the coupon code BUYANOTHER2021 to save 30% on your next ebook.

Void where prohibited, restricted, or otherwise unwelcome. Do not use ebooks near water. If rash persists, see a doctor. Doesn't apply to *The Pragmatic Programmer* ebook because it's older than the Pragmatic Bookshelf itself. Side effects may include increased knowledge and skill, increased marketability, and deep satisfaction. Increase dosage regularly.

And thank you for your continued support,

The Pragmatic Bookshelf

Kotlin and Android Development featuring Jetpack

Start building native Android apps the modern way in Kotlin with Jetpack's expansive set of tools, libraries, and best practices. Learn how to create efficient, resilient views with Fragments and share data between the views with ViewModels. Use Room to persist valuable data quickly, and avoid NullPointerExceptions and Java's verbose expressions with Kotlin. You can even handle asynchronous web service calls elegantly with Kotlin coroutines. Achieve all of this and much more while building two full-featured apps, following detailed, step-by-step instructions.

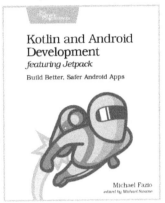

Michael Fazio
(444 pages) ISBN: 9781680508154. $49.95
https://pragprog.com/book/mfjetpack

Learn to Program, Third Edition

It's easier to learn how to program a computer than it has ever been before. Now everyone can learn to write programs for themselves—no previous experience is necessary. Chris Pine takes a thorough, but lighthearted approach that teaches you the fundamentals of computer programming, with a minimum of fuss or bother. Whether you are interested in a new hobby or a new career, this book is your doorway into the world of programming.

Chris Pine
(230 pages) ISBN: 9781680508178. $45.95
https://pragprog.com/book/ltp3

Intuitive Python

Developers power their projects with Python because
it emphasizes readability, ease of use, and access to a
meticulously maintained set of packages and tools.
The language itself continues to improve with every
release: writing in Python is full of possibility. But to
maintain a successful Python project, you need to know
more than just the language. You need tooling and in-
stincts to help you make the most out of what's available to you. Use this book as your guide to help you
hone your skills and sculpt a Python project that can
stand the test of time.

David Muller
(140 pages) ISBN: 9781680508239. $26.95
https://pragprog.com/book/dmpython

Modern CSS with Tailwind

Tailwind CSS is an exciting new CSS framework that
allows you to design your site by composing simple
utility classes to create complex effects. With Tailwind,
you can style your text, move your items on the page,
design complex page layouts, and adapt your design
for devices from a phone to a wide-screen monitor.
With this book, you'll learn how to use the Tailwind
for its flexibility and its consistency, from the smallest
detail of your typography to the entire design of your
site.

Noel Rappin
(90 pages) ISBN: 9781680508185. $26.95
https://pragprog.com/book/tailwind

Essential 555 IC

Learn how to create functional gadgets using simple but clever circuits based on the venerable "555." These projects will give you hands-on experience with useful, basic circuits that will aid you across other projects. These inspiring designs might even lead you to develop the next big thing. The 555 Timer Oscillator Integrated Circuit chip is one of the most popular chips in the world. Through clever projects, you will gain permanent knowledge of how to use the 555 timer will carry with you for life.

Cabe Force Satalic Atwell
(104 pages) ISBN: 9781680507836. $19.95
https://pragprog.com/book/catimers

Resourceful Code Reuse

Reusing well-written, well-debugged, and well-tested code improves productivity, code quality, and software configurability and relieves pressure on software developers. When you organize your code into self-contained modular units, you can use them as building blocks for your future projects and share them with other programmers, if needed. Understand the benefits and downsides of seven code reuse models so you can confidently reuse code at any development stage. Create static and dynamic libraries in C and Python, two of the most popular modern programming languages. Adapt your code for the real world: deploy shared functions remotely and build software that accesses them using remote procedure calls.

Dmitry Zinoviev
(64 pages) ISBN: 9781680508208. $14.99
https://pragprog.com/book/dzreuse

The Pragmatic Bookshelf

The Pragmatic Bookshelf features books written by professional developers for professional developers. The titles continue the well-known Pragmatic Programmer style and continue to garner awards and rave reviews. As development gets more and more difficult, the Pragmatic Programmers will be there with more titles and products to help you stay on top of your game.

Visit Us Online

This Book's Home Page
https://pragprog.com/book/lmelixir
Source code from this book, errata, and other resources. Come give us feedback, too!

Keep Up to Date
https://pragprog.com
Join our announcement mailing list (low volume) or follow us on twitter @pragprog for new titles, sales, coupons, hot tips, and more.

New and Noteworthy
https://pragprog.com/news
Check out the latest pragmatic developments, new titles and other offerings.

Save on the ebook

Save on the ebook versions of this title. Owning the paper version of this book entitles you to purchase the electronic versions at a terrific discount.

PDFs are great for carrying around on your laptop—they are hyperlinked, have color, and are fully searchable. Most titles are also available for the iPhone and iPod touch, Amazon Kindle, and other popular e-book readers.

Send a copy of your receipt to support@pragprog.com and we'll provide you with a discount coupon.

Contact Us

Online Orders:	*https://pragprog.com/catalog*
Customer Service:	*support@pragprog.com*
International Rights:	*translations@pragprog.com*
Academic Use:	*academic@pragprog.com*
Write for Us:	*http://write-for-us.pragprog.com*
Or Call:	+1 800-699-7764